THE CAMBRIDGE BIBLE COMMENTARY

NEW ENGLISH BIBLE

GENERAL EDITORS
P. R. ACKROYD, A. R. C. LEANEY, J. W. PACKER

THE FIRST AND SECOND BOOKS OF THE MACCABEES

THE FIRST AND SECOND BOOKS OF THE

MACCABEES

COMMENTARY BY

JOHN R. BARTLETT

Lecturer in Divinity, Trinity College, Dublin

CAMBRIDGE
AT THE UNIVERSITY PRESS
1973

Published by the Syndics of the Cambridge University Press
Bentley House, 200 Euston Road, London NW1 2DB
American Branch: 32 East 57th Street, New York, N.Y.10022

© Cambridge University Press 1973

Library of Congress Catalogue Card Number: 72-87436

ISBNS:
0 521 08658 2 hard cover
0 521 09749 5 paperback

Printed in Great Britain
at the University Printing House, Cambridge
(Brooke Crutchley, University Printer)

GENERAL EDITORS' PREFACE

The aim of this series is to provide the text of the New English Bible closely linked to a commentary in which the results of modern scholarship are made available to the general reader. Teachers and young people have been especially kept in mind. The commentators have been asked to assume no specialized theological knowledge, and no knowledge of Greek and Hebrew. Bare references to other literature and multiple references to other parts of the Bible have been avoided. Actual quotations have been given as often as possible.

The completion of the New Testament part of the series in 1967 provides a basis upon which the production of the much larger Old Testament and Apocrypha series can be undertaken. The welcome accorded to the series has been an encouragement to the editors to follow the same general pattern, and an attempt has been made to take account of criticisms which have been offered. One necessary change is the inclusion of the translators' footnotes since in the Old Testament these are more extensive, and essential for the understanding of the text.

Within the severe limits imposed by the size and scope of the series, each commentator will attempt to set out the main findings of recent biblical scholarship and to describe the historical background to the text. The main theological issues will also be critically discussed.

Much attention has been given to the form of the volumes. The aim is to produce books each of which will be read consecutively from first to last page. The introductory material leads naturally into the text, which itself leads into the alternating sections of the commentary.

The series is accompanied by three volumes of a more general character. *Understanding the Old Testament* sets out to provide the larger historical and archaeological background, to say something about the life and thought of the people of the Old Testament, and to answer the question 'Why should we study the Old Testament?'. *The Making of the Old Testament* is concerned with the formation of the books of the Old Testament and Apocrypha in the context of the ancient near eastern world, and with the ways in which these books have come down to us in the life of the Jewish and Christian communities. *Old Testament Illustrations* contains maps, diagrams and photographs with an explanatory text. These three volumes are designed to provide material helpful to the understanding of the individual books and their commentaries, but they are also prepared so as to be of use quite independently.

P. R. A.

A. R. C. L.

J. W. P.

CONTENTS

CONTENTS

LIST OF MAPS AND CHARTS

THE FOOTNOTES TO THE
N.E.B. TEXT

The footnotes to the N.E.B. text are designed to help the reader either to understand particular points of detail – the meaning of a name, the presence of a play upon words – or to give information about the actual text. Where the Hebrew text appears to be erroneous, or there is doubt about its precise meaning, it may be necessary to turn to manuscripts which offer a different wording, or to ancient translations of the text which may suggest a better reading, or to offer a new explanation based upon conjecture. In such cases, the footnotes supply very briefly an indication of the evidence, and whether the solution proposed is one that is regarded as possible or as probable. Various abbreviations are used in the footnotes:

(1) Some abbreviations are simply of terms used in explaining a point: *ch(s)*., chapter(s); *cp*., compare; *lit*., literally; *mng*., meaning; *MS(S)*., manuscript(s), i.e. Hebrew manuscript(s), unless otherwise stated; *om*., omit(s); *or*, indicating an alternative interpretation; *poss*., possible; *prob*., probable; *rdg*., reading; *Vs(s)*., Versions.

(2) Other abbreviations indicate sources of information from which better interpretations or readings may be obtained.

Aq.   Aquila, a Greek translator of the Old Testament (perhaps about A.D. 130) characterized by great literalness.

Aram.   Aramaic – may refer to the text in this language (used in parts of Ezra and Daniel), or to the meaning of an Aramaic word. Aramaic belongs to the same language family as Hebrew, and is known from about 1000 B.C. over a wide area of the Middle East, including Palestine.

Heb.   Hebrew – may refer to the Hebrew text or may indicate the literal meaning of the Hebrew word.

Josephus   Flavius Josephus (A.D. 37/8–about 100), author of the *Jewish Antiquities*, a survey of the whole history of his people, directed partly at least to a non-Jewish audience, and of various other works, notably one on the *Jewish War* (that of A.D. 66–73) and a defence of Judaism (*Against Apion*).

Luc. Sept.   Lucian's recension of the Septuagint, an important edition made in Antioch in Syria about the end of the third century A.D.

Pesh.   Peshitta or Peshitto, the Syriac version of the Old Testament. Syriac is the name given chiefly to a form of Eastern Aramaic used by the Christian community. The translation varies in quality, and is at many points influenced by the Septuagint or the Targums.

Sam.   Samaritan Pentateuch – the form of the first five books of the Old Testament as used by the Samaritan community. It is written in Hebrew in a special form of the Old Hebrew script, and preserves an important form of the text, somewhat influenced by Samaritan ideas.

Scroll(s)   Scroll(s), commonly called the Dead Sea Scrolls, found at or near Qumran from 1947 onwards. These important manuscripts shed light on the state of the Hebrew text as it was developing in the last centuries B.C. and the first century A.D.

Sept.   Septuagint (meaning 'seventy'; often abbreviated as the Roman numeral LXX), the name given to the main Greek version of the Old Testament. According to tradition, the Pentateuch was translated in Egypt in the third century B.C. by 70 (or 72) translators, six from each tribe, but the precise nature of its origin and development is not fully known. It was intended to provide Greek-speaking Jews with a convenient translation. Subsequently it came to be much revered by the Christian community.

Symm.   Symmachus, another Greek translator of the Old Testament (beginning of the third century A.D.), who tried to combine literalness with good style. Both Lucian and Jerome viewed his version with favour.

Targ.   Targum, a name given to various Aramaic versions of the Old Testament, produced over a long period and eventually standardized, for the use of Aramaic-speaking Jews.

Theod.   Theodotion, the author of a revision of the Septuagint (probably second century A.D.), very dependent on the Hebrew text.

Vulg.   Vulgate, the most important Latin version of the Old Testament, produced by Jerome about A.D. 400, and the text most used throughout the Middle Ages in western Christianity.

[...]   In the text itself square brackets are used to indicate probably late additions to the Hebrew text.

(Fuller discussion of a number of these points may be found in *The Making of the Old Testament* in this series.)

KINGS OF EGYPT

('Lagides' or 'Ptolemies')

Ptolemy I Soter	304–285
Ptolemy II Philadelphus	285–246
Ptolemy III Euergetes	246–221
Ptolemy IV Philopator	221–203
Ptolemy V Epiphanes	203–180
Ptolemy VI Philometor	180–145
Ptolemy VII Neos Philometor	145
Ptolemy VIII Euergetes II	145–116

KINGS OF SYRIA

('Seleucids')

Seleucus I Nicator	312–280
Antiochus I Soter	280–262
Antiochus II Theos	262–246
Seleucus II Callinicus	246–226
Seleucus III Ceraunus	226–223
Antiochus III 'the Great'	223–187
Seleucus IV Philopator	187–175
Antiochus IV Epiphanes	175–164
Antiochus V Eupator	164–161
Demetrius I Soter	161–150
Alexander Balas	150–145
Antiochus VI Epiphanes	145–142
Trypho	142–138
Demetrius II Nicator	145–138
Antiochus VII Sidetes	138–129

THE SELEUCIDS

The Seleucids from Antiochus III onwards were related in the following way:

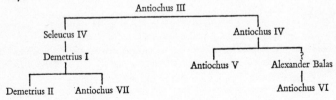

THE MACCABAEAN FAMILY ('the Hasmonaeans')

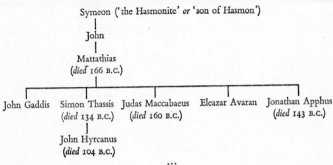

xiii

HIGH PRIESTS OF JERUSALEM

(from the time of Alexander the Great)

Jaddua	about 330
Onias I	(dates unknown)
Simon I	,,
Eleazar (brother of Simon I)	,,
Manasseh (uncle of Eleazar)	,,
Onias II (son of Simon I)	about 245–220
Simon II	about 220–200
Onias III	*died* 172–171
Jason (brother of Onias III)	175–172
Menelaus ('of the clan Bilgah')	172–163
Alcimus ('a priest of the family of Aaron')	161–159
(vacancy for seven years)	159–152
Jonathan (son of Mattathias, 'a priest of the Joarib family')	152–143
Simon (son of Mattathias)	143–134
John Hyrcanus	134–104

Unless otherwise stated, each high priest is the son of his predecessor. Our evidence for the earlier high priests in this list comes mainly from Josephus.

THE FIRST AND SECOND BOOKS
OF THE
MACCABEES

✳   ✳   ✳   ✳   ✳   ✳   ✳   ✳   ✳   ✳   ✳   ✳   ✳

Before one begins to read a book written in a long past age,
some explanation of things that the writer took for granted
and of the way in which he approached his task is often helpful. The next few pages give, very briefly, some background
information about the world to which the Maccabees belonged
and about the writers who have left us some account of the
Maccabees. Most of the material here concerns both 1 and 2
Maccabees, but something will be said about each book
separately before the reader turns to the text and commentary.

THE WORLD OF THE MACCABEES

1 Maccabees writes of events from the accession of the Syrian
king Antiochus IV in 175 B.C. to the death of the high priest
Simon in 134 B.C. 2 Maccabees writes of a more limited period,
175–160 B.C. Both books, therefore, are concerned with what
went on in the middle of the second century B.C. in a province
of the Syrian empire called Judaea. The stage is set by the
opening verses of 1 Maccabees; the death of Alexander the
Great in 323 B.C. and the consequent division of his empire
(which stretched from Greece to India) meant to Judaea that,
as so often before, she became an area whose possession was
a matter of dispute between the two powers of the Euphrates
and Nile valleys. From 312 B.C. Seleucus I ruled in Syria and
Babylon, and Ptolemy I, son of Lagus, ruled Egypt; each was
the founder of a dynasty, the 'Seleucids' and the 'Ptolemies'
(sometimes called the 'Lagides'). Egypt controlled Judaea

until 198 B.C. when Antiochus III, having defeated Ptolemy V's general, Scopas, at Paneion near the source of the Jordan, took it over. From now till the end of Antiochus VII's reign Judaea was technically a Syrian province, though gradually becoming more and more independent. This gaining of independence was the work of the Maccabees (sometimes called the 'Hasmonaeans'; see the genealogy on p. xi). This family emerged from a country district of Judaea in 167 B.C. to lead resistance to the policies of Syria and her Jewish supporters.

It may help the reader to refer from time to time to the charts of Syrian and Egyptian kings, contemporary Jewish high priests, and the Maccabaean family, on pp. xi–xii.

Political independence, however, was not the only point at issue in the Maccabaean struggle. Before the arrival of Alexander the Great, Judaea was a province of the Persian empire, ruled by a governor appointed by Persia and by a high priest appointed on hereditary principles. Such joint rule was made necessary by the Jewish devotion to the law of Moses and the Jerusalem temple, and Persia appears to have made special provision for the Jews to live within the Persian empire under their own internal law. At one stage a Jewish scribe, Ezra, was appointed to enforce 'the law of your God and the law of the king' (Ezra 7: 26). Special provision for the conscience of Jewish subjects became a regular feature of imperial rule; both the Syrian emperor Antiochus III and the Roman Julius Caesar and his successors followed this course in ruling the Jews. The occasional breakdown of this provision was usually due to internal troubles within Judaea rather than to imperial ill-will.

The later years of Persian rule, however, saw the increase of something which did in due course produce internal division among the Jews. This was the influence of Greece. This influence was not new; from the seventh century B.C. onwards Greek pottery and other exports had been known on the Palestinian coast. In the fourth century B.C. Jewish coins were minted bearing an owl on one side and a human bearded head on the other in imitation of the coins of Athens. But the arrival of Alexander in 331 B.C. and the subsequent settling of Greek or hellenized soldiers in colonies throughout the east opened new doors to the Greek way of life with its commerce, its art and literature, its athletic training, its town-planning, its inquiring and inventive spirit. Greeks were beginning to discover Palestine; about Alexander's time a Greek we call Pseudo-Skylax described the coast of Palestine in his *Periplous* ('sailing round'). Excavation has found Greek or Phoenician coins and pottery in virtually every city of the coast and coastal plains. Alexander initiated a period of the building of new Greek towns in the east, of which the greatest was his own foundation of Alexandria in Egypt. Seleucus I founded Seleucia-on-Tigris and Antioch, his capital. Jerash, whose beautiful remains are still to be seen in north Jordan, was probably one of the many towns founded by the Seleucids. Ptolemy II made the ancient Acco on the coast into a new city, renamed Ptolemais (1 Macc. 5: 15); ancient Rabbah, chief city of the Ammonites (modern Amman), he renamed Philadelphia. Bethshan became Scythopolis (cp. 1 Macc. 5: 52; 2 Macc. 12: 29). Marisa (1 Macc. 5: 66) and Adora in Idumaea (1 Macc. 13: 20) were busy, hellenized commercial towns, as were Joppa, Ascalon and Gaza on the coast (most of these can be found on the map on p. 50). Thus contact between the Jews, surrounded by hellenized cities, and the Greek world was bound to grow, and 1 Macc. 5 and 2 Macc. 12 tell us of Jews who lived in these cities.

There was in particular a large and growing settlement of Jews in Alexandria, perhaps originally transported there by Ptolemy I, though, as we know from Jer. 42–4 and from the Elephantine papyri (see *Old Testament Illustrations* in this series, pp. 99–101), there had been Jews in Egypt since the sixth century B.C. These Jews were allowed, under the Ptolemies, to keep their own way of life, but many were deeply influenced by the hellenistic way of life they met at Alexandria, which was a centre of learning and literature with a famous library, as well as being a centre of trade and commerce. In the reign of Ptolemy II the Jewish law was translated into Greek for the benefit of Alexandrian Jews who could no longer read Hebrew fluently. This was the beginning of what is called the 'Septuagint' translation (see *The Making of the Old Testament* in this series, pp. 147–51).

In the third century B.C. Egypt was responsible for the administration of Palestine, and Egypt's tax- and trade-interests gave scope for the rise of a new class of person among the Jews – the businessman in public life. Ptolemy II's finance minister Apollonius sent his agent Zeno in 259 B.C. on a trade mission, and from Zeno's correspondence we read of his contact with one Tobiah, a land-owner and military garrison commander in Transjordan and probably a descendant of Nehemiah's adversary Tobiah, an Ammonite (Neh. 2: 10). Tobiah married the sister of the Jewish high priest Onias II, and was clearly a man of some importance. His son Joseph was probably also an Egyptian official. In about 240 B.C. Onias II ceased to pay tribute to Egypt, perhaps hoping that Seleucus II's recent victories over Egypt would mean a change of master for the Jews. On this occasion, it was Joseph who negotiated with Ptolemy, and in fact he seems to have taken over from the high priest the duties of collecting and paying the Jewish taxes to Egypt and of representing the Jewish people at Ptolemy's court. For twenty-two years he was tax-collector for Coele-syria, Phoenicia, Judaea and Samaria. The success of this latter-day Joseph in Egypt did two things: it diminished the power and status of high priest in the eyes of foreign rulers, and it created a second family rivalling the high priest's in power and influence, the 'sons of Tobiah'. It was a son of Joseph called Hyrcanus (2 Macc. 3: 11) who (by bribery) took over Joseph's job, thus alienating his elder brothers. And so by the beginning of the second century B.C., when Syria took over the rule of Judaea, there were in Judaea, as one might expect, two political parties: Hyrcanus and his followers supported Egypt, while his brothers and the then high priest,

Simon II, supported Syria. High priests did not always support Syria, however; thus Simon's successor, Onias III, in whose high-priesthood the real trouble began, supported Egypt.

Families like that of Tobiah, linked with the ruling high-priestly family yet involved in commerce and in contact with the Greek world, made a difference to Judaea. Josephus (*Jewish Antiquities* XII. 4. 10; for this work see p. 11) says that Joseph 'brought the Jewish people from poverty and a state of weakness to more splendid opportunities of life', though Jesus son of Sirach, writing in the book known as Ecclesiasticus, about 180 B.C., was quick to point to the disadvantages of the growth of a new monied class:

> Do not lift a weight too heavy for you,
> keeping company with a man greater and richer than
>   yourself.
> How can a jug be friends with a kettle?
> If they knock together, the one will be smashed.
> A rich man does wrong, and adds insult to injury;
> a poor man is wronged, and must apologize into the
>   bargain.
> If you can serve his turn, a rich man will exploit you,
> but if you are in need, he will leave you alone.
>
>   (Ecclus. 13 : 2–4)

The gulf which Jesus son of Sirach portrays between rich and poor may reflect a growing gulf between the old country peasantry and the new monied, cosmopolitan aristocracy. And with this development came also the entry into Judaea of Greek ways of thought, which had what might be called a 'secularizing' effect on the Jewish traditions. Opposition to this also may be seen in Ecclesiasticus:

> Do not pry into things too hard for you
> or examine what is beyond your reach.
> Meditate on the commandments you have been given;
> what the Lord keeps secret is no concern of yours.
> Do not busy yourself with matters that are beyond you;

even what has been shown you is above man's grasp.
Many have been led astray by their speculations,
and false conjectures have impaired their judgement.

(Ecclus. 3: 21–4)

Ecclesiasticus urges respect for the Jewish law (which is
equated with wisdom) and for the priesthood; above all he
praises the scholar who studies the law, of whom he gives a
portrait in 39: 1–11. The author himself, according to the
prologue, 'had applied himself industriously to the study of
the law, the prophets, and the other writings of our ancestors',
and he may have been an earlier member of the Hasidaeans
who supported the Maccabaean movement (see 1 Macc. 2: 42
and the note on that verse).

Behind the Maccabaean struggle, then, lay factors like
these – the rival claims of Syria and Egypt to Judaea, the particular status within an empire of Jewish law, the influence of
the Greek world on Jewish society, the rival families and loyal-
ties within Judaea, the growing division in Judaea between
rich and poor, rulers and people, often parallel with the division between hellenizers and orthodox. In such a situation
trouble could begin very easily.

THE DATING OF EVENTS IN 1 AND 2 MACCABEES

Some events are described by both 1 and 2 Maccabees, but
they are not always easy to date, because, first, the two books
do not always give the same order of events, and secondly,
the two books use slightly different dating systems. Both books
date events by 'the Greek era' (1 Macc. 1: 10), which began
with the start of the reign of Seleucus I. But there were two
ways of reckoning this:

(1) the official Syrian usage (the 'Seleucid' era). This
counted the years from the first day of the month Dios (October) 312 B.C. This is followed, at least in the dating of some
events, by 1 Maccabees;

(2) the traditional Babylonian usage (the 'Babylonian' era). This counted the years from the first day of Nisan (April) 311 B.C. The Jews followed this usage, though their calendar varied by a few days from the Babylonian calendar. This system is used in 2 Maccabees, and also in 1 Maccabees when the author was drawing on Jewish, not Syrian, archives. These dates may be those given in 1 Macc. 1: 20, 29, 54, 59; 2: 70; 4: 52; 7: 43; 9: 3, 54; 10: 21; 13: 41, 51; 14: 27; 16: 14.

The months are sometimes numbered, and this helps us decide which system is in use. Thus 1 Macc. 10: 21 mentions the Feast of Tabernacles in the seventh month of year 160. As this feast takes place in autumn, clearly the 'Babylonian' era is being used here. Apart from numbers, the months are referred to by Jewish or Greek names, which are given below:

1	Nisan	Artemisios	(approx. April)
2	Iyyar	Daisios	(May)
3	Sivan	Panemos	(June)
4	Tammuz	Loos	(July)
5	Ab	Gorpiaios	(August)
6	Elul★	Hyperberetaios	(September)
7	Tishri	Dios	(October)
8	Marchesvan	Apellaios	(November)
9	Kislev★	Audynaios	(December)
10	Tebeth	Peritios	(January)
11	Shebat★	Dystros★	(February)
12	Adar★	Xanthicus★	(March)

Names actually used in 1 and 2 Maccabees are asterisked.

A further aid to certain dates is found in the first-century A.D. Jewish writing, the *Megillath Ta'anith*, the 'Scroll of Fasting', which lists days (and the events commemorated on them) on which fasting was not allowed. The following dates relevant to 1 and 2 Maccabees are mentioned:

23 Iyyar: the sons (i.e. men) of the citadel left Jerusalem (cp. 1 Macc. 13: 51)

27 Iyyar: the crown-tax was withdrawn from Judah and Jerusalem (cp. 1 Macc. 13: 39)

17 Sivan: the tower of Sur was captured (perhaps the capture of Bethsura is meant, cp. 1 Macc. 11: 66)

23 Marchesvan: the *sirouga* was hidden away from the temple court (cp. 1 Macc. 4: 43-6)

3 Kislev: the *simoth* were taken out of the temple court (cp. 1 Macc. 4: 43-6)

25 Kislev: the eight days of Hanukkah begin (cp. 1 Macc. 4: 52)

28 Shebat: King Antiochus left Jerusalem (cp. 1 Macc. 6: 63)

13 Adar: the day of Nicanor (cp. 1 Macc. 7: 49; 2 Macc. 15: 36)

28 Adar: the Jews heard the good news that keeping the commands of the law was no longer forbidden (cp. 2 Macc. 11: 25)

(The meaning of *sirouga* and *simoth* is uncertain, but they are probably connected with the defiled altar of burnt offering.)

THE SYRIAN ADMINISTRATION

1 and 2 Maccabees contain several references to various officials of the Syrian empire, and a description of its administration may be found helpful.

The empire was divided into provinces called 'satrapies', a name inherited from the Persian administration (cp. 2 Macc. 9: 25). Among these were Cilicia (2 Macc. 4: 36), Persia (1 Macc. 3: 31), Media (see the note on 2 Macc. 9: 3), the 'upper provinces' (which perhaps included the lower regions of Mesopotamia and Babylonia as well as the higher regions of Persia and Media, 1 Macc. 3: 37), Syria Seleucis (northern Syria, around Antioch), and the province we hear most of, Coele-syria and Phoenicia. Most of these provinces will be found on the maps on pp. 79 and 146. These provinces were

ruled by 'governors' (Greek *strategoi*, 2 Macc. 4: 4), and for
Coele-syria and Phoenicia we know of four by name: under
Seleucus IV, Apollonius (2 Macc. 4: 4), under Antiochus IV,
Ptolemaeus son of Dorymenes (2 Macc. 4: 45 ff.) and Ptole-
maeus Macron (2 Macc. 10: 11 ff.), and under Demetrius I,
Bacchides (1 Macc. 7: 8).

The province was subdivided into 'eparchies' – probably
the regions of Phoenicia, Coele-syria, Idumaea (of which
Gorgias was *strategos*, 2 Macc. 12: 32) and 'the coastal zone'
(of which Simon was made *strategos*, 1 Macc. 11: 59, and later
Kendebaeus *epistrategos*, 1 Macc. 15: 38) or possibly Transjordan. These eparchies in turn were subdivided into 'parts'
(Greek *merides*), each governed by a 'meridarch'; thus Apollonius was meridarch of Samaria (cp. 1 Macc. 3: 10 ff., Josephus,
Antiquities XII. 5. 5) and Jonathan became meridarch of Judaea
(1 Macc. 10: 65). Below them were more local governors; we
hear of Philip and Andronicus, the 'commissioners' (Greek
epistatai) of Jerusalem and Mount Gerizim (2 Macc. 5: 22).
Presumably there were administrative officials in charge of
'toparchies' such as the three districts of Samaria (1 Macc.
11: 34).

Alongside the civil administration was the army; indeed, the
civil administrator often had military rank as well. We hear
of an army officer Seron (1 Macc. 3: 13) and of the 'distinguished commander' Nicanor (1 Macc. 7: 26), of mercenary
troop commanders (2 Macc. 4: 29; 12: 2) and commanders
of the elephant corps (2 Macc. 14: 12), and of the garrison
commander in Jerusalem, Sostratus (2 Macc. 4: 29). But
Nicanor could be made a *strategos* of Judaea (2 Macc. 14: 12),
Bacchides was governor of a province (1 Macc. 7: 8), Gorgias
of an eparchy (2 Macc. 12: 32), and Apollonius was a meridarch (1 Macc. 3: 10), yet all these led troops in the field, as
might the king and his chief minister in person.

At the head of the empire was the king, assisted by his
Friends. The Friends had their own internal hierarchy; thus
Alexander enrolled Jonathan 'in the first class of the order'

9

(1 Macc. 10: 65), and Demetrius II later 'appointed him head of the first class' (1 Macc. 11: 27). Friends closest to the king might be called 'the King's Kinsmen' (cp. 1 Macc. 10: 89; 11: 31 f.) or 'intimate friend' (2 Macc. 9: 29). From these Friends might be selected the chief ministers of state, men like Heliodorus, the 'chief minister' (2 Macc. 3: 7). The 'minister' Andronicus was left as 'regent' when Antiochus IV went to Cilicia (2 Macc. 4: 31), and later Lysias is similarly left as 'viceroy of the territories between the Euphrates and the Egyptian frontier' (1 Macc. 3: 32) or as 'vicegerent' (2 Macc. 11: 1) and as 'guardian' of the heir to the throne. The Friend Philip was appointed 'regent over his whole empire' (1 Macc. 6: 14).

ANCIENT WRITERS WHO DESCRIBE THIS PERIOD

1 and 2 Maccabees are not the only ancient books which describe the achievements of the Maccabees or the political history of this period. We have other sources, both Jewish and Greek, with which to compare the material found in 1 and 2 Maccabees. The most important are the following:

(1) *The Book of Daniel.* It is now generally agreed that this book was written at the height of the Maccabaean struggle, shortly before the death of Antiochus. It uses stories and legends about an ancient figure called Daniel, and the literary device of the vision, to encourage men to resist Antiochus. The kingdoms of this world, including his, will soon be swept away by the arrival of God's kingdom (cp. Dan. 2: 44). 'The kingly power, sovereignty, and greatness of all the kingdoms under heaven shall be given to the people of the saints of the Most High' (7: 27) – that is, to the Jews.

Certain passages refer particularly to Antiochus, who is seen as an arrogant persecutor of the Jews who will be punished by God (7: 24–5; 8: 23 ff.; 9: 26–7), but in ch. 11 Daniel hears from an angel a summary of events from the rise of Alexander the Great to the death of Antiochus. No names are given, but on the whole the details are quite recognizable. The kings of Egypt and Syria are respectively 'the king of the south' and 'the king of the north', and their rivalry in the third and second century B.C. is accurately described. Verses 2–9 deal with third-century B.C. wars and diplomacy; verses 10–19 with Antiochus III, his victory over Egypt and defeat by Rome. Verse 20 refers to the events of 2 Macc. 3, in the reign of Seleucus IV. Verses 21–39 describe in some detail the reign of Antiochus IV and parallel closely much of the material in 1 and 2 Maccabees. Verses 40–5 picture the end of Antiochus, but the picture does not agree with what we learn from 1 and 2 Maccabees, and it is probable that the author of Daniel was here looking ahead and guessing.

Not all the allusions in Dan. 11, however, are clear, and the reader should consult the commentary on Daniel in this series for further information. 1 Macc. 2: 60 refers to the story of Daniel in the lions' pit (cp. Dan. 6), and the famous phrase 'the abomination of desolation' (1 Macc. 1: 54) may be taken from Dan. 11: 31.

(2) *Josephus*. See the note under 'The footnotes to the N.E.B. text' on p. ix above. There is a short account of the Maccabaean period in the *Jewish War* I. 1–2, which perhaps follows the work of Herod the Great's court historian, Nicolaus of Damascus, who in turn was following 1 Maccabees and Polybius (see below).

Much more important to us is the *Jewish Antiquities*, written about A.D. 93. Books XII and XIII cover the period from Alexander the Great to the death of Queen Alexandra in 67 B.C. The main source used by Josephus is 1 Maccabees, at least until the death of Jonathan is reached. Whether Josephus used the final chapters (13–16) of 1 Maccabees is disputed. If he did not, was it because he had no copy of these chapters? If he did possess these chapters, did other sources seem more important to him? His other sources again included Polybius and Nicolaus, and occasionally the geographer Strabo.

(3) *Polybius*. Polybius was a Peloponnesian Greek (208–

127 B.C.), who was deported to Rome in 168 B.C. He wrote a 'Universal History', covering the period from 220 to 145 B.C., but out of forty books only the first five survive. This is unfortunate for us, for Polybius was a personal friend of Demetrius I, and helped him escape from Rome in 161 B.C. (see the note on 1 Macc. 7: 1–4).

(4) *Diodorus Siculus.* Diodorus (about 80–20 B.C.) came from Sicily and wrote a 'library of history' in forty volumes. Books XXI–XL dealt with events from 301 to 61 B.C., but little is left; there are fragments about Antiochus IV and Demetrius I in Book XXXI, and about Demetrius II and Trypho in Book XXXIII. But Diodorus is not always reliable.

(5) *The Dead Sea Scrolls.* It is possible that some of the material found at Qumran has a bearing on the events of the Maccabaean period. The site of Qumran was occupied for a short period in the mid-second century B.C. – the beginning of this occupation is variously dated by scholars from about 165 B.C. to about 130 B.C. The origins of the community are often connected with the disillusionment of the Hasidaeans (see the note on 1 Macc. 2: 42) with the high-priesthood first of Alcimus and then of Jonathan, in 161 and 152 B.C. respectively. If this is the case, we might find references to persons and events of the Maccabaean age in the writings which come from Qumran, especially in the community's biblical commentaries, such as that on Habakkuk, and in the description of the community's origin in the 'Damascus Document'. In particular, Jonathan has often been cast for the role of the 'Wicked Priest' (cp. the note on 1 Macc. 10: 21). But much here is still obscure, and it is dangerous to rely too heavily on allusions in the Qumran literature for help in filling out the details of 1 and 2 Maccabees. On Qumran the reader should consult the companion volumes to this series, especially *The Making of the Old Testament*, pp. 101–4, and *Old Testament Illustrations*, pp. 139–40.

N.B. The books known as 3 and 4 Maccabees do not in fact describe the history of the Maccabees. 3 Maccabees tells

how Jews in Egypt in about 217 B.C. were rescued mira-
culously from being trampled on by elephants which Ptolemy
IV had deliberately turned on them. Josephus tells a similar
story about Ptolemy IX, Lathyrus. The book, like Esther and
2 Maccabees, ends in the institution of a festival. 4 Maccabees
uses material from 2 Maccabees, especially the stories of
Eleazar and the seven brothers, to demonstrate that reason
must triumph over emotion. Both books probably come
from Alexandria in the last century B.C. or the first century
A.D. and are not included in the Apocrypha.

THE FIRST BOOK OF THE

MACCABEES

✳ ✳ ✳ ✳ ✳ ✳ ✳ ✳ ✳ ✳ ✳ ✳ ✳

THE ORIGINAL TEXT AND ITS DATE

The book has been preserved for us in several ancient languages. Our oldest manuscript containing it is the Codex Sinaiticus, originally a Bible written in Greek for fourth-century Christians in Egypt. Another Greek Bible, the Codex Alexandrinus, from fifth-century Alexandria, and the Codex Venetus from the eighth or ninth century also contain 1 Maccabees. These manuscripts are in 'uncial' (i.e. capital) letters. There are also later Greek manuscripts written in a cursive hand, most of which show the influence of the revision of the Septuagint text by Lucian of Antioch in A.D. 312; one, however, may be derived from an earlier text. The Latin version of 1 Maccabees is not from the hand of Jerome, who about A.D. 400 produced the Latin Vulgate, but from the 'Old Latin' version, which may be ultimately derived from a second-century A.D. Greek text. The Greek was also translated into Syriac; two different versions of this exist. But even if we could reconstruct for certain what the text was in the third century A.D., that still leaves about three centuries or more of the text's transmission, about which we know virtually nothing, before we get back to the earliest Greek text.

But the Greek text, it seems, was itself a translation from the original Hebrew version (which no longer exists). The Christian scholar Origen (died A.D. 254) notes that the Maccabaean books bore a title *Sarbeth Sabanaiel*, perhaps an Aramaic translation of the original Hebrew title. But its meaning is debated, because the wording seems to have become corrupted, and several restorations of the original are possible. 'Prince' (or 'Book') 'of the house of Sabaniel' is a starting point; but who was Sabaniel? For his name, therefore, some restore 'Israel' or 'the Hasmonaeans' (this being the family to which Mattathias and his sons belonged). Within the book itself the strange name 'Asaramel' (14: 28) makes us suspect that the Greek translator did not always understand his Hebrew original. The book is certainly written in a Hebrew style, which was modelled on that of the historical books of the Old Testament such as 1 and 2 Samuel and 1 and 2 Kings. This is less clear in the N.E.B. than in the Greek translation, but the N.E.B. does reveal the Hebrew nature of the poetic passages (see, e.g., 1: 25-8, 37-40).

THE AUTHOR'S APPROACH TO THE WORK

The author's Jewish background is abundantly clear from his use of the Old Testament. 1 Macc. 2: 52-60 contains a list of Old Testament men of faith from Abraham to Daniel; Judas and his battles are described in terms which remind us of Saul and David and the battles against the Philistines in 1 and 2 Samuel (see, e.g., the notes on 3: 10-24, 42-60). The poetic passages (1: 25-8, 37-40; 2: 7-11; 3: 3-9, 45) and 14: 4-15 (which may also be poetry) are full of Old Testament allusion. Respect is shown to the idea of prophecy, whose day is past (9: 27), though there is a lively hope that a 'true prophet' will appear (4: 46; 14: 41). But above all the author is concerned with the law and the temple; 'be zealous for the law' is the text and closing thought of the sermon of the dying Mattathias (2: 49-68) and a major theme of the whole book, and the restoration of the temple is equally vital.

Yet the writing is not moralistic or pietistic in style; the author does not openly pass his own judgements on events. Nor does he portray events as controlled by the miraculous intervention of God, whose name, on the whole, he avoids using. In both these features he differs markedly from the author of 2 Maccabees. Jewish confidence in God is quietly but very firmly expressed in Judas' speeches before battle (cp. 3: 18–22, 58–60; 4: 8–11) and in the steady success of the Maccabaean movement which reaches its climax in the person and work of Simon. The author never doubts that the Maccabees are in the right and that the hellenizing party is in the wrong.

The author's use of Hebrew, his attempt to write his history in Old Testament historical style, and the scope of his narrative all show that he was directly motivated by strong nationalistic feelings. For him the trouble began with those in Israel who wanted to ally with the surrounding Gentiles (1: 11). The law and the temple and all that goes with them mark off the Jew from the Gentile, and the book shows how the re-establishment of the law and the temple go hand in hand with the re-establishment of the nation. This emphasis is clearly shown in the inscription dedicated to Simon (14: 27–49): Simon and his family 'risked their lives...in order that the temple and law might be preserved, and they brought great glory to their nation. Jonathan rallied the nation... Then Simon came forward and fought for his nation...When the people saw Simon's patriotism and his resolution to win fame for his nation, they made him their leader and high priest.' And further, as 5: 62 shows, the author believes that Simon's is the only 'family to whom it was granted to bring deliverance to Israel'.

THE HISTORICAL VALUE OF I MACCABEES

Such strong beliefs will certainly affect a historian's presentation of his subject, and the modern historian of the Maccabaean age must ask himself, 'How trustworthy is I Maccabees as a source for these events?' In fact, I Maccabees' sober account of events has won much respect from historians; if it does not contain the whole truth, it contains enough of it for a fairly clear picture of these years to be reconstructed. The author is careful with dating, and apparently well informed.

Interestingly, a comparison of 1 Maccabees with 2 Maccabees shows both how much other material of historical value might have been included (see especially 2 Macc. 3–5) and how much pious legend 1 Maccabees omitted (e.g. 2 Macc. 6: 18 – 7: 42). The author does not turn Jewish defeats into victories, as 2 Maccabees does (compare 2 Macc. 13: 9–24). Like other ancient authors, the author of 1 Maccabees was not in a position to give us the actual words of any speaker; he had no tape-recorder and relied on the memories of men who were probably not all first-hand witnesses. He can only give us the gist of what was said, or invent some suitable speech. More difficult to assess are the documents he quotes. He refers to 'annals', at least for the time of John Hyrcanus (16: 24), and he may have been able to draw on similar archives for previous years. He quotes or refers to the following documents (for detailed explanation the reader should see the commentary on each):

(1)	8: 23–30	Jewish–Roman treaty terms
(2)	8: 31–2	A Roman letter to Demetrius I
(3)	10: 18–20	Alexander's letter to Jonathan
(4)	10: 25–45	Demetrius I's offer to the Jews
(5)	11: 30–7	Demetrius I's letter to Jonathan, enclosing a copy of Demetrius' letter to Lasthenes
(6)	11: 57	Antiochus VI writes to Jonathan
(7)	12: 4	Roman letters to local authorities
(8)	12: 5–18	Jonathan's letter to Sparta
(9)	12: 19–23	Sparta's letter to Onias
(10)	13: 36–40	Demetrius II's letter to Simon
(11)	14: 20–3	Sparta's letter to Simon
(12)	14: 27–47	Jewish inscription dedicated to Simon
(13)	15: 2–9	Antiochus VII's letter to Simon
(14)	15: 15–21	Letter of Lucius, Roman consul, to Ptolemy and others.

Not all these are equally reliable. No. 4 has suspicious features (see the commentary), and so have nos. 8, 9, 11 (the Spartan correspondence). Nos. 1 and 14, which involve Rome, have certain problems of dating to be considered, though much of the phrasing, in no. 1 especially, seems to have a genuine Roman background. The various letters between Syria and the Jews are difficult to evaluate. In general, their contents are realistic, and the author of 1 Maccabees may here be using genuine archives. How much he has 'touched up' the letters we do not know. But we must remember that these letters, probably written originally in Greek or Aramaic, were translated by the author of 1 Maccabees into Hebrew, then re-translated into Greek – not necessarily into the original Greek.

THE AUTHOR

Finally, what sort of person was the author of 1 Maccabees? We do not know his name (we do not in fact know the name of many of the writers of the Old Testament or Apocrypha). What we have already said about his work suggests that he was an educated Jew, working probably in Jerusalem. He appears to be a little more interested in the political and military aspects than the religious; it has often been noted that he does not show the strict attitude to the sabbath or the interest in the resurrection shown by 2 Maccabees, and that he does not criticize the hellenizing high priests Jason and Menelaus as 2 Maccabees does. He perhaps sympathized, then, more with the Sadducean tradition than with the Hasidaean and Pharisaic tradition, more with the political rulers of his day than with the pietistic movements. But he was not a cynical academic. Though he criticizes, he never sneers. He was a man of judgement and ability who has made an important contribution to our knowledge of a complicated but interesting period of history.

✷　　✷　　✷　　✷　　✷　　✷　　✷　　✷　　✷　　✷　　✷　　✷　　✷

Antiochus and the Jewish revolt

THE HELLENISTIC BACKGROUND

ALEXANDER of Macedon, the son of Philip, marched **1**
from the land of Kittim, defeated Darius, king of
Persia and Media, and seized his throne, being already
king of Greece.[a] In the course of many campaigns he cap- **2**
tured fortified towns, slaughtered kings, traversed the **3**
earth to its remotest bounds, and plundered innumerable
nations. When at last the world lay quiet under his rule,
his pride knew no limits; he built up an extremely power- **4**
ful army, and ruled over countries, nations, and dominions; all paid him tribute.

The time came when he fell ill, and, knowing that he **5**
was dying, he summoned his generals, nobles who had **6**
been brought up with him from childhood, and divided
his empire among them while he was still alive. Alexander **7**
had reigned twelve years when he died. His generals took **8**
over the government, each in his own province. On his **9**
death they were all crowned as kings, and their descendants succeeded them for many years. They brought untold miseries upon the world.

✳ These verses summarize 136 years of Near-Eastern power
politics with a bias to the effect that the Jews' troubles are to
be blamed entirely on the Greeks. Alexander the Great
(356–323 B.C.) began his conquest of Persia in 334 B.C. By
331 B.C. he controlled modern Turkey, Syria and Egypt; by

[a] being...Greece: *probable meaning; Gk. obscure.*

325 B.C. he had reached India; in 323 B.C. he died at Babylon. His conquests and settlements improved communications between East and West, though Greek influence was visible in Judaea before his coming (see pp. 2 f.). In 312 B.C. Seleucus took Babylon and later Syria, while Ptolemy took Egypt. The Greek era (verse 10) is really the Seleucid era, beginning with 312 B.C. Seleucus and Ptolemy and their successors disputed possession of Judaea, which lay between them; the story is told in Dan. 11 (see p. 10). Control of Judaea finally passed to the Seleucid king Antiochus III in 198 B.C., and it is with the Jews under his successors (for whom see p. xi) that 1 and 2 Maccabees are concerned.

1. *Philip* II of Macedon (359–336 B.C.) conquered Greece in 338 B.C. and prepared to attack his major enemy, Persia. He was assassinated in 336 B.C., and his son Alexander 'the Great' magnificently effected Philip's plans. The *Kittim*, originally a people from Cyprus, are used in the Old Testament for various conquerors from the west; *the land of Kittim* here means Macedon. *Media* was the mountain region south of the Caspian Sea.

3. *his pride knew no limits* may refer to Alexander's readiness to be worshipped as a god.

5 f. *divided his empire:* Alexander died so suddenly that this is unlikely; in fact, the generals took what they could get.

7. *reigned twelve years:* actually, from 336 to 323 B.C.

9. *untold miseries* reflects the strongly nationalistic view of Jews who suffered from the hellenizing policy of their rulers in Jerusalem and Antioch. The Ptolemies and Seleucids were not entirely bad, but their policy (for which see pp. 1–6) probably helped the towns and tradesmen more than the country and its peasants. In Judaea the revolt began in the country village of Modin. ✲

ANTIOCHUS AND THE HELLENISTS

A scion of this stock was that wicked man, Antiochus 10 Epiphanes, son of King Antiochus. He had been a hostage in Rome before he succeeded to the throne in the year 137 of the Greek era.[a]

At that time there appeared in Israel a group of rene- 11 gade Jews, who incited the people. 'Let us enter into a covenant with the Gentiles round about,' they said, 'because disaster upon disaster has overtaken us since we segregated ourselves from them.' The people thought this 12 a good argument, and some of them in their enthusiasm 13 went to the king and received authority to introduce non-Jewish laws and customs. They built a sports-stadium in 14 the gentile style in Jerusalem. They removed their marks 15 of circumcision and repudiated the holy covenant. They intermarried with Gentiles, and abandoned themselves to evil ways.

✷ The author sees Antiochus Epiphanes as another Alexander, attempting to unify his empire (see verse 41 below). Thus he leaps straight from Alexander to Antiochus, omitting important details, some of which are preserved in 2 Macc. 3 and 4. Alongside the *wicked* Antiochus, however, as a second immediate cause of the Jews' troubles, the author describes the *renegade Jews*, who have independently *appeared in Israel* with a new political policy for Israel. The author oversimplifies this, by emphasizing its *non-Jewish* influence on Israel's religion (verses 13 ff.).

10. The Seleucid king *Antiochus IV* (175–164 B.C.), *son of King Antiochus* III, used the title *Theos Epiphanes*, 'God Manifest', on some of his coins, but there is little evidence to suggest

[a] *That is* 175 B.C.

that Antiochus attached much importance to his divine status or used it to unite his empire in worship of him. The title was often simply 'Epiphanes', which may mean little more than 'Illustrious'.

Rome had made him a *hostage* for the behaviour of his father after the Peace of Apamea in 188 B.C.

11. The *group of renegade* hellenizers are shown as a minority who *incited the people*, who later 'thronged to their side in large numbers' (verse 52), but would otherwise have remained loyal and orthodox. The new policy was to end the segregation of Jew and Gentile so forcibly demanded by Ezra and Nehemiah nearly three centuries earlier. What *disaster upon disaster* refers to is not clear, for Persian and Greek rulers had on the whole respected the Jews. Antiochus III had praised Jewish subjects settled in Babylon for their loyalty, and had respected Jewish law. Probably the hellenizers appealed to the hope of improved economic circumstances from closer links with other peoples: the hellenizers were men like Hyrcanus, son of Joseph, of the developing merchant class (see p. 4).

13. *some...went to the king:* see 2 Macc. 4: 7–17. Their leader was Jason, brother of the high priest Onias.

14. The *sports-stadium* was the training ground for the citizens of a Greek city-state; its introduction to Jerusalem implied not just a new way of life but a new political constitution, that of a Greek city-state with a citizen body and council. This would give Jerusalem a higher status and greater opportunities for trade and contact with other cities within the Syrian empire.

15. Under this new constitution, *circumcision*, sabbath-keeping and segregation from the Gentiles were no longer demanded. A Jew could still practise the Law of Moses, but the Law of Moses was no longer the law governing Jerusalem. Thus the *covenant* between God and Israel for which the Mosaic Law provided the terms was *repudiated* in the eyes of non-hellenizing Jews. *intermarried with* might also be translated 'allied with', and to Antiochus there was a great advantage in

having a hellenized ally in Jerusalem as a bulwark against
Egypt (this factor lies behind Antiochus' visit to Joppa and
Jerusalem described in 2 Macc. 4: 21 ff.). *

ANTIOCHUS IN EGYPT

When he was firmly established on his throne, Antio- 16
chus made up his mind to become king of Egypt and so to
rule over both kingdoms. He assembled a powerful force 17
of chariots, elephants, and cavalry, and a great fleet, and
invaded Egypt. When battle was joined, Ptolemy king of 18
Egypt was seized with panic and took to flight, leaving
many dead. The fortified towns were captured and the 19
land pillaged.

* These events are cryptically described in Dan. 11: 25–7.
In 172 B.C. Ptolemy VI, a minor, was enthroned in Egypt. In
170 B.C., his guardians, on the grounds that Palestine had been
promised to Egypt as the dowry of Antiochus IV's sister,
Cleopatra, on her marriage to Ptolemy V but never given,
declared war on Syria. Antiochus sent a diplomat to Rome to
present his case, and invaded Egypt (169 B.C.).

16. *to rule over both kingdoms* had always been the aim of
both Egyptian and Syrian rulers. Twenty-four years later
Ptolemy VI himself briefly 'wore two crowns' (see 11: 13).

17. The Syrian army's elephants are mentioned several
times; the Persians used Indian elephants against Alexander
in 331 B.C., and Hannibal of Carthage used African elephants
against Rome (218–202 B.C.); after his defeat, Hannibal went
to the court of Antiochus III.

18. Antiochus caught Ptolemy, and finally left him king at
Memphis and a rival king in Alexandria.

19. Antiochus failed to take Alexandria, but he left a Syrian
garrison at Pelusium on the coast between Egypt and Palestine. *

ANTIOCHUS ROBS THE TEMPLE

20 On his return from the conquest of Egypt, in the year
143,[a] Antiochus marched with a strong force against
21 Israel and Jerusalem. In his arrogance he entered the temple
and carried off the golden altar, the lamp-stand with all its
22 equipment, the table for the Bread of the Presence, the
sacred cups and bowls, the golden censers, the curtain, and
the crowns. He stripped off all the gold plating from the
23 temple front. He seized the silver, gold, and precious
24 vessels, and whatever secret treasures he found, and took
them all with him when he left for his own country. He
had caused much bloodshed, and he gloated over all he
had done.

25   Great was the lamentation throughout Israel;
26   rulers and elders groaned in bitter grief,
    Girls and young men languished;
    the beauty of our women was disfigured.
27   Every bridegroom took up the lament,
    and every bride sat grieving in her chamber.
28   The land trembled for its inhabitants,
    and all the house of Jacob was wrapped in shame.

✵ 1 Maccabees dates this event (cp. Dan. 11: 28) after Antiochus' first Egyptian campaign in 169 B.C.; 2 Macc. 5: 15–21
dates it (wrongly) a year later. Antiochus was not at war with
Judaea; but the high priest Menelaus probably owed him
tribute. He needed money to pay his army, and he was following the practice of Seleucus IV (see 2 Macc. 3) and his father
Antiochus III (who died robbing a temple). Temples were an

[a] *That is* 169 B.C.

obvious target with their sacred vessels and the deposits made
by rich men like Hyrcanus (2 Macc. 3: 10–11).

21. *arrogance:* Antiochus' attitude is similarly described in
Dan. 7: 8, 25. His father, himself a Gentile, had decreed that
no foreigner should enter the sanctuary's precincts. But in a
Greek city, such as Jerusalem now was (technically, at least),
a visiting king's presence in the city temple would cause no
surprise. The *golden altar* (of incense) and the other equipment
and furnishings of the temple are described in Exod. 39: 32 ff.,
and 1 Kings 6: 2–36. Antiochus' theft was later made good
by Judas (4: 49).

22. The *crowns* were probably memorial offerings or diplomatic gifts laid up in the temple (for such a diplomatic gift
see 13: 37).

24. *much bloodshed:* but in fact there was no bloodshed in
Jerusalem on this occasion. The phrase may refer generally to
Antiochus' whole campaign, or, by confusion, to his second
campaign (2 Macc. 5: 11 ff.), or may exaggerate Antiochus'
evil deeds.

25. *lamentation:* the destruction of Jerusalem and her temple
in 586 B.C. had evoked the book of Lamentations; so here the
author introduces a similar song of lament. Compare also
verses 37–40; 2: 7–11; 3: 45. For a prose description of the
feeling raised by the proposed robbery of the temple by
Heliodorus, see 2 Macc. 3: 14–21.

27. *bridegroom...bride:* Jer. 7: 34 speaks of the silencing of
the voices of bride and groom in the day of Jerusalem's ruin. ✳

THE OCCUPATION OF JERUSALEM

Two years later, the king sent to the towns of Judaea a 29
high revenue official, who arrived at Jerusalem with a
powerful force. His language was friendly, but full of 30
guile. For, once he had gained the city's confidence, he

suddenly attacked it. He dealt it a heavy blow, and killed
31 many Israelites, plundering the city and setting it ablaze.
32 He pulled down houses and walls on every side; women
and children were made prisoners, and the cattle seized.

33 The city of David was turned into a citadel, enclosed by
34 a high, stout wall with strong towers, and garrisoned by
impious foreigners and renegades. Having made them-
35 selves secure, they accumulated arms and provisions, and
deposited there the massed plunder of Jerusalem. There
36 they lay in ambush, a lurking threat to the temple and a
perpetual menace to Israel.

37 They shed the blood of the innocent round the temple;
they defiled the holy place.
38 The citizens of Jerusalem fled for fear of them;
she became the abode of aliens,
and alien herself to her offspring;
her children deserted her.
39 Her temple lay desolate as a wilderness;
her feasts were turned to mourning,
her sabbaths to a reproach,
her honour to contempt.
40 The shame of her fall matched the greatness of her
renown,
and her pride was bowed low in grief.

∗ Between the robbing of the temple and the events now
related much has happened which 1 Maccabees passes over.
In 168 B.C. Antiochus fought a second campaign in Egypt (cp.
2 Macc. 5: 1) which ended abruptly when the Roman legate
in person ordered Antiochus to withdraw (cp. Dan. 11: 30).
Meanwhile in Jerusalem something like civil war had been

raging (see 2 Macc. 5: 5–10), and Antiochus, thinking that Judaea had rebelled (there were always Egyptian sympathizers in Jerusalem, such as the high priest Onias), on his return from Egypt took Jerusalem, and much blood was shed (2 Macc. 5: 11–14, Dan. 11: 30). Antiochus returned to Antioch leaving commissioners in Jerusalem (2 Macc. 5: 21 ff.). At this point we turn to 1 Macc. 1: 29 ff., which describes the punishment of Jerusalem for rebellion.

29. *Two years later:* in fact, 168 B.C. *high revenue official:* the underlying Hebrew phrase *sar ham-missim* was perhaps a mistake for the Hebrew *sar ham-mussim*; cp. 2 Macc. 5: 24, 'the general of the Mysian mercenaries' (from north-west Asia Minor). The officer's name was Apollonius (2 Macc. 5: 24).

30. The most likely reason for Apollonius' behaviour is that between Antiochus' departure and Apollonius' arrival the opponents of the hellenizing party had gained control of the city, at least in part. Alternatively, Apollonius is completing Antiochus' earlier suppression. In either case his task was to give control of Jerusalem to the hellenizing party, and this involved the use of considerable force (verses 31–2). If 'high revenue official' is right, Apollonius perhaps introduced new forms of taxation, perhaps those mentioned in 10: 29–30, to replace the arrangements made with Menelaus (2 Macc. 4: 24).

33–4. The *city of David*, originally the hill of Ophel south of the temple, was by now the name for the area west of the temple. This, or part of it, became a walled *citadel* (the building of it probably took some months and lasted into spring, 167 B.C.) garrisoned by Jewish hellenists (*renegades*) and Syrian soldiers (*impious foreigners*). This garrison changed not only the political but also the religious situation in Jerusalem. Some scholars think the citadel itself was the new city of Jerusalem; but in any case both Jewish hellenists and Syrian garrison soldiers would expect to worship in the city's temple, and 2 Macc. 6: 4–7 describes the nature of their activities there, as much Syrian as Jewish.

35. This garrison, like others, was clearly maintained at local expense; later, there was a threat to allot land to its members (3: 36). After many attempts, military and diplomatic, to oust it, the garrison was finally removed in 141 B.C. (13: 49 ff.).

37–40: a lament (cp. verses 25–7) full of allusions to Old Testament passages, designed to make the reader feel the magnitude of the disaster and the shame of Jerusalem's new situation.

37. The verse comments on the events of verses 20–36, in words similar to those of Ps. 79: 1–3:

> O God, the heathen have set foot in thy domain,
>> defiled thy holy temple
>> and laid Jerusalem in ruins...
> Their blood is spilled all round Jerusalem like water.

38. *abode of aliens:* cp. the complaint in Lam. 5: 2. *deserted her:* if this is not just poetic exaggeration, by then already citizens had fled: 2 Macc. 5: 27 puts the flight of Judas and his companions to the desert at this point.

39. *her feasts...mourning:* cp. Amos 8: 10,

> I will turn your pilgrim-feasts into mourning
> and all your songs into lamentation.

40. Cp. Lam. 1: 6,

> All majesty has vanished
>> from the daughter of Zion. ✳

ANTIOCHUS' DECREE

41 The king then issued a decree throughout his empire:
42 his subjects were all to become one people and abandon their own laws and religion. The nations everywhere complied with the royal command, and many in Israel ac-
43 cepted the foreign worship, sacrificing to idols and profan-

ing the sabbath. Moreover, the king sent agents with 44
written orders to Jerusalem and the towns of Judaea. Ways
and customs foreign to the country were to be introduced.
Burnt-offerings, sacrifices, and libations in the temple 45
were forbidden; sabbaths and feast-days were to be profaned; the temple and its ministers to be defiled. Altars, 46,47
idols, and sacred precincts were to be established; swine
and other unclean beasts to be offered in sacrifice. They 48
must leave their sons uncircumcised; they must make themselves in every way abominable, unclean, and profane,
and so forget the law and change all their statutes. The 49,50
penalty for disobedience was death.

Such was the decree which the king issued to all his 51
subjects. He appointed superintendents over all the people,
and instructed the towns of Judaea to offer sacrifice, town
by town. People thronged to their side in large numbers, 52
every one of them a traitor to the law. Their wicked conduct throughout the land drove Israel into hiding in every 53
possible place of refuge.

* Why did Antiochus deliberately outlaw religious practices
such as sacrifice, sabbath-keeping, circumcision, which with the
temple, the priesthood and the law had been since the exile
the hallmark of Judaism over against other nations? The
hellenizing Jews wanted to remove Jewish exclusivism (cp. 1:
11) and therefore needed to remove the symbols of it. Antiochus, however, was a cultured Greek, tolerant of foreign
beliefs, and his motives for such a decree were surely political.
In his eyes, the Jewish people, opposing the hellenizing party,
were rebellious, and rebellion on the borders of Egypt was
dangerous. The rebellion seemed to be based on the people's
allegiance to their own law and on their rejection of the

constitution agreed on between Antiochus and the hellenizing party. Therefore, the Jewish law must be declared illegal and the Jewish cult made to conform to the city's new constitution.

41. *throughout his empire* is wrong but perhaps reflects the belief of a persecuted community. The decree was aimed solely at the Palestinian Jews, including those of the coastal cities like Ptolemais (cp. 2 Macc. 6: 8). Josephus (*Antiquities* XII. 5. 5) says that the decree applied to the Samaritans also, who promptly disclaimed their Jewishness, but this may be a piece of anti-Samaritan Jewish polemic.

42. *to become one people:* but there is no evidence that Antiochus intended to secure cultural and religious uniformity among his *subjects*. There is perhaps an echo here of the hellenizers' propaganda that the Israelites are to become like the other peoples, and renounce their segregation and abandon their law.

44. Such *Ways and customs* had already been introduced (verses 13-15).

45. The point of the decree was the suppression of the Jewish law, with all it involved.

47. The establishing of *Altars, idols, and sacred precincts* meant the turning of the exclusive Jewish temple courts into a typical gentile sanctuary, an area with a shrine and altar, open to every citizen. The eating of *swine* with *other unclean beasts* is forbidden in the Old Testament (Lev. 11: 7) and such animals could not be offered to God.

48. As this verse shows, we have not the actual words of Antiochus' decree, but only a description of it from one Jewish viewpoint.

51. The *superintendents* perhaps included the Athenian (see 2 Macc. 6: 1) sent to supervise the operation. People were made *to offer sacrifice* as a sign of their loyalty; Antiochus probably had no idea that this was precisely the wrong test of loyalty to propose to a Jew.

52. *People* conformed *in large numbers*; in the towns especially, there was probably a fair measure of sympathy with the

new, liberal, hellenizing ways. From the orthodox standpoint, such people were each *a traitor to the law*.

53. The true *Israel* is restricted to the minority, who go into hiding. ✳

THE DECREE'S EFFECTS

On the fifteenth day of the month Kislev in the year 54 145,*a* 'the abomination of desolation' was set up on the altar. Pagan altars were built throughout the towns of Judaea; incense was offered at the doors of houses and in 55 the streets. All scrolls of the law which were found were 56 torn up and burnt. Anyone discovered in possession of a 57 Book of the Covenant, or conforming to the law, was put to death by the king's sentence. Thus month after 58 month these wicked men used their power against the Israelites whom they found in their towns.

On the twenty-fifth day of the month they offered 59 sacrifice on the pagan altar which was on top of the altar of the Lord. In accordance with the royal decree, they 60 put to death women who had had their children circumcised. Their babies, their families, and those who had 61 circumcised them, they hanged by the neck. Yet many in 62 Israel found strength to resist, taking a determined stand against eating any unclean food. They welcomed death 63 rather than defile themselves and profane the holy covenant, and so they died. The divine wrath raged against 64 Israel.*b*

✳ The author describes the devastating results of the decree which outlawed the Jewish law. The honour in which the

[a] *That is* 167 B.C.
[b] The divine...Israel: *or* Israel lived under a reign of terror.

covenant, the law and the temple were held in this period is shown by the book Ecclesiasticus, whose author thought of the covenant and law as God's wisdom (24: 23) and the temple and its high priest as the medium of God's blessing to Israel (50: 20–1). The hellenizing party were trying to destroy the prestige and Jewishness of both.

54. The decree was issued in summer 167 B.C., and on 7 December (for *Kislev* see p. 7) '*the abomination of desolation*' (*Heb. shiqqus meshomem*) *was set up on the altar*. The *abomination* was perhaps an altar; verse 59 refers to 'the pagan altar which was on top of the altar of the Lord'. The Hebrew phrase (used also in Dan. 12: 11: a Greek version later appears in Mark 13: 14) puns on the Syrian god Baal Shamim (Lord of Heaven) whom the hellenizers could identify with the Jewish God of Heaven (Ezra 7: 12). 2 Macc. 6: 2 says that Antiochus had the Jerusalem sanctuary dedicated to 'Olympian' – i.e. heavenly – 'Zeus'. This was not to introduce a new god (as far as Antiochus was concerned) but rather to give the Jewish God a Greek name. To Antiochus and the hellenizers in Jerusalem Zeus Olympios, Baal Shamim, Zeus God of Hospitality on Mount Gerizim (2 Macc. 6: 2) and the Jewish God of Heaven were identifiable as the same god, under their local names. The general effect and intention was to turn the Jewish worship into something more like the worship of the Greek world.

55. Local altars and street shrines had once been common in Israel (cp. Jer. 44: 15 ff.), but since Josiah's reformation in 621 B.C. sacrificial worship had been restricted to the Jerusalem temple, as the 'Book of the Covenant' (verse 57, here probably the books Genesis–Deuteronomy) demanded, at least in Deut. 12: 1–12.

58. *month after month* suggests monthly visits of inspection, probably on the 'monthly celebration of the king's birthday' (2 Macc. 6: 7). Jewish loyalty was tested by new cultic obligations.

59. 17 December 167 B.C. Such *sacrifice* would be acceptable to the hellenizing, but not to the more conservative, Jews.

32

60. Compare 2 Macc. 6: 10.

62. Clearly, the observation of ritual cleanliness was becoming very difficult, if not impossible.

63. People *died* for their beliefs: see 2 Macc. 6: 18 – 7: 42.

64. The author sees all this as divine punishment on Israel; the N.E.B.'s alternative interpretation of the verse is tempting, but 3: 5 blames the divine wrath against Israel on 'the lawless', i.e. the hellenizing Jews. ✳

THE FAMILY OF MATTATHIAS

At this time a certain Mattathias, son of John, son of **2** Symeon, appeared on the scene. He was a priest of the Joarib family from Jerusalem, who had settled at Modin. Mattathias had five sons, John called Gaddis, Simon called **2, 3** Thassis, Judas called Maccabaeus, Eleazar called Avaran, **4, 5** and Jonathan called Apphus.

✳ The story of Mattathias' reaction to the decree does not appear in 2 Maccabees, but is prominent in 1 Maccabees, whose author favoured the Hasmonaean kings descended from Mattathias.

1. The priestly family of *Joarib* is mentioned in 1 Chron. 9: 10; 24: 1 ff. ('Jehoiarib'). Mattathias was a country priest (cp. John the Baptist's father) who lived at Modin, some 27 km (17 miles) north-west of Jerusalem, and would come up to Jerusalem to perform his day's service in the temple during the week's course allotted to his family.

2. Of his *five sons*, only Jonathan and Simon seem to have used their priestly rights; in fact, they became high priests though they were not of a high-priestly family. But all five died in battle, or by treachery.

3–5. The meaning of the nicknames is not always clear. *Maccabaeus* may mean 'hammer' or 'the name given by the Lord'. ✳

33

MATTATHIAS' LAMENT

6 When Mattathias saw the sacrilegious acts committed in
7 Judaea and Jerusalem, he said:

> 'Oh! Why was I born to see this,
>> the crushing of my people, the ruin of the holy city?
>> They sat idly by when it was surrendered,
>> when the holy place was given up to the alien.

8 Her temple is like a man robbed of honour;
9 its glorious vessels are carried off as spoil.
>> Her infants are slain in the street,
>> her young men by the sword of the foe.

10 Is there a nation that has not usurped her sovereignty,[a]
>> a people that has not plundered her?

11 She has been stripped of all her adornment,
>> no longer free, but a slave.

12 Now that we have seen our temple with all its beauty and
13 splendour laid waste and profaned by the Gentiles, why
14 should we live any longer?' So Mattathias and his sons
tore their garments, put on sackcloth, and mourned
bitterly.

---

* As in the other laments (cp. 1: 25–8, 37–40), any event
of the period referred to in this poem is probably much
coloured by traditional themes of lamentation.

7. *the crushing…the ruin…* perhaps refer in particular to the
events of 1: 29–32. *sat idly by:* the people did not resist the
hellenization of the temple.

9. *spoil:* see 1: 20–3, and 2 Macc. 4: 32; 5: 21. *infants…
slain:* see 1: 61.

[a] *Or* occupied her palaces.

11. Jerusalem is pictured as a beautiful woman, deprived of her children and adornments (verses 9–11); compare Lam. 1: 1, written in similar circumstances:

How solitary lies the city, once so full of people!
Once great among nations, now become a widow;
once queen among provinces, now put to forced labour!

Compare also Lam. 2: 21:

There in the streets young men and old
lie on the ground.
My virgins and my young men have fallen
by sword and by famine;
thou hast slain them in the day of thy anger,
slaughtered them without pity.

14. *tore their garments…sackcloth:* traditional signs of mourning. *

CONFRONTATION AT MODIN

The king's officers who were enforcing apostasy came 15
to the town of Modin to see that sacrifice was offered, and 16
many Israelites went over to them. Mattathias and his sons
stood in a group. The king's officers spoke to Mattathias: 17
'You are a leader here,' they said, 'a man of mark and
influence in this town, with your sons and brothers at
your back. You be the first now to come forward and 18
carry out the king's order. All the nations have done so, as
well as the leading men in Judaea and the people left in
Jerusalem. Then you and your sons will be enrolled
among the King's Friends; you will all receive high
honours, rich rewards of silver and gold, and many further benefits.'

To this Mattathias replied in a ringing voice: 'Though 19
all the nations within the king's dominions obey him and

forsake their ancestral worship, though they have chosen
20 to submit to his commands, yet I and my sons and brothers
21 will follow the covenant of our fathers. Heaven forbid
22 we should ever abandon the law and its statutes. We will
not obey the command of the king, nor will we deviate
one step from our forms of worship.'

23   As soon as he had finished, a Jew stepped forward in
full view of all to offer sacrifice on the pagan altar at
24 Modin, in obedience to the royal command. The sight
stirred Mattathias to indignation; he shook with passion,
and in a fury of righteous anger rushed forward and
25 slaughtered the traitor on the very altar. At the same time
he killed the officer sent by the king to enforce sacrifice,
26 and pulled the pagan altar down. Thus Mattathias showed
his fervent zeal for the law, just as Phinehas had done by
27 killing Zimri son of Salu. 'Follow me,' he shouted through
the town, 'every one of you who is zealous for the law
28 and strives to maintain the covenant.' He and his sons took
to the hills, leaving all their belongings behind in the town.

* According to 1 Maccabees, the flash-point of the Jewish
rebellion was the courageous stand of Mattathias against the
order to show one's loyalty by sacrificing in the new style
away from the temple. The author perhaps dramatizes the
occasion a little, and illustrates its significance for the Jew by
comparing Mattathias' action with that of Phinehas in Num.
25.

15. The *king's officers* are perhaps the deputies of the
'superintendents' of 1: 51.

17. Flattery is followed (verse 18) by persuasion.

18. *All the nations* is an exaggeration, but the reference to
the leading men in Judaea and the people left in Jerusalem indicates

that many influential people had hellenized. Now follows a bribe: for *King's Friends* see pp. 9 f.

19–22. Mattathias' reply emphasizes the traditional Jewish devotion to the *ancestral worship* and the *covenant of our fathers, the law and its statutes* compromised by the hellenizers' attempts to desegregate Judaism and deliberately attacked by the decree.

23. After Mattathias' words, the Jew's action appears not only as apostasy but also as a direct challenge to Mattathias' leadership.

26. Phinehas, grandson of Aaron the priest, had taken decisive action against a man who compromised Israelite exclusivism by having intercourse with a foreign woman who worshipped the Moabite Baal of Peor (Num. 25). The first law of the covenant was 'You shall have no other god to set against me' (Deut. 5: 7), and Deuteronomy commanded violent action against any who urged apostasy: 'you shall put him to death; your own hand shall be the first to be raised against him and then all the people shall follow' (Deut. 13: 9). Similarly, 'You shall demolish all the sanctuaries where the nations whose place you are taking worship their gods...You shall pull down their altars' (Deut. 12: 2–3). Jewish law supported Mattathias' action, and history and example are much appealed to in his death-bed speech (2: 49–70). Phinehas' action is quoted in Ecclus. 45: 23–4, and the picture there given may have helped the author of 1 Maccabees make the comparison:

Phinehas son of Eleazar ranks third in renown
for being zealous in his reverence for the Lord,
and for standing firm with noble courage,
when the people were in revolt;
by so doing he made atonement for Israel.
Therefore a covenant was established with him,
assuring him command of the sanctuary and of the nation,
conferring on him and his descendants
the high-priesthood for ever.

28. the *hills* or 'wilds' (verse 29), particularly those descending towards the Dead Sea, of Judaea were traditionally the refuge of outlaws. 2 Macc. 5: 27, however, puts the flight of Judas and his companions after the attack of Apollonius on Jerusalem and before the decree. ✳

A MATTER OF PRINCIPLE

29 At that time many who wanted to maintain their reli-
30 gion and law went down to the wilds to live there. They took their sons, their wives, and their cattle with them,
31 for their miseries were more than they could bear. Word soon reached the king's officers and the forces in Jerusalem, the city of David, that men who had defied the king's
32 order had gone down into hiding-places in the wilds. A large body of men went quickly after them, came up with them, and occupied positions opposite. They prepared to
33 attack them on the sabbath. 'There is still time,' they shouted; 'come out, obey the king's command, and your
34 lives will be spared.' 'We will not come out,' the Jews replied; 'we will not obey the king's command or profane
35 the sabbath.' Without more ado the attack was launched;
36 but the Israelites did nothing in reply; they neither hurled
37 stones, nor barricaded their caves. 'Let us all meet death with a clear conscience,' they said; 'we call heaven and earth to testify that there is no justice in this slaughter.'
38 So they were attacked and massacred on the sabbath, men, women, and children, up to a thousand in all, and their cattle with them.

39   Great was the grief of Mattathias and his friends when
40 they heard the news. They said to one another, 'If we all do as our brothers have done, if we refuse to fight the

Gentiles for our lives as well as for our laws and customs, then they will soon wipe us off the face of the earth.' That day they decided that, if anyone came to fight against 41 them on the sabbath, they would fight back, rather than all die as their brothers in the caves had done.

✻ Mattathias' family was not the only group that took to the hills. A large group of outlaws chose death rather than break the Sabbath law; the result was that Mattathias and his group decided to defend themselves on the Sabbath if need arose. The preservation of the true people of God is seen as a principle overriding even the command to keep the Sabbath.

30. This was a large communal group who seem to have been retreating from the situation rather than organizing active resistance.

38. For a similar incident compare 2 Macc. 6: 11. ✻

COUNTER-ATTACK

It was then that they were joined by a company of 42 Hasidaeans, stalwarts of Israel, every one of them a volunteer in the cause of the law; and all who were refugees 43 from the troubles came to swell their numbers, and so add to their strength. Now that they had an organized force, 44 they turned their wrath on the guilty men and renegades. Those who escaped their fierce attacks took refuge with the Gentiles.

Mattathias and his friends then swept through the 45 country, pulling down the pagan altars, and forcibly cir- 46 cumcising all the uncircumcised boys found within the frontiers of Israel. They hunted down their arrogant 47 enemies, and the cause prospered in their hands. Thus they 48 saved the law from the Gentiles and their kings, and broke the power of the tyrant.

✻ Mattathias' group is joined by another dissident group within Israel, and by 'refugees from the troubles', and together they begin terrorist attacks on hellenizing Jews.

42. *Hasidaeans:* Hebrew *ḥasidim*, those who show loyalty (*ḥesed*) to the faith; compare Ps. 31: 23, 'Love the LORD, all you his loyal servants.' Here they are mentioned as an already existing party. They seem to have belonged to the scribal class, the interpreters of the law. Under Antiochus III, when the Jews were allowed to live according to their ancestral law, such a body was important for the daily administration of justice. When Antiochus IV suspended the Jewish law, the Hasidaeans naturally took sides with the opposition. Dan. 11: 33 says of them: 'Wise leaders of the nation will give guidance to the common people; yet for a while they will fall victims to fire and sword, to captivity and pillage.' 2 Macc. 14: 6 reports a complaint that the Hasidaeans, led by Judas Maccabaeus, 'are keeping the war alive and fomenting sedition, refusing to leave the kingdom in peace'.

44. *organized force:* it has been suggested that the Hasidaeans provided much of the intellectual leadership. *guilty men and renegades:* the rebels attacked the hellenizing Jews and the outward signs of their way of life, which clearly was well established. The rebels would be seen as violent extremists, upsetting the security of the nation, and many citizens emigrated – *took refuge with the Gentiles* – to bring up their families in peace.

48. The author and the rebels, however, interpret the campaign differently. ✻

THE LAST WORDS OF MATTATHIAS

The time came for Mattathias to die, and he said to his 49
sons: 'Arrogance now stands secure and gives judgement
against us; it is a time of calamity and raging fury. But 50
now, my sons, be zealous for the law, and give your lives
for the covenant of your fathers. Remember the deeds 51
they did in their generations, and great glory and eternal
fame shall be yours. Did not Abraham prove steadfast 52
under trial, and so gain credit as a righteous man? Joseph 53
kept the commandments, hard-pressed though he was,
and became lord of Egypt. Phinehas, our father, never 54
flagged in his zeal, and his was the covenant of an everlasting priesthood. Joshua kept the law, and he became a 55
judge in Israel. Caleb bore witness before the congrega- 56
tion, and a share in the land was his reward. David was a 57
man of loyalty, and he was granted the throne of an everlasting kingdom. Elijah never flagged in his zeal for the 58
law, and he was taken up to heaven. Hananiah, Azariah, 59
and Mishael had faith, and they were saved from the
blazing furnace. Daniel was a man of integrity, and he was 60
rescued from the lions' jaws. As generation succeeds 61
generation, follow their example; for no one who trusts
in Heaven shall ever lack strength. Do not fear a wicked 62
man's words; all his success will end in filth and worms.
Today he may be high in honour, but tomorrow there 63
will be no trace of him, because he will have returned to
the dust and all his schemes come to nothing. But you, my 64
sons, draw your courage and strength from the law, for
by it you will win great glory.

'Now here is Symeon, your brother; I know him to be 65

wise in counsel: always listen to him, for he shall be a
66 father to you. Judas Maccabaeus has been strong and
brave from boyhood; he shall be your commander in the
67 field, and fight his people's battles. Gather to your side
all who observe the law, and avenge your people's wrongs.
68 Repay the Gentiles in their own coin, and always heed
the law's commands.'

69 Then Mattathias blessed them, and was gathered to his
70 fathers. He died in the year 146,[a] and was buried by his
sons in the family tomb at Modin. All Israel raised a loud
lament for him.

* Mattathias, like other great Israelites of the past, such as
Jacob (Gen. 49), Moses (Deut. 33), Samuel (1 Sam. 12), or
like Jacob's sons in *The Testaments of the Twelve Patriarchs*, a
book originating in late, pre-Christian Judaism, is given a long
final speech. In it he describes how Israel's past heroes were
rewarded for their loyalty to the law and covenant. This list
has obvious similarities with the list of famous men in Ecclus.
44–9, which perhaps our author knew. The list of men of
faith in Heb. 11 is a Christian example of the same sort of
thing. The speech ends with a commendation of his sons
Symeon and Judas as leaders, and general instructions for
conduct of the fight.

50. *be zealous for the law…covenant:* the *law* in particular is
constantly referred to throughout the speech.

52. The law did not exist before Moses, so *Abraham* gained
credit as a righteous man by proving *steadfast under trial* – whether
by his readiness to sacrifice Isaac or by his trust in God's
unbelievable promise of heirs. Compare the use of Abraham
as an example in Ecclus. 44: 19 ff.:

> He kept the law of the Most High;
> he entered into covenant with him,

[a] *That is* 166 B.C.

> setting upon his body the mark of the covenant;
> and, when he was tested, he proved faithful. (verse 20)

(For Paul's rather different use of the same material, see Rom. 4: 1–22, Gal. 3: 1–9.)

53. *Joseph kept the commandments* in spite of misfortunes.

54. *Phinehas* is here seen as a Maccabaean ancestor in the priesthood and perhaps as justifying the later Maccabaean assumption of the high priesthood (see also verse 26 and the comment there).

55–6. *Joshua* and *Caleb* appear in Num. 14: 5–10 as the minority group which encouraged the Israelites to enter Canaan in spite of the giants, and the pair appear side by side in Ecclus. 46: 1–10.

57. What David's *loyalty* refers to is not clear – perhaps a general picture such as that given by Ecclus. 47: 1–11 is in mind – but *an everlasting kingdom* was promised by Nathan in 2 Sam. 7.

58. Elijah's *zeal for the law* appeared when he rebuked Ahab's transgression of the tenth commandment and Jezebel's transgression of the first (1 Kings 21: 17–29). *taken up to heaven:* see 2 Kings 2: 11.

59. The story of *Hananiah, Azariah and Mishael* is told in The Song of the Three, added between Dan. 3: 23 and 24 in the book's Greek version, and is reminiscent of the stories of Dan. 6 and 2 Macc. 6 and 7. We have here evidence that such stories were told to encourage the faithful during the Maccabaean crisis.

60. *Daniel*'s resistance under persecution made a good example for the Maccabees, and the book of Daniel as it stands was addressed primarily to the Maccabaean crisis.

62. The *wicked man* (compare 'the man doomed to perdition', 2 Thess. 2: 3–4) is Antiochus; as described here, his end is reminiscent of Herod's (cp. Acts 12: 20–3), but see 1 Macc. 6: 8–16 and 2 Macc. 9: 11–29.

63. This verse raises the age-old question of why the wicked

seem to prosper; the answer here given reminds us of Ps. 37: 35–6:

> I have watched a wicked man at his work,
> rank as a spreading tree in its native soil.
> I passed by one day, and he was gone;
> I searched for him, but he could not be found.

65. *Symeon*, presumably Simon of verse 3, for whose later leadership see chapters 13–16, is *wise in counsel, a father*. The latter title is sometimes found used of a priest, prophet or leader (cp., e.g., 2 Kings 2: 12). Simon is given greater honour here than either Judas or Jonathan (for 1 Maccabees' low estimate of Jonathan, the other son to become leader, see below on 13: 25 ff.).

69. *blessed them, and was gathered to his fathers:* like a Jacob or Moses of old (Gen. 49, Deut. 33).

70. *the family tomb:* see the comment on 13: 25–30. 1 Maccabees makes much of Mattathias as the founder of the Hasmonaean dynasty, but 2 Maccabees, written from a different standpoint, does not even mention him. ✲

The war under Judas and Jonathan

IN PRAISE OF JUDAS

3 THEN JUDAS MACCABAEUS came forward in his
2 father's place. He had the support of all his brothers and his father's followers, and they carried on the fight for Israel with zest.

3   He enhanced his people's glory.
        He put on his breastplate like a giant,
        and girt himself with weapons of war.

44

He fought battle on battle;
he guarded his army with his sword.
He was like a lion in his exploits,　　　　　4
like a lion's whelp roaring for prey.
He hunted and tracked down the lawless;　　5
he blasted the troublers of his people.
The lawless cowered in fear of him;　　　　6
all evil-doers were confounded.
The cause of freedom prospered in his hands;
he provoked many kings to anger.　　　　7
But he made Jacob glad by his deeds;
he is remembered for ever in blessing.
He passed through the towns of Judaea;　　8
he destroyed the godless there.
He turned wrath away from Israel;
his fame spread to the ends of the earth,　　9
and he rallied a people near to destruction.

* The author of 1 Maccabees had a taste for Hebrew poetry (cp. 2: 7–11, the present passage, 3: 45, and perhaps 2: 49–68 which some think is verse: these may be his own compositions). In style 3: 3–9 reminds us again of the roll of honour in Ecclus. 44–9; compare, e.g., the passage on Joshua (Ecclus. 46: 1–6):

He lived up to his name
as a great liberator of the Lord's chosen people,
able to take reprisals on the enemies who attacked them,
and to put Israel in possession of their territory.
How glorious he was when he raised his hand
and brandished his sword against cities!
Never before had a man made such a stand,
for he was fighting the Lord's battles. (verses 1–3)

1. *Judas Maccabaeus:* see the comment on 2: 1 ff.

45

5. *the lawless...the troublers of his people* are the hellenizing Jews who despise the Jewish law, and their Syrian supporters.

6–7. The author sees the struggle as one for *freedom*, against Antiochus and his successors (*many kings*).

8. But the *godless* (i.e. 'renegade', hellenizing Jews, verse 15) in *the towns of Judaea* were the real enemies; this was civil war between hellenizers and conservatives as much as war with Antiochus. Judas was probably not as popular with Israel at the time as he was in retrospect. ⁎

SYRIAN AID FOR THE HELLENIZERS

10 Apollonius now collected a gentile force and a large
11 contingent from Samaria, to fight against Israel. When Judas heard of it, he marched out to meet him, and defeated and killed him. Many of the Gentiles fell, and the
12 rest took to flight. From the arms they captured, Judas took the sword of Apollonius, and used it in his campaigns for the rest of his life.

13 When Seron, who commanded the army in Syria, heard that Judas had mustered a large force, consisting of all his
14 loyal followers of military age, he said to himself, 'I will win a glorious reputation in the empire by making war on
15 Judas and his followers, who defy the royal edict.' Seron was reinforced by a strong contingent of renegade Jews, who marched up to help him take vengeance on Israel.
16 When he reached the pass of Beth-horon, Judas advanced
17 to meet him with a handful of men. When his followers saw the host coming against them, they said to Judas, 'How can so few of us fight against so many? Besides, we have had nothing to eat all day, and we are exhausted.'
18 Judas replied: 'Many can easily be overpowered by a

few; it makes no difference to Heaven to save by many or by few. Victory does not depend on numbers; strength 19 comes from Heaven alone. Our enemies come filled with 20 insolence and lawlessness to plunder and to kill us and our wives and children. But we are fighting for our lives and 21 our religion. Heaven will crush them before our eyes. 22 You need not be afraid of them.'

When he had finished speaking, he launched a sudden 23 attack, and Seron and his army broke before him. They 24 pursued them down the pass of Beth-horon as far as the plain; some eight hundred of the enemy fell, and the rest fled to Philistia.

* This passage describes the growing Syrian involvement in the Jerusalem government's attempts to suppress Judas' terrorism.

10. *Apollonius* (for whose earlier part in affairs see 1: 29, 2 Macc. 5: 24) was now meridarch (civil governor) of the *Samaria* region, which was divided into toparchies (cp. 11: 34). Samaria and Jerusalem were not friendly, as Jesus son of Sirach shows:

> Two nations I detest,
> and a third is no nation at all:
> the inhabitants of Mount Seir, the Philistines,
> and the senseless folk that live at Shechem.
>
> (Ecclus. 50: 25–6)

Their differences went back to different tribal origins, different historical and religious development, and diplomatic failures; and in 128 B.C. John Hyrcanus (Judas' nephew) was to destroy the Samaritan sanctuary on Mount Gerizim near Shechem. The division remained into New Testament times and beyond. Apollonius' army contained Samaritans and Gentiles, probably from the non-Jewish coastal cities like Joppa which resented the growing Jewish involvement in economic affairs.

12. *took the sword:* the words remind us of David, who took Goliath's sword (1 Sam. 17: 51). The author perhaps means us to see Judas as a new David.

13. *Seron* was a professional soldier sent from Syria, but as the Syrian army was in this year (166 B.C.) engaged in a full-scale review at Daphne near Antioch, the major part of his force was probably the 'strong contingent of renegade Jews' (verse 15).

16. *Beth-horon*, about 18 km (11 miles) north-west of Jerusalem, controls the road from Modin and the coastal plain to Jerusalem, and featured in military campaigns from Joshua's time onwards. It was later fortified by Bacchides (9: 50). Josephus describes the later rout of a Roman army there: 'In the wide spaces the Jews pressed them less vigorously, but when they were crowded together in the defiles of the descending road, one group got in front of them and barred their egress, others pushed the rearmost down into the ravine, and the main body lined the high ground overlooking the waist of the pass and showered missiles on the massed Romans' (*Jewish War*, II. 19. 8).

17 f. *so few…nothing to eat:* common disadvantages of guerrilla troops. Judas encouraged them by referring to the words of Jonathan in his attack on the Philistines: 'He can bring us safe through, whether we are few or many' (1 Sam. 14: 6).

24. *the plain:* the pursuit is westwards, downhill. The reference to *Philistia* (the Philistines had long since disappeared) shows how conscious the author is of the work of Judas as part of Israel's perpetual struggle against foreigners. ✳

THE POLICY OF ANTIOCHUS

25 Thus Judas and his brothers began to be feared, and
26 alarm spread to the Gentiles all round. His fame reached the ears of the king, and the story of his battles was told

in every nation. When King Antiochus heard this news, 27 he flew into a rage and ordered all the forces of his empire to be assembled, an immensely powerful army. He 28 opened his treasury and gave a year's pay to his troops, ordering them to be prepared for any duty. But he found 29 that his resources were running low; his tribute, too, had dwindled as a result of the disaffection and violence he had brought upon the world by abolishing traditional laws and customs. He now saw with alarm that he might be 30 short of money, as had happened once or twice before, both for his normal expenses and for the gifts he had been accustomed to distribute with an even more lavish hand than any of his predecessors on the throne.

For a time he was much perplexed; then he decided to 31 go to Persia, collect the tribute due from the provinces, and raise a large sum of ready money. He left Lysias, a 32 distinguished member of the royal family, as viceroy of the territories between the Euphrates and the Egyptian frontier. He also appointed him guardian of his son Antio- 33 chus until his return. He transferred to Lysias half the 34 armed forces, together with the elephants, and told him all that he wanted done, especially to the population of Judaea and Jerusalem. Against these Lysias was to send a 35 force, and break and destroy the strength of Israel and those who were left in Jerusalem, to blot out all memory of them from the place. He was to settle foreigners in all 36 their territory, and allot the land to the settlers. The other 37 half of the forces the king took with him, and set out from Antioch, his capital, in the year 147.[a] He crossed the Euphrates and marched through the upper provinces.

[a] *That is* 165 B.C.

1. The campaigns of 166–163 B.C. (1 Macc. 3: 38–5: 68).

✳ I Maccabees makes Antiochus' difficulties with a small guerrilla movement in Judaea the king's major preoccupation and a major reason for his tribute-collecting expedition to the east. The real reason for this, however, was to ensure the loyalty of the eastern provinces. A senior general and administrator is sent to Judaea with a larger military force and with new measures designed to weaken Jewish nationalism.

26. *told in every nation:* a more realistic picture is probably that of 2 Macc. 8: 5-7.

27. *rage:* Antiochus' quick temper was well known, but it was balanced by his equally unpredictable generosity (cp. verse 30). *all the forces...assembled* may refer to the army review at Daphne in 166 B.C., held mainly to impress the Greek world with Antiochus' power after his failure in Egypt in 168 B.C. Antiochus was an able emperor, called by one scholar 'the last great Seleucid', capable of bold and intelligent policies. His mistaken estimate of the Jewish situation and its consequences, and the biased picture given by 1 and 2 Maccabees and Daniel, have given us a one-sided picture.

29. *as a result...laws and customs:* see the commentary on 1: 41-53.

30. *short of money...gifts:* in 173 B.C. Antiochus paid the last instalments of the fine demanded by Rome by the treaty of Apamea, and his Egyptian expeditions in 170-168 B.C., in spite of captured booty, were expensive, as was also the review at Daphne. It was said that he was *lavish* and eccentric with personal gifts, sometimes throwing money to the crowd.

31. *Persia* at the head of the Persian Gulf was among the most easterly of Antiochus' provinces (see also the commentary on 6: 1).

32. *Lysias...of the royal family* (i.e. one of the king's senior courtiers, cp. 'King's Kinsmen', pp. 9 f.) was now given control over what had been the Persian satrapy of Beyond-Euphrates (Ezra 5: 6).

33. *Antiochus* Eupator ('of a good father'), then aged about nine years. See 7: 2-4.

35–6. *to blot out all memory of them from the place:* the policy
was to undermine Jewish nationalism, by military success and
by allotting Jewish land to foreign settlers (see also 2 Macc. 11:
3, Dan. 11: 39). This was normal practice in conquered territories; the Assyrians had done it in Samaria (2 Kings 17: 24 ff.)
and Antiochus III had settled Jews among the rebellious peoples
of Lydia and Phrygia (in what is now Turkey). Elizabeth I of
England and Cromwell did much the same in Ireland.

37. *Antioch*, on the River Orontes in Syria. In spring 165
B.C. Antiochus set out for Armenia, Babylon and Persia; for
upper provinces, see p. 8. ✲

PREPARATIONS FOR BATTLE

38 Lysias chose Ptolemaeus son of Dorymenes, with Nicanor and Gorgias, all three powerful members of the order
39 of King's Friends, and sent with them forty thousand
infantry and seven thousand cavalry to invade Judaea
and devastate the country as the king had commanded.
40 They set out with all their forces and encamped near
41 Emmaus in the lowlands. The merchants of the region,
impressed by what they heard of the army, took a large
quantity of silver and gold, with a supply of fetters, and
came into the camp to buy the Israelites for slaves. The
army was also reinforced by troops from Syria and
Philistia.

42   Judas and his brothers saw that their plight had become
grave, with the enemy encamped inside their frontiers.
They learnt, too, of the commands which the king had
43 given for the complete destruction of the nation. So they
said to one another, 'Let us restore the shattered fortunes
of our nation; let us fight for our nation and for the holy
44 place.' They gathered in full assembly to prepare for

battle, and to pray and seek divine mercy and compassion.

> Jerusalem lay deserted like a wilderness; 45
> none of her children went in or out.
> Her holy place was trampled down;
> aliens and heathen lodged in her citadel.
> Joy had been banished from Jacob;
> and flute and harp were dumb.

They assembled at Mizpah, opposite Jerusalem, for in 46 former times Israel had a place of worship at Mizpah. That day they fasted, put on sackcloth, sprinkled ashes 47 on their heads, and tore their garments. They unrolled the 48 scroll of the law, seeking the guidance which Gentiles seek from the images of their gods. They brought the priestly 49 vestments, the firstfruits, and the tithes; they presented Nazirites who had completed their vows, and they cried 50 to Heaven: 'What shall we do with these Nazirites, and where shall we take them? Thy holy place is trodden 51 down and defiled, and sorrow and humiliation have come upon thy priests. And see, the Gentiles have gathered 52 against us to destroy us. Thou knowest the fate they plan for us; how can we withstand them unless thou help us?' 53 Then the trumpets sounded, and a great shout went up. 54

Judas then appointed leaders of the people, officers over 55 thousands, hundreds, fifties, and tens. As the law com- 56 mands, he ordered back to their homes those who were building their houses or were newly wed or who were planting vineyards, or who were faint-hearted. Thereupon 57 the army moved and took up their positions to the south of Emmaus, where Judas thus addressed them: 'Prepare 58 for action and show yourselves men. Be ready at dawn to

fight these Gentiles who are massed against us to destroy
59 us and our holy place. Better die fighting than look on
while calamity overwhelms our people and the holy place.
60 But it will be as Heaven wills.'

✻ See also 2 Macc. 8: 8–11 and the comment there. Both 1 and
2 Maccabees mention Ptolemaeus, Nicanor and Gorgias, the
threatened selling of Jews as slaves, and the subsequent Jewish
victories, but they disagree on some important points. Perhaps two or more encounters have been confused.

38. *Lysias chose...*: 2 Macc. 8: 8 f. makes Philip, commissioner in Jerusalem, appeal to Ptolemaeus, governor of Coele-
syria and Phoenicia, who sends Nicanor and Gorgias against
the Jews. 1 Maccabees, however, recounts a campaign in
which the only general named is Gorgias, 2 Maccabees a
campaign in which the enemy general is Nicanor.

39. 2 Macc. 8: 9 numbers the army at 'at least twenty
thousand',

40. *Emmaus* was about 13 km (8 miles) south of Modin and
about 35 km (22 miles) west-north-west of Jerusalem. 2
Maccabees gives no location.

41. *The merchants of the region* are from the pro-Syrian
coastal cities such as Joppa and Jamnia. For *Syria* (whose troops
are perhaps included in those of verse 39) some scholars would
read 'Edom' (i.e. Idumaea, cp. 4: 29; 5: 3). The people of
Edom and Philistia were ancient enemies of the Jews.

42–60. This description of battle-preparation has Israel's
ancient traditions well in mind (cp. e.g. 'in former times',
verse 46).

44. Jewish prayer before battle is particularly stressed in
2 Maccabees; for another example, see 2 Chron. 20: 5–12.

45. This lament is reminiscent of several Old Testament
passages, such as Isa. 1 or Ps. 79. It may be a quotation from a
psalm otherwise unknown to us.

46. It was at *Mizpah* 13 km (8 miles) north of Jerusalem

that the Israelites under Samuel once gathered to face a Philistine invasion (1 Sam. 7: 5 f.) and fasted all day confessing their sins.

48. They consult *the law*, not mentioned in the ancient traditions of battle-preparation (see Deut. 20), but important to the Maccabees (see also on 2 Macc. 8: 23). Possession of such a *scroll of the law* at this time carried the death-penalty (1: 57). *seeking the guidance...gods* is the best sense that can be made of a difficult text, and contrasts Jewish reverence for the law with the idolatry of their enemies. 2 Chron. 20: 4 says that before battle 'Judah gathered together to ask counsel of the LORD; from every city of the land they came to consult him'.

49. The use of *priestly vestments*, the presentation of *first-fruits* and *tithes*, and the release of *Nazirites* from their *vows* all belonged to the temple and its ritual, and would be a powerful visual reminder of the need to fight 'for the holy place' (verses 43, 59). The Nazirites were men consecrated to God, originally for life, but in later times for limited periods only (see Num. 6: 1–21). But mention of Nazirites in this context would remind the reader of men like Samson, a champion of Israel against the Philistines.

54. *the trumpets sounded* as traditionally in preparation for battle; cp. Num. 10: 9, Judg. 7: 18, 22.

55 ff. Judas is shown as a faithful adherent to the Law. He *appointed* his *officers* as Moses once did (Deut. 1: 15), sent home certain categories of men (cp. Deut. 20: 5–8), and made a speech like those described in 1 and 2 Chronicles (e.g. 2 Chron. 20: 15–17).

58 f. Like heroes of old, Judas' men must be ready to die for *our people and the holy place*. ✶

THE BATTLE

Gorgias, taking a detachment of five thousand men and **4** a thousand picked cavalry, set out by night to attack the 2 Jewish army and fall upon them unawares; his guides

3 were men from the citadel. But Judas had word of this,
and he and his soldiers moved out to attack the king's
4 army in Emmaus, while its forces were still divided.
5 Gorgias reached the camp of Judas during the night, but
found no one there. He set out to search for them in the
hills, thinking, 'These Jews are running away from us.'

6 At daybreak, there was Judas in the plain with three
thousand men, though they had not all the armour and
7 the swords they wanted. They saw the Gentiles' camp
strongly fortified with breast-works, while mounted
guards, seasoned troops, patrolled round it.

8 Judas said to his men: 'Do not be afraid of their great
9 numbers or panic when they charge. Remember how our
fathers were saved at the Red Sea, when Pharaoh and his
10 army were pursuing them. Let us cry now to Heaven to
favour our cause, to remember the covenant made with
11 our fathers, and to crush this army before us today. Then
all the Gentiles will know that there is One who saves and
liberates Israel.'

12 When the foreigners looked up and saw them advancing
13 to the attack, they marched out of their camp to give
14 battle. Judas and his men sounded their trumpets and
closed with them. The Gentiles broke, and fled to the
15 plain. All the rearmost fell by the sword. The pursuit was
pressed as far as Gazara and the lowlands of Idumaea,
Azotus and Jamnia; about three thousand of the enemy
were killed.

* The battle is in fact won by the superior strategy and
bravery of Judas and his men. Gorgias, helped by hellenizing
Jews from the citadel with their local knowledge, tried to

surprise Judas' camp, but his mistaken strategy on finding the camp empty gave Judas the chance to attack a divided enemy. The account contains many reminiscences of Old Testament stories.

2. *his guides...from the citadel* in Jerusalem were probably hellenizing Jews.

3. *Emmaus:* see 3: 40.

5. *in the hills* suggests that Gorgias moved south-east towards Jerusalem.

6 f. The Jewish disadvantages, in numbers and equipment, are made plain. To judge from 3: 39 and 4: 1 the camp contained 35,000 infantry and 6,000 cavalry; the figure given for casualties (verse 15) is correspondingly high. For different figures, cp. 2 Macc. 8: 9, 24.

8 f. Judas' speech recalls the defeat of *Pharaoh and his army* (Exod. 14); the parallel speech in 2 Macc. 8: 16–20 adds reference to other occasions when God had helped Israel.

10. Secondly, Judas recalls the *covenant made with our fathers* (i.e. Abraham, Isaac and Jacob). This covenant basically promised land and descendants in perpetuity (cp. Gen. 17: 6–8), while the covenant with Moses promised 'You shall be my kingdom of priests, my holy nation' (Exod. 19: 6) and laid certain obligations on the nation which it was to keep as a token of its loyalty to the God of Israel. It was this loyalty which was at stake in the hellenizers' cry, 'Let us enter into a covenant with the Gentiles round about' (1: 11).

11. Judas reaffirms the covenant election of Israel against the universalistic attitude of the hellenizers. In the present situation, Judas' vision is limited to Israel's salvation, and we do not find the wider vision of Second Isaiah:

> Look to me and be saved,
> > you peoples from all corners of the earth (Isa. 45: 22).

15. *Gazara* (Gezer), *Azotus* (Ashdod) and *Jamnia* (Jabneh, where later Gorgias appears quartered, 5: 58 f.) were once

coastal Philistine cities, the last two by now perhaps lying in *the lowlands of Idumaea*, named after Edomite peoples who settled there in the period from about 700 to 400 B.C. ✶

OUTCOME OF THE BATTLE

16 Judas and his force then broke off the pursuit and re-
17 turned. He said to the people: 'Curb your greed for spoil;
18 there is more fighting before us; Gorgias and his force are in the hills near by. Stand firm now against our enemies and fight; after that, plunder as you please.'

19 Before Judas had finished speaking, an enemy patrol
20 appeared, reconnoitring from the hills. They saw that their army was in flight, and that their camp was being set on fire; the smoke that met their gaze showed what
21 had happened. They were filled with panic as they took in the scene, and when they saw the army of Judas in the
22 plain, ready for battle, they all fled to Philistia.

23 Then Judas turned back to plunder the camp, and there they got much gold and silver, violet and purple stuffs,
24 and great riches. On their return they sang songs of thanksgiving and praised Heaven, 'for it is right, because his
25 mercy endures for ever'. That day saw a great deliverance for Israel.

26 Those of the Gentiles who escaped with their lives went
27 and reported to Lysias all that had happened. On hearing the news he was overwhelmed with disappointment, because Israel had not suffered the disaster he had hoped for, and the issue was not what the king had ordered.

* The Syrian defeat is completed by the flight of Gorgias' troops, and Judas' plundering of the Syrian camp.

16 ff. Judas lies between Gorgias' troops and the main Syrian force, and controls the situation.

21 f. *Philistia* is the obvious direction for the flight, for part of the Syrian army came from there (3: 41), and there they could join up with the fugitives of the main force (verse 15). 2 Macc. 8: 25–6 says that the pursuit stopped on the eve of the sabbath.

23. *violet and purple stuffs:* the famous products of the *murex trunculus* of the Phoenician sea-coast (cp. Ezek. 27: 7, of Tyre, 'your awnings were violet and purple').

24. *...because his mercy endures for ever:* this refrain suggests that one of the songs of thanksgiving was Ps. 136, which describes the acts of God on Israel's behalf:

> He remembered us when we were cast down,
>> his love endures for ever,
> and rescued us from our enemies;
>> his love endures for ever (Ps. 136: 23–4).

25. *great deliverance:* another Old Testament reminiscence. See Judg. 15: 18, 1 Sam. 14: 45 where the same phrase (translated 'great victory') is used of defeats of the Philistines. According to 2 Macc. 8: 35, Nicanor was 'lucky to reach Antioch after losing his whole army'. *

A MAJOR EXPEDITION BY LYSIAS

In the following year he gathered sixty thousand picked 28 infantry and five thousand cavalry to make war on the Jews. They marched into Idumaea, and encamped at 29 Bethsura, where Judas met them with ten thousand men. When he saw the strength of the enemy's army, he 30 prayed: 'All praise to thee, the Saviour of Israel, who didst break the attack of the giant by thy servant David. Thou

didst deliver the army of the Philistines into the power of
31 Saul's son, Jonathan, and of his armour-bearer. In like
manner put this army into the power of thy people Israel.
Humble their pride in their forces and their mounted men.
32 Strike them with panic, turn their insolent strength to
33 water, make them reel under a crushing defeat. Overthrow them by the sword of those who love thee, and let
all who know thy name praise thee with songs of thanksgiving.'

34   So they joined battle, and Lysias lost about five thou-
35 sand men in the close fighting. When he saw his own
army routed and Judas's army full of daring, ready to live
or die nobly, he departed for Antioch, and there collected
a force of mercenaries, in order to return to Judaea with
a much larger army than before.[a]

∗ Lysias the viceroy appears in person to defeat Judas, and
like his predecessors is defeated. For the author of 1 Maccabees, this is clearly the climax of the first round between Syria
and the Maccabees. But Lysias' feebleness as here described,
and the similarity of this campaign with Lysias' second campaign in 163 B.C. (6: 28–63; 2 Macc. 13: 1–26), together with
problems of dating, have made some scholars think that this
first campaign is fictional, a reduplication of the second.

28. *In the following year:* the Seleucid year 148 (cp. 3: 37),
i.e. October 165–September 164 B.C. If the campaign occurred,
its date was late 165 B.C. The negotiations of 2 Macc. 11: 16 ff.
began about this time or a little after. For Lysias' numbers,
cp. 2 Macc. 11: 1–5.

29. *Idumaea:* Lysias approaches Jerusalem not directly from
the north but by the south. Idumaea had already helped Syria
(see note on 3: 41) and would later harass the Jews (5: 3;

[a] in order…before: *probable meaning; Gk. obscure.*

2 Macc. 10: 14–15); but *Bethsura*, on the borders of Idumaea, 28 km (17½ miles) from Jerusalem, a Jewish administrative centre (Neh. 3: 16) in the Persian period, resisted Lysias (2 Macc. 11: 5), presumably having some Maccabaean sympathies. *ten thousand men:* at the last battle (4: 6) only three thousand.

30. 1 Maccabees again reminds us of earlier famous victories against the Philistines, when the enemy's size and numbers had terrified the Israelites (cp. 1 Sam. 13: 5). *the giant:* cp. 1 Sam. 17: 5 f. *Thou didst deliver…*: cp. 1 Sam. 14: 1–23.

35. *to return to Judaea:* see 1 Macc. 6: 28–50; 2 Macc. 13: 18–22. However, it is at this point that according to 2 Macc. 11: 14–38 some negotiations took place. For details, see the commentary on that passage. In late 165 B.C. or early 164 B.C., negotiations opened between Lysias and the Jews – probably the official hellenizing Jewish leaders – who saw that if they were to regain control, the extremists would have to be appeased. We have a letter (2 Macc. 11: 16–21) dated October 165 B.C. or early 164 B.C. from Lysias, referring to some Jewish document containing proposals which Lysias is not fully competent to grant; he must refer some of them to the king. We have a letter from the Roman legates (2 Macc. 11: 34–8), on their way to peace talks in Antioch, in answer to an approach from the Jews. We have a letter from Antiochus IV to the Jewish Senate and people declaring an amnesty (for the limited period of a fortnight) and a relaxation of the edict about food laws (2 Macc. 11: 27–33). We have a reference to the support of the governor-general of Coele-syria and Phoenicia for peaceful relations with the Jews (2 Macc. 10: 12). But the negotiations, whether conducted with the Maccabaeans directly or indirectly through the hellenizers, achieved no settlement. The Maccabees were so far undefeated, and the concessions were too small; in particular, the Jerusalem temple and cult were still controlled by the hellenizing party. The removal of that control is now described. *

THE CLEANSING OF THE TEMPLE AND REDEDICATION
OF THE ALTAR

36 But Judas and his brothers said: 'Now that our enemies
have been crushed, let us go up to Jerusalem to cleanse
37 the temple and rededicate it.' So the whole army was
38 assembled and went up to Mount Zion. There they found
the temple laid waste, the altar profaned, the gates burnt
down, the courts overgrown like a thicket or wooded
39 hill-side, and the priests' rooms in ruin. They tore their
40 garments, wailed loudly, put ashes on their heads, and fell
on their faces to the ground. They sounded the ceremonial trumpets, and cried aloud to Heaven.

41 Then Judas detailed troops to engage the garrison of the
42 citadel while he cleansed the temple. He selected priests
43 without blemish, devoted to the law, and they purified
the temple, removing to an unclean place the stones which
44 defiled it. They discussed what to do with the altar of
45 burnt-offering, which was profaned, and rightly decided
to demolish it, for fear it might become a standing reproach to them because it had been defiled by the Gen-
46 tiles. They therefore pulled down the altar, and stored
away the stones in a fitting place on the temple hill, until
a prophet should arise who could be consulted about
47 them. They took unhewn stones, as the law commands,
and built a new altar on the model of the previous one.
48 They rebuilt the temple and restored its interior, and
49 consecrated the temple courts. They renewed the sacred
vessels and the lamp-stand, and brought the altar of in-
50 cense and the table into the temple. They burnt incense
on the altar and lit the lamps on the lamp-stand to shine

within the temple. When they had put the Bread of the 51 Presence on the table and hung the curtains, all their work was completed.

Then, early on the twenty-fifth day of the ninth month, 52 the month Kislev, in the year 148,[a] sacrifice was offered as 53 the law commands on the newly made altar of burnt-offering. On the anniversary of the day when the Gentiles 54 had profaned it, on that very day, it was rededicated, with hymns of thanksgiving, to the music of harps and lutes and cymbals. All the people prostrated themselves, wor- 55 shipping and praising Heaven that their cause had prospered.

They celebrated the rededication of the altar for eight 56 days; there was great rejoicing as they brought burnt-offerings and sacrificed peace-offerings and thank-offerings. They decorated the front of the temple with golden 57 wreaths and ornamental shields. They renewed the gates and the priests' rooms, and fitted them with doors. There 58 was great merry-making among the people, and the disgrace brought on them by the Gentiles was removed.

Then Judas, his brothers, and the whole congregation 59 of Israel decreed that the rededication of the altar should be observed with joy and gladness at the same season each year, for eight days, beginning on the twenty-fifth of Kislev.

At that time they encircled Mount Zion with high walls 60 and strong towers to prevent the Gentiles from coming and trampling it down as they had done before. Judas set 61 a garrison there; he also fortified Bethsura, so that the people should have a fortress facing Idumaea.

[a] *That is* 164 B.C.

✲ The date of this event is December 164 B.C., nine months or so after the treaty negotiations described above. 2 Macc. 9, 10: 1–13 says that Antiochus IV died in these months before the temple-cleansing; 1 Maccabees, however, places the event after the cleansing in the year 149, i.e. between autumn 164 B.C. and autumn 163 B.C. In fact, a recently published king-list from Babylon shows that Antiochus' death was known there sometime between 19 November and 19 December in 164 B.C. He died, therefore, much the same time as Judas cleansed the temple, though the news of his death probably did not reach Jerusalem until after that event.

37. *up to Mount Zion:* cp. 'Zion my holy mountain' (Ps. 2: 6); the temple hill took its name from the 'stronghold of Zion' which was the original 'City of David' just south of the temple hill (see 2 Sam. 5: 7).

38. The damage was probably done in the fighting in 168 B.C. 2 Macc. 1: 8 says that Jason's men had set the porch on fire, and 2 Macc. 8: 33 says that one Callisthenes had set fire to the sacred *gates. altar profaned:* see on 1: 54 above. It has been suggested that this verse refers in fact to a deliberate change in the nature of the place. The temple building with its porch, common hall and holy of holies had been laid waste, the gates of the courts burnt, and trees, forbidden by Deut. 16: 21, allowed to grow. The area now represented a typical Syrian–Canaanite sanctuary with altar, sacred trees, and open space, of the sort condemned by Deuteronomy and the prophets (cp. Deut. 12: 2, Hos. 4: 13 ff.).

39–40. The Maccabaean reaction to this sight was a lament, with all its attendant physical actions (cp. 3: 46–54 for similar behaviour).

41. *the citadel* was garrisoned by government forces, overlooking the temple from the west (see above on 1: 33).

42. *priests without blemish:* the Talmud (a compilation of Jewish oral teaching and comment on it, from the early centuries A.D.) lists 147 physical blemishes making a man unfit for the priesthood. *devoted to the law:* necessary because the

Jerusalem priests (see 2 Macc. 4: 14–17) had been prominent among the hellenizers.

43. *stones which defiled it:* probably those used on top of the 'altar of burnt-offering' to make 'the abomination of desolation' (1: 54).

46. They hesitated to destroy such a sacred object, temporarily profaned, and looked for some prophetic judgement on the matter. *until a prophet should arise* suggests that they thought that in one sense the age of prophecy had passed, but that after these difficult times a 'true prophet' (14: 41) might be expected, presumably as the herald of God's day of judgement. We are reminded of Deut. 18: 14: 'These nations whose place you are taking listen to soothsayers and augurs, but the LORD your God does not permit you to do this. The LORD your God will raise up a prophet from among you like myself, and you shall listen to him', or Mal. 4: 5: 'Look, I will send you the prophet Elijah before the great and terrible day of the LORD comes.'

47. With respect for the prophetic word goes respect for the *law*, in accordance with which the new altar is fashioned (Exod. 20: 25, Josh. 8: 31).

49. New vessels and pieces of furniture were made; a description of them can be found in Exod. 25–7.

51. *Bread of the Presence:* twelve loaves, offered to God as a food-offering every sabbath, and eaten by the priests. See Lev. 24: 5–9.

52. The date is 14 December 164 B.C., appropriately three years to the day after the first heathen sacrifice (cp. 1: 59; 4: 54).

54. For similar music-making, compare the account of the dedication of the walls of Jerusalem, Neh. 12: 27–43.

56. *eight days:* this, with other details of the temple-cleansing and altar-rededication, recalls the purification of the temple under Hezekiah (2 Chron. 29) and the original dedication by Solomon (1 Kings 7 and 8). *burnt-offerings* were gifts to God in which a whole animal was burnt; *peace-offerings* were sacrifices combining the ideas of gift and communion; some of the animal was eaten by the worshippers; *thank-offerings*

(Lev. 7: 11 ff.) were a type of peace-offering, requiring the additional offering of unleavened cakes mixed with oil. Sin-offerings and guilt-offerings (Lev. 4; 6: 24 – 7: 10) are not here mentioned, but in post-exilic times the burnt-offering itself acquired an expiatory value simply because by it a man made a gift of something he valued to God.

59. *each year:* annual observation may have been difficult in the years immediately after 164 B.C., for Jerusalem was the scene of fighting and the government forces continued (until 141 B.C.) to hold the citadel. 2 Maccabees begins with two documents inviting the Egyptian Jews to keep the feast; John 10: 22 refers to it as a winter feast under its Greek name *enkainia* (the word for 'rededication' in verse 56 is the related word *enkainismos*). 2 Macc. 10: 6–8; 1: 9 say that it was like the Feast of Tabernacles (cp. Lev. 23: 33–43) which was the feast at which Solomon's temple (1 Kings 8: 2, 65) and the post-exilic altar (Ezra 3: 4) were dedicated, with people carrying garlanded wands, branches, and palm fronds. Perhaps, however, the feast was also meant as a counter to the celebration of the king's birthday on the twenty-fifth day of each month, and the procession was an answer to the festal processions of the Greek god Dionysus (2 Macc. 6: 7). 2 Macc. 1: 8 refers to the lighting of lamps, and the theme of fire plays a great part in the second letter in 2 Macc. 1. Josephus calls the feast 'Lights', and Jews light an extra lamp on each day of the feast to this day.

60–1. Two vital military provisions are made: the temple area is fortified against the citadel, whose occupants are roundly called *Gentiles*, and *Bethsura* (see verse 29) is fortified against *Idumaea* to its immediate south. ✵

GENTILES AND JEWS

5 When the Gentiles round about heard that the altar had been rebuilt and the temple rededicated, they were furious, 2 and determined to wipe out all those of the race of Jacob

who lived among them. Thus began the work of massacre and extermination among the people.

✻ These verses set the scene for the following events. By the time of the Maccabees there were for various reasons many Jews living in the surrounding, predominantly gentile, areas. In 721 B.C., Israelites had been deported to Assyria (2 Kings 17); and in 597 and 586 B.C. Judaeans to Babylon (Ezek. 1, 2 Kings 24). In 586 B.C. some Judaeans had fled to Egypt (Jer. 43). In 312 B.C. Ptolemy I took some Jewish captives to Egypt and under Ptolemy II the Greek translation of the Jewish scriptures was started in Alexandria. In the second half of the third century B.C. we hear of Jewish families like the Tobiad family (see p. 4). These last were hellenizers, with interests in the Greek cities, and were representative of the new type of wealthy, aristocratic Jew whose progressive policies suited Antiochus IV well. They were anathema, however, to conservative men like Jesus son of Sirach and the Hasidaeans (see 2: 42, and comment there).

Thus we are not surprised to read in this chapter and in 1 Macc. 5 and 2 Macc. 12 of Jews in Gilead, Galilee, the coastal towns, Ammon and the land of Tob. They do not seem to have been popular; indeed, the Philistines and Idumaeans were ready to join Syrian expeditions against Judaea, and traders were ready to enslave Jews. On the other hand, the Maccabaeans, unlike the hellenizing Jews, saw the Gentiles as pagans and as a threat to Jewish nationalism. Thus they attacked temples, altars and images (5: 44, 68) as well as cities and forts (5: 65). Their attacks were not simply to rescue hellenizing Jews who lived abroad. Similarly the Gentiles' annoyance (verse 1) is based on Jewish national resurgence as well as religious and cultural differences. ✻

AGAINST IDUMAEANS AND AMMONITES

3 Judas then made war on the descendants of Esau in Idumaea and attacked Acrabattene, because they had hemmed Israel in. There he inflicted on them a severe and
4 humiliating defeat, and took spoils from them. He remembered also the wrong done by the Baeanites, who with their traps and road-blocks were continually am-
5 bushing the Israelites. He first confined them to their forts and took up positions against them; then he solemnly committed them to destruction and set the forts ablaze
6 with all their occupants. He crossed over to the Ammonites, and came upon a strong and numerous force under
7 the command of a certain Timotheus. He fought many battles with them, and they broke before him and were
8 crushed. After capturing Jazer and its dependent villages, he returned to Judaea.

✻ These verses summarize Judas' battles against the Idumaeans (see also 5: 65; 2 Macc. 10: 14–23) and the Ammonites (see also 2 Macc. 8: 31–3). The precise order of these campaigns is not so clear as these verses suggest, but their date is probably 163 B.C.

3. *Acrabattene* was perhaps the region of 'the ascent of Akrabbim' (Num. 34: 4) near the south-west end of the Dead Sea; some scholars, however, locate it between Samaria and Jericho, which fits well with the indications of verse 6, though not with the reference to *the descendants of Esau*.

4. The *Baeanites*, otherwise unknown, may have lived between Acrabattene and Jericho, ready to attack travellers on the Jerusalem–Jericho road.

5. *forts:* see comment on 2 Macc. 10: 18.

6. *Ammonites:* the capital was Rabbah (2 Sam. 12: 26),

under hellenistic Egyptian rule in the third century B.C. renamed Philadelphia after Ptolemy II Philadelphus; it belonged
to the 'Ten Towns' (Decapolis) of Mark 7: 31. Hyrcanus had
his estates in the Ammonite region, and here the hellenizing
high-priest Jason was exiled (2 Macc. 4: 26). *Timotheus* was
either a local ruler, or the Syrian commander in Transjordan:
2 Macc. 8: 30 links him with the Syrian general Bacchides.

7. *many battles:* see the commentary on 2 Macc. 10: 24 ff.

8. *Jazer,* perhaps the Gazara of 2 Macc. 10: 32, was in the
region of modern *es-salt*, west of Amman, and east of the
River Jordan. *

GENTILE ATTACKS IN GILEAD AND GALILEE

Then the Gentiles in Gilead gathered against the Israel- 9
ites within their territory, intending to destroy them; but
they took refuge in the fortress of Dathema, and sent this 10
letter to Judas and his brothers:

> The Gentiles round us have gathered to wipe us out.
> They are preparing to come and seize the fortress where 11
> we have taken refuge; Timotheus is in command of
> their army. So come at once and rescue us from their 12
> clutches, for many of our number have already fallen.
> All our fellow-Jews in the region of Tubias have been 13
> massacred, their wives and their children taken captive,
> and their property carried off. About a thousand men
> there have lost their lives.

While the letter was being read, other messengers with 14
their garments torn arrived from Galilee. 'Ptolemais, Tyre 15
and Sidon,' they said, 'and all heathen Galilee have
mustered their forces to make an end of us.'

✻ These verses describe the particular background to the campaigns of Judas and his brother Simon in Gilead and Galilee. For the places referred to, see the accompanying map on p. 50.

9. *Dathema* (cp. verse 29): *tell hamad*, in the basin of the River Yarmuk, in biblical Bashan.

13. *the region of Tubias* (cp. 2 Macc. 12: 17) is perhaps *et-taiyibeh* between modern Bosra and Deraa; compare 'the land of Tob' (Judg. 11: 3).

15. *Ptolemais* (modern Akko, restored by, and named after, Ptolemy II of Egypt, 261 B.C.). *Tyre and Sidon* were independent cities, friendly to the Seleucids, on the Phoenician coast. To their east, for administrative purposes partitioned between them, lay the Galilaean hills. *Galilee* was *heathen* (cp. Isa. 9: 1, 'Galilee of the Nations') until Aristobulus in 104–103 B.C. forcibly circumcised part of the population. Even in Jesus' time, Galilaeans were suspect in the eyes of some Jerusalem Jews (cp. John 7: 52). 2 Macc. 6: 8 says that Ptolemais had already, in 167 B.C., shown its readiness to persecute Jews. ✻

JUDAS' PREPARATIONS: SIMON INVADES GALILEE

16 When Judas and the people heard this, a full assembly was called to decide what they should do for their fellow-
17 countrymen in distress and under enemy attack. Judas said to Simon his brother, 'Choose your men, and go and rescue your countrymen in Galilee, while I and my brother
18 Jonathan march into Gilead.' The rest of his forces he left for the defences of Judaea, with Josephus son of Zacharias,
19 and Azarias, leading citizens, and gave them this order: 'Take charge of the people of Jerusalem, but on no account
20 join battle with the Gentiles until we return.' Simon was allotted three thousand men for the march on Galilee, and Judas eight thousand for the march on Gilead.

Simon invaded Galilee and, after many battles, broke 21
the resistance of the Gentiles. He pursued them as far as 22
the gate of Ptolemais, killed nearly three thousand of them,
and stripped their corpses. He took back with him the 23
Jews from Galilee and Arbatta, their wives and children,
and all their property, and brought them to Judaea with
great jubilation.

* As Maccabaean operations expand, the military ability
of Judas is revealed ever more clearly, and new leaders
emerge.

17. *Simon* (cp. 2: 65) is in some ways the real hero of the
author of 1 Maccabees; Jonathan (cp. 2: 5), who later takes
Judas' place as leader, is less admired. See the commentary on
13: 25–30.

18. *Josephus son of Zacharias* is perhaps mentioned with his
father and with Simon in 2 Macc. 10: 19 in connection with
an unfortunate episode in the Idumaean campaign. *Azarias*
appears elsewhere only in the sequel, in verses 55–62 below.

20. 4: 29 numbers Judas' men at 10,000; here we have a total
of 11,000 in addition to those left to defend Judaea (verse 18;
compare verse 60).

22. Simon's campaign is successful. The final battlefield is
not named, though the area where the River Kishon breaks
into the plain of Akko seems likely.

23. *Arbatta:* south-west of Galilee and the Esdraelon
valley. *

JUDAS AND JONATHAN IN GILEAD

Meanwhile Judas Maccabaeus and his brother Jonathan 24
crossed the Jordan and made a three days' march through
the desert. They came upon some Nabataeans, who met 25
them peacefully, and gave them an account of all that
had happened to their fellow-Jews in Gilead: many of 26

them were held prisoner in Bozrah and Bezer, in Alema, Casphor, Maked, and Carnaim – all large fortified towns;
27 some in the other towns of Gilead. 'Your enemies', they told them, 'are marshalling their forces to storm your fortresses tomorrow so as to capture them and destroy all the Jews in them in a single day.'

28   Then Judas and his army suddenly turned aside to Bozrah by way of the desert, captured the town, and put all the males to the sword. He plundered all their pro-
29 perty and set fire to the town. From there he made a night-march and came within reach of the fortress of
30 Dathema. When dawn broke they saw in front of them an innumerable host, bringing up scaling-ladders and siege-engines and engaging the defenders, to capture the
31 fortress. Judas saw that battle was already joined, and a cry went up to heaven from the town, with trumpeting
32 and loud shouting. Judas said to his men: 'Now is the time to fight for our brothers.'

33   They marched out in three columns to take the enemy in the rear. Then they sounded the trumpets and cried
34 aloud in prayer, and the army of Timotheus recognized that it was Maccabaeus and took to flight before him. He inflicted a severe defeat on them, and nearly eight thousand of the enemy fell that day.

35   Judas then turned aside to Alema,*a* attacked and cap-tured it, and killed all the males. He plundered the town
36 and set it on fire. From there he moved on and occupied Casphor, Maked, Bezer, and the other towns of Gilead.

[a] *Some witnesses read* Maapha.

✲ With this passage should also be read 2 Macc. 12: 10–31 and the commentary there. The campaign's progress might be easier to follow if we were more certain where the various places mentioned lay.

24. *three days' march through the desert* – perhaps about 120 km (75 miles) or a little less – would bring Judas' men to the general region of north Gilead.

25. *Nabataeans:* Petra in ancient Edom was their centre, and their caravans went north to Damascus (cp. Paul's experiences, 2 Cor. 11: 32), west to Gaza, and south to Arabia. 2 Macc. 5: 8 mentions one of their earliest kings, 'Aretas the ruler of the Arabs', whose name has been found on an inscription along the Petra–Gaza road. Possibly this meeting is another version of the event described in 2 Macc. 12: 10–12.

26. For the cities, see the map on p. 50. Probably each had its own small Jewish community. *Bozrah* is well known, 110 km (about 70 miles) south of Damascus on the road to Amman. The people here were perhaps responsible for the Jewish massacre in the nearby region of Tubias (verse 13).

27. *your fortresses* is a little puzzling; only Dathema (verse 29) is mentioned as a fortress under siege, and the existence of Jewish military fortresses in this area seems unlikely.

29. *Dathema* (if it is *tell hamad*) is 50 km (just over 30 miles) from Bozrah; such a night-march would hardly leave Judas' troops fresh for a battle. Some have suggested that for *Bozrah* in verse 28 we should read 'Bezer', some that verse 28 belongs with verse 35, and others that Judas sent one part of the army to Bozrah while he went to Dathema.

30. For a similar picture of an ancient siege, see Ezek. 4: 2 ff.; 21: 22.

35. *Alema* (cp. verse 26): this name is probably right. The *Maapha* of some witnesses (see the footnote) may reflect the influence on the text of the better known 'Mizpeh of Gilead' (Judg. 11: 29). If Alema is right, then 1 Maccabees describes the capture (see verses 36, 44) of all the towns mentioned in verse 26. ✲

JUDAS AND JONATHAN IN GILEAD (CONTINUED)

37 After these events, Timotheus gathered another army, and took up position opposite Raphon, on the other side 38 of the ravine. Judas sent spies to their camp, and they reported that all the Gentiles in the neighbourhood had 39 rallied in very great strength to Timotheus, who had also hired Arab mercenaries to help them; they were encamped on the far side of the ravine, ready to engage him in battle. So Judas marched to meet them.

40 As Judas and his army were approaching the flooded ravine, Timotheus said to his officers: 'If Judas crosses over to our side first, we shall not be able to stand up to him; 41 he will certainly get the better of us. If, however, his courage fails him and he takes up a position on the other side of the river, then we will cross over and get the better 42 of him.' When Judas reached the ravine, he stationed the officers of the muster on its bank, with instructions that no one should be allowed to take up a fixed position, but 43 that all should advance to battle. Thus Judas forestalled the enemy by crossing to attack them, with all his people following. The Gentiles broke before him; they all threw away their arms and took refuge in the temple at Car- 44 naim. Judas captured the town and burnt the temple together with all its occupants: Carnaim was completely subdued and could no longer withstand him.

* Compare 2 Macc. 12: 20–6. The narrative describes the events leading up to the capture of Carnaim.

37. *Timotheus* (cp. verse 34) is the enemy general throughout Judas' Transjordanian campaigns (see also verses 6–8).

Raphon is *er-rafeh*, 15 km (9½ miles) west of Carnaim (see verses 43 f.).

38–9. For Timotheus' use (customary with the Seleucid armies) of mercenaries, see 2 Macc. 10: 24; for his use of Arab support, see 2 Macc. 12: 10 ff.

40–1. Why the advantage would go to whichever side crossed the *flooded ravine* (flooded by the spring rain) is not clear; in fact, Timotheus probably lost the battle by letting Judas take the initiative (verse 43).

43. *took refuge in the temple at Carnaim:* see 2 Macc. 12: 21, 26. A temple was always a place of sanctuary, though it was not always respected as such. *Carnaim* (cp. Gen. 14: 5, 'Ashteroth-karnaim') was *tell ashterah* or *sheik sa'ad. Carnaim* means 'horns', and the name refers to the distinctive feature of the local version of the ancient goddess Astarte worshipped there. ✳

THE RETURN TO JERUSALEM

Then Judas gathered together all the Israelites in Gilead 45 to escort them to Judaea. They amounted to an immense host, small and great, women and children, with their property. They came as far as Ephron, a large and strongly 46 fortified town on the road: it was impossible to pass by it on either side; the only route was through the town. But the townsmen kept them out, barricading their gates 47 with boulders. Judas sent them a conciliatory message: 48 'We have to pass through your territory to reach our own. No one shall do you any harm: we shall only march through.' But they refused to open their gates to him.

Judas issued orders to the whole host for everyone to 49 halt where he was. Then the fighting men took up battle 50 positions and attacked the town all that day and all the night, until it fell into their hands. They put every male 51

to the sword, razed the town to the ground and plundered
it, and then marched through it over the bodies of the
52 dead. They crossed the Jordan to the great plain opposite
53 Bethshan, while Judas brought up the stragglers and encouraged the people all along the road till he arrived in
54 Judaea. They went up to Mount Zion with gladness and
jubilation, and offered burnt-offerings, because they had
returned in safety without the loss of a single man.

✻ The account is closely paralleled by 2 Macc. 12: 27–31.

46. *Ephron:* perhaps *et-taiyibeh* about 14½ km (9 miles) east
of the Jordan, opposite Bethshan (verse 52).

52. *Bethshan:* see the note on 2 Macc. 12: 29.

54. 2 Macc. 12: 31 says that they returned to Jerusalem in
time for Pentecost, May 163 B.C.

1 and 2 Maccabees have in common that this whole campaign began with an encounter with the Nabataeans (or
Arabs) and ended with a victory over Timotheus and the
capture of Carnaim, Ephron, and the return to Jerusalem by
Bethshan. In the middle, 1 Maccabees describes the capture of
Bozrah, the relief of Dathema, and the capture of Alema,
Casphor, Maked, Bezer, and other towns. 2 Maccabees describes an attack on Caspin (cp. Casphor, 1 Macc. 5: 36), a
visit to Charax, the home of the Tubian Jews, and the destruction of an unnamed enemy garrison. It is doubtful if we can
draw an accurate picture of the progress of this campaign.
Possibly 2 Macc. 10: 32–8, ending with the death of
Timotheus, also belongs to this context.

However, even if numbers are exaggerated (at least in 2
Maccabees), the places captured more like villages than fortified cities, and Antiochus' death had created the opportunity,
we can only admire the boldness of Judas' strategy, and its
execution. Clearly the author of 1 Maccabees admired these
exploits, for he seems to be comparing them with similar
great events of Israel's history. Judas defeats the Edomites

(Idumaeans) and Ammonites like a David of old (2 Sam. 8); he rescues allies in Gilead as Saul once did (1 Sam. 11); he marches his army by night (verse 29), dividing it into three companies and frightening the enemy with trumpet-blasts (verses 33–4), like a Gideon of old (Judg. 7); like Moses, he asks for passage through foreign territory (Num. 20: 14–21, cp. verse 48), and like Joshua he conquers the territory of Sihon and Og (Jazer, verse 8, cp. Num. 21: 32; Carnaim, verse 44, cp. Deut. 1: 4) and then crosses the Jordan (verse 52). Pagan peoples and their places of worship are religiously destroyed, as Deuteronomy had commanded of the Canaanites (Deut. 7). The Jews are threatened with extermination 'in a single day' (verse 27; cp. Esther 3: 13), and they rejoiced at the conclusion of the rescue (verse 54; cp. Esther 9: 17–19). The chapter is full of allusions to the Old Testament; the campaign is thus put on a level with the mighty acts of old. *

EXPLOITS IN IDUMAEA AND PHILISTIA

Now while Judas and Jonathan were in Gilead, and 55 Simon their brother in Galilee was besieging Ptolemais, the two commanders, Josephus son of Zacharias, and 56 Azarias, heard of their exploits in battle. 'We too', they 57 said, 'must make a name for ourselves: let us go and fight the Gentiles in our neighbourhood.' So they gave orders 58 to their forces and marched against Jamnia. Gorgias came 59 out of the town with his men to meet them in battle; and 60 Josephus and Azarias were routed and pursued to the frontier of Judaea. Some two thousand of the people fell that day. So the Israelites suffered a heavy defeat, because 61 their commanders, thinking to play the hero themselves, had not obeyed Judas and his brothers. They were not, 62 however, of that family to whom it was granted to bring deliverance to Israel.

63 Judas and his brothers won a great reputation in all Israel and among the Gentiles, wherever their fame was
64 heard, and crowds flocked to acclaim them.

65 After this, Judas marched out with his brothers and made war on the descendants of Esau to the south. He struck at Hebron and its villages, demolished its fortifica-
66 tions, and burnt down its forts on all sides. He then set out to invade Philistine territory, marching through
67 Marisa. On that day several priests, who had ill-advisedly gone into action wishing to distinguish themselves, fell in
68 battle. Then Judas turned aside to Azotus in Philistia. He pulled down their altars, burnt the images of their gods, carried off the spoil from their towns, and returned to Judaea.

✳ Verses 55–62 are the sequel to Judas' orders in verse 19 above, and describe how inexperienced Maccabaean commanders played into the hands of an experienced Syrian general. Verses 65–8 describe sorties made by Judas against hellenistic towns to the south and south-west of Jerusalem.

58. *Jamnia* (cp. 4: 15), once the Philistine city of Jabneh (2 Chron. 26: 6), appears several times as a Syrian base (cp. 10: 69; 15: 40); here it seems to be the base of Gorgias, 'the general in charge of Idumaea' (2 Macc. 12: 32).

62. For the author of 1 Maccabees, only one family, the Hasmonaean, descendants of the Maccabees, could *bring deliverance to Israel*. This Maccabaean defeat took place in Judas' absence, and so before Pentecost 163 B.C.

65. *descendants of Esau*: i.e. the Idumaeans, as in verse 3, but this time *to the south*, at Hebron.

66. *Philistine*: like the 'descendants of Esau', the Philistines as a recognizable national group had long since disappeared, but the use of the Old Testament terms again sets this struggle in

2. The last campaign of Antiochus (1 Macc. 6: 1–4).

the context of other great struggles of the past. *Marisa* was a hellenistic town about half-way between Jerusalem and Gaza. Cp. 2 Macc. 12: 35.

67. The *battle* may be that described in 2 Macc. 12: 32–7, and the reference to the *priests* who fell may be closely related to the events described in 2 Macc. 12: 38–45. 1 Maccabees describes not a victory but a defeat, though the author takes care to lay the blame (by implication) not on Judas but on those who *fell in battle*. 2 Macc. 12: 35, however, portrays a victory which ends in Gorgias' flight for refuge to Marisa, though even here there are hints of Jewish difficulties (verses 34–6, 38). 2 Macc. 12: 38 suggests a Jewish withdrawal to Adullam, about 16 km (10 miles) from Marisa towards Jerusalem, and an expedition from there to pick up the bodies of the fallen, and 2 Maccabees gives another explanation, also exonerating Judas, for their deaths.

68. *Azotus* (cp. 4: 15) is Ashdod on the coast, north-west of Marisa. Note once again the destruction of the pagan *images.* ✳

THE DEATH OF ANTIOCHUS

6 As King Antiochus marched through the upper provinces he heard that there was a city in Persia called
2 Elymais, famous for its wealth in silver and gold. Its temple was very rich, full of gold shields, coats of mail, and arms, left there by Alexander son of Philip, king of Macedon
3 and the first to be king over the Greeks. Antiochus came and tried to capture and plunder the city, but failed because
4 his plan had become known to the citizens. They gave battle and put him to flight, and he withdrew to Babylon in bitter disappointment.

5 A messenger met him in Persia with the news that the armies which had invaded Judaea were in full retreat.
6 Lysias had marched up with an exceptionally strong force, only to be flung back before the enemy, and the strength of the Jews had grown by the capture of arms, equipment,
7 and spoils from the Syrian armies they had defeated. They had pulled down the abomination he had built on the altar in Jerusalem, and surrounded their temple with high walls as before, and had even fortified Bethsura.

8 When the king heard this news, he was thrown into such deep dismay that he took to his bed, ill with grief at the
9 miscarriage of his plans. There he lay for many days, his bitter grief breaking out again and again, and he realized
10 that he was dying. So he summoned all his Friends and said to them: 'Sleep has deserted me; the weight of care
11 has broken my heart. At first I said to myself, "Why am

I overwhelmed by this flood of trouble, I who was kind
and well-loved in the day of my power?" But now I 12
remember the wrong I did in Jerusalem, when I took all
her vessels of silver and gold, and when I made an un-
justified attempt to wipe out the inhabitants of Judaea.
It is for this, I know, that these misfortunes have come 13
upon me; and here I am, dying of grief in a foreign land.'

He summoned Philip, one of his Friends, and appointed 14
him regent over his whole empire, giving him the crown, 15
the royal robe, and the signet-ring, with authority to take
his son Antiochus and bring him up to be king. King 16
Antiochus died there in the year 149.[a]

When Lysias learnt that the king was dead, he placed 17
the young Antiochus, whom he had brought up from
boyhood, on the throne in succession to his father, and
gave him the name of Eupator.

✻ See also 2 Macc. 1: 13–17 and 2 Macc. 9. 1 Maccabees
puts the death of Antiochus after Judas' recapture of the
temple, and 2 Maccabees before, but it is now clear that it
happened about November or early December 164 B.C. (see
the commentary on 4: 36–61). This chapter picks up the story
from 3: 37, where after crossing the Euphrates in spring 165
B.C. Antiochus 'marched through the upper provinces'. After
some activity on the coast of the Persian Gulf, he marched
inland to the regions of Elymais and Persia; 1 and 2 Maccabees agree in describing an unsuccessful attack, illness, and
death, though the geographical details they give are confused.
Both 1 and 2 Maccabees tell the story from a distinctly Jewish
point of view.

1. *upper provinces*: see p. 8. *Elymais* was a mountain region

[a] *That is* 163 B.C.

(not a *city*) lying roughly west of (not *in*) *Persia*. There is perhaps some confusion here with Antiochus III, who died raiding the temple of Bel in Elymais. 2 Macc. 1: 11–17 says that Antiochus IV was killed plundering the temple dedicated to a goddess Nanaea (no location is given). For Seleucid kings' plundering of temples to aid their finances, see the commentary on 1: 20–8.

2. *Alexander:* cp. 1: 1.

3. *the city:* 2 Macc. 9: 1–3 tells of Antiochus' retreat to Ecbatana after an unsuccessful attempt to plunder the temples of Persepolis, and his death in the mountains of a foreign land. The Greek historian Polybius (a contemporary of Antiochus) says that he died at Gabae (Isfahan), half way between Persepolis and Ecbatana. In fact, he died at a place called Tabae, between Persia and Media. Possibly, then, *the city* which he tried to take was the great Persepolis, the city founded by Cyrus as the Persian capital.

4. A retreat to *Babylon* after a campaign in Elymais or Persia, followed by a return to Persia (verse 5, cp. 56) for Antiochus' illness and death, seems most unlikely. Antiochus refounded Babylon, but its mention here is out of place.

5–7. The news that reaches Antiochus summarizes events described in 4: 28–61, but if Antiochus died in November or early December 164 B.C., he could not have heard of Judas' rededication of the temple and his fortifications. For the doubts concerning the historicity of Lysias' campaign (verse 6), see the commentary on 4: 28 ff. In any case, the author was hardly well placed to know what was reported to Antiochus. The news is given in Jewish terms; thus, the building of the *abomination...on the altar* (verse 7: see 1: 54) is ascribed to Antiochus in person.

8. 2 Macc. 9: 7 blames Antiochus' illness (for its physical causes, at least) on a chariot accident. Polybius speaks of insanity.

11. *kind and well-loved:* Antiochus was on the whole popular; his son was called 'Eupator' (verse 17), 'of a good father'.

1 Maccabees presents only one aspect of Antiochus' career, and that with considerable prejudice.

13. *in a foreign land:* these words underline for the Jewish writer the severity of the punishment.

14. Antiochus, like Alexander (cp. 1: 5), makes his final arrangements. *Philip* was an 'intimate friend' of Antiochus (2 Macc. 9: 29); the Greek word behind this description is used of Manaen in Acts 13: 1, where it is translated 'who had been at the court of Prince Herod'. For the title *Friend* see pp. 9 f. Philip was perhaps the royal official at Babylon who dedicated an altar to Antiochus Epiphanes in 169–168 B.C. (He is not the Philip mentioned in 2 Macc. 5: 22; 8: 8.) He is appointed in place of Lysias (see 3: 32) as guardian of and *regent* for Antiochus' son, Antiochus V Eupator, now between nine and twelve years old, who was killed three years later by Demetrius I (7: 1–4) when apparently still in Lysias' care.

15. *crown:* in fact, a white woollen band. The *royal robe* was purple, and the *signet-ring* (cp. Esther 3: 10) bore the device of an anchor, the dynasty's emblem. For Philip's further career, see 6: 63, and the note on 2 Macc. 9: 29.

16. *the year 149* would have begun in October 164 B.C.; Antiochus died early in the year, and did not survive to 163 B.C.

17. Lysias placed Eupator on the throne, and Eupator, who probably had little choice, appointed Lysias, already governor-general of Coele-syria and Phoenicia, as vicegerent (2 Macc. 10: 11). ✵

RENEWED ATTACK FROM SYRIA

Meanwhile the garrison of the citadel were confining the 18 Israelites to the neighbourhood of the temple, and giving continual support to the Gentiles by their harassing tactics. Judas therefore determined to make an end of them. He 19 gathered all the people together to lay siege to the citadel

20 in the year 150,[a] erecting emplacements and siege-engines against the enemy.

21 Now some of the besieged garrison escaped and were 22 joined by a number of renegade Israelites. They went to the king and said: 'How long must we wait for you to do 23 justice and avenge our comrades? We were willing to serve your father, to follow his instructions and to obey 24 his decrees, and what was the result? Our own country-men became our enemies. They actually killed as many of 25 us as they could find, and robbed us of our property. Nor are we the only ones to suffer at their hands. They have 26 attacked all their neighbours as well. At this very moment they are besieging the citadel in Jerusalem and mean to capture it; and they have fortified both the temple and 27 Bethsura. Unless your majesty quickly overpowers them they will go to yet greater lengths, and you will not be able to keep them in check.'

28 When the king heard this he was furious. He assembled all his Friends, the commanders of his army, and his 29 cavalry officers. He was joined by mercenary troops from 30 other kingdoms and from the islands. His forces numbered one hundred thousand infantry, twenty thousand cavalry, 31 and thirty-two war-elephants. They passed through Idu-maea and laid siege to Bethsura. They kept up the attack for a long time and erected siege-engines, but the defenders made a sortie and set fire to them, and fought back manfully.

* Though Judas had campaigned vigorously in Transjordan and Idumaea in the first half of 163 B.C., he and his supporters

[a] *That is* 162 B.C.

were in fact a militant minority, holding two small fortified
sites (the temple and Bethsura) in a country whose government was still pro-Syrian and supported by Syrian troops.
This section describes the Jerusalem government's new attempt, at the beginning of the new reign, to put down the
Maccabaean rebels.

18. The *garrison...were confining the Israelites to the neighbourhood of the temple* and (so Josephus adds, *Antiquities* XII. 9. 3)
attacking men going to sacrifice there. Naturally, confining
the Maccabaean garrison on the temple site would give *support
to the Gentiles* (those attacked by the Maccabees throughout
the country) by keeping Maccabaean troops occupied.

20. *the year 150:* i.e. the year beginning autumn 163 or
spring 162 B.C.; the N.E.B. footnote takes the period common
to both reckonings. But summer 162 B.C. seems a little late:
it would mean that Philip (verses 55, 63) waited a whole year
or more before coming to Antioch to take up his regency.
This is possible, but unlikely, and the reference of verse 49 to
a sabbatical year (which by calculation from a known sabbatical year in autumn 38–37 B.C. may be dated to autumn
164–163 B.C.) suggests that this attack on the citadel may be
dated to autumn 163 B.C., at the beginning of the year 150.
Indeed, 2 Macc. 13: 1 puts this event in 'the year 149'. Most
probably, then, the attack can be dated summer or autumn
163 B.C.

The reference to 'all the people' (verse 19), and the erection
of *emplacements and siege-engines* (for these see the note on
verse 31), show that the Maccabees now had sufficient support
to be a serious danger to the government.

21. *renegade Israelites:* probably hellenizing government
officials, perhaps including Menelaus (2 Macc. 13: 3). They
complain that they are suffering for their loyalty by death or
loss of property (verse 24).

25. *all their neighbours:* see chapter 5.

26. See verses 19 f., and 4: 60–1.

28. For the expedition see also 2 Macc. 13: 9–26. Both

1 and 2 Maccabees give some place to the king's initiative, though he can hardly have been more than twelve years old. But the guiding hand of Lysias is seen at several points (cp. verses 38, 55, 57–9; 2 Macc. 13: 2, 4, 26).

29. *mercenary troops* (cp. 2 Macc. 13: 2, an additional 'Greek force') from places like Pergamum, Bithynia, Pontus, Cappadocia (*other kingdoms*), Cyprus, Rhodes, Crete (*islands*) and elsewhere were often used by the Seleucids. Later, Demetrius II used Jewish mercenaries in Antioch itself (11: 44–8).

30. 2 Macc. 13: 2 says that the Greek force consisted of 110,000 infantry, 5,300 cavalry, 22 elephants, and 300 scythed chariots. At his army review in 166 B.C. Antiochus had 42 elephants. Verses 35 and 38 suggest that Lysias had well over 16,000 cavalry at his disposal. Both accounts thus suggest a massive army; the Syrians do not underestimate Judas, and in this campaign have military success.

31. The Syrian strategy is to take Bethsura before marching on Jerusalem (cp. 4: 28 ff.). (2 Macc. 13: 9–17 describes a preliminary night-attack by Judas on the Syrian army near Modin.) At Bethsura, an American excavation in 1931 revealed traces of Maccabaean fortifications and found remains of arrow-heads, spear-heads, daggers and fire-torches. Siege-engines (cp. 5: 30; 6: 20, 51–2) had been known for centuries; the Assyrians had used them, and they were used by Demetrius 'the Besieger' at the siege of Rhodes in 305–304 B.C. The hellenistic age was ingenious in the contriving of military machines and counter-defences (cp. 6: 52); at Rhodes a revolving crane was designed to lift the enemy's siege-engines into the city. ✳

THE BATTLE OF BETHZACHARIA

32 Judas now withdrew from the citadel and encamped at
33 Bethzacharia, opposite the camp of the king. Early next morning the king broke camp and rushed his army along the road to Bethzacharia; there his forces were drawn up

for battle and the trumpets were sounded. The elephants 34
were roused for battle with the juice of grapes and of mul-
berries. The great beasts were distributed among the 35
phalanxes; by each were stationed a thousand men, equipped with coats of chain-mail and bronze helmets. Five
hundred picked horsemen were also assigned to each
animal. These had been stationed beforehand where the 36
beast was; and wherever it went, they went with it, never
leaving it. Each animal had a strong wooden turret 37
fastened on its back with a special harness, by way of
protection, and carried four[a] fighting men as well as an
Indian driver. The rest of the cavalry Lysias stationed on 38
either flank of the army, to harass the enemy while themselves protected by the phalanxes. When the sun shone 39
on the gold and bronze shields, they lit up the hills, which
flashed like torches.

Part of the king's army was deployed over the heights, 40
and part over the low ground. They advanced confidently
and in good order. All who heard the din of this marching 41
multitude and its clashing arms shook with fear. It was a
very great and powerful array indeed.

Judas advanced with his army and gave battle, and six 42
hundred of the king's men were killed. Eleazar Avaran, 43
seeing that one of the elephants wore royal armour and
stood out above all the rest, thought that the king was
riding on it. So he gave his life to save his people and win 44
everlasting renown for himself. He ran boldly towards it, 45
into the middle of the phalanx, dealing death right and
left, while they fell back on either side before him. He 46

[a] *Probable reading; Gk.* thirty-two (*compare verse 30*).

got in underneath the elephant, and thrust at it from below and killed it. It fell to the ground on top of him, and there he died.

* The battle was clearly a Syrian victory (see verse 47), but I Maccabees plays down the Maccabaean defeat by emphasizing the magnificent power of the Syrian army and the brave self-sacrifice of one of the Maccabees. 2 Maccabees omits any mention of this battle.

32. Judas is forced to raise the siege of the citadel, thus leaving a dangerous garrison threatening his rear. *Bethzacharia* was south of Jerusalem, 10 km (6 miles) north of Bethsura.

34–7. Antiochus appears to have stimulated his elephants with alcohol, which sounds a somewhat dangerous expedient, especially if the elephants were surrounded by horses. Stories of intoxicated elephants being roused against the Jews in Egypt in the mid-second century B.C. are found in a book known as 3 Maccabees (see above, pp. 12 f.) and in Josephus (*Against Apion* II. 5), and in these stories the elephants in fact do turn on their masters. Here, however, the beasts were stationed in the battle line like so many towers, from each of which three or four men (not *thirty-two*, a scribal slip perhaps caused by a backward glance at verse 30) could shoot down on the opposing ranks.

38. The tactics are classical Macedonian tactics. The *phalanx* had been adopted by Philip of Macedon and his son Alexander the Great, and its weight and solidity made it irresistible until it met the Roman legions. It consisted of heavy infantry in parallel columns, sixteen ranks deep, armed with swords and long spears.

40. The author cannot help showing his admiration for the disciplined advance of the Syrian army.

43. *Eleazar Avaran* (cp. 2: 5) was one of Judas' younger brothers. The elephant's *royal armour*, protecting chest and flanks, probably did not indicate the king's mount, which

would be a more mobile horse. 2 Macc. 13: 15, which describes the stabbing of 'the leading elephant', may derive from the same incident.

44. Eleazar is portrayed as one of 'the heroes of our nation's history', one of those who 'made themselves a name by their exploits' (Ecclus. 44: 1, 3). (For a more theological interpretation of deaths in the Maccabaean cause, see 2 Macc. 7: 38.)

45. For a single man to reach *the middle of the phalanx* was a real achievement. ✶

THE SIEGE OF THE TEMPLE

When the Jews saw the strength and impetus of the 47 imperial forces, they fell back before them. Part of the 48 king's army marched up to Jerusalem to renew the engagement, and the king put Judaea and Mount Zion into a state of siege. He made peace with the people of Beth- 49 sura, who abandoned the town, having no more food there to withstand a siege, as it was a sabbatical year when the land was left fallow. Thus the king occupied Bethsura 50 and detailed a garrison to hold it.

He then attacked the temple and subjected it to a long 51 siege; he set up emplacements and siege-engines, with flame-throwers, catapults for discharging stones and barbed missiles, and slings. But the defenders too con- 52 structed engines to counter his engines, and put up a prolonged resistance. There was no food, however, in the 53 stores[a] because of the sabbatical year; those who from time to time had arrived in Judaea as refugees from the Gentiles had eaten up all that remained of the provisions. There 54 were only a few men left in the temple, because the famine

[a] *Some witnesses read* in the temple.

had been too severe for them, and they had scattered to their own homes.

* After their victory, the Syrians occupy the Maccabaean garrison at Bethsura and besiege the Maccabaean-held temple. 1 Maccabees again contrasts the Syrian resources with the Maccabaean lack of them by way of minimizing the Maccabaean misfortunes, but he cannot disguise that they were in great difficulty. 2 Maccabees omits or alters this material.

48. *the king put Judaea and Mount Zion into a state of siege:* Judaea was probably put under military control; only Mount Zion, i.e. the temple, was actually besieged.

49. *Bethsura,* now isolated, and provisionless, capitulates and is garrisoned by Antiochus. (2 Macc. 13: 18–22 again gives the impression that the king's siege is a failure, even though a Jewish soldier betrayed Judas' despatch of relief supplies.)

51. *siege-engines:* see the commentary on verse 31. *barbed missiles* translates the Greek *skorpidia*, scorpions.

52. The defenders' counter-engines remind us of the 'machines designed by engineers for use upon towers and bastions, made to discharge arrows and large stones' credited to King Uzziah in the eighth century B.C. by 2 Chron. 26: 15.

53. The *sabbatical year* which ended in autumn 163 B.C. meant that there had been no sowing or harvest that spring and summer (cp. verse 49, and Lev. 25: 3 f.), and so *there was no food...in the stores* (Greek *aggeiois,* for which some witnesses read *agiois,* meaning *temple*). *refugees from the Gentiles:* cp. 5: 23, 54.

54. The verse reveals, once again, that Antiochus was not fighting all Israel, but a resistance group whose numbers were probably drawn largely from the country peasantry and fluctuated according to circumstances. *

SYRIA OFFERS TERMS

Lysias heard that Philip, whom King Antiochus had 55
appointed before he died to educate his son Antiochus for
the kingship, had returned from Persia and Media with 56
the late king's expeditionary force, and that he was seeking
to take over the government. So he hastily gave orders for 57
departure, saying to the king, his commanders, and his
troops: 'Every day we are growing weaker, provisions
are low, the place we are besieging is strong, and the
affairs of the empire are pressing. So let us offer these men 58
terms and make peace with them and their whole nation.
Let us guarantee their right to follow their laws and cus- 59
toms as they used to do, for it was our abolition of these
very customs and laws that roused their resentment, and
produced all these consequences.'

The proposal met with the approval of the king and the 60
commanders, and an offer of peace was sent and accepted.
The king and his commanders bound themselves by oath 61
and on the agreed terms the besieged emerged from their
stronghold. But when the king entered Mount Zion and 62
saw how strongly the place was fortified, he went back
on the oath he had sworn, and gave orders for the surrounding wall to be demolished. He then set off at top 63
speed for Antioch, where he found Philip in possession;
a battle ensued, and the city was taken by storm.

* New political circumstances rather than lack of military
success force Lysias to offer terms; their effect is to repeal the
'decree' of 1: 41–50. In spite of his assurances, Lysias destroys
the temple fortifications, and returns to Antioch to deal with
his rival, Philip.

55–6. See 6: 14 f. 2 Macc. 13: 23, however, says that Philip, left in Antioch by Antiochus V, 'had gone out of his mind'.

57. *provisions are low:* a besieging army expected to live off the land, and the sabbatical year affected the Syrians as well as the Maccabaeans. But the most telling reason for abandoning the siege is the pressure of *the affairs of the empire*.

58. *them and their whole nation* perhaps reveals the two Jewish groups involved – the Maccabaean, and the rest of the people, led by the hellenizing government.

59. *to follow their laws and customs as they used to do:* i.e. the 'decree' of 1: 51 ff. is repealed. The letter of 2 Macc. 11: 22–6, which notes that the Jews prefer their own laws to Greek ways and decrees that the temple shall be restored to the Jews, who should regulate their lives according to their ancestral customs, belongs to this situation. It was written by Antiochus V to Lysias, probably early in 162 B.C. This would be a blow to the ruling hellenizing party, who did not regain the initiative until after Antiochus' death (7: 5 ff.).

62. The Maccabaeans lost their fortified stronghold, however, and Jerusalem remained under the military control of the Syrian garrison in the citadel. But by the terms of the peace, the temple services, restored to their traditional forms by the Maccabees in 164 B.C. (4: 36–59) and since then performed under threat from the citadel, were now given official approval. It was an uneasy peace, however; hellenizers and Maccabaeans alike were frustrated, and above all there was no high priest, for Lysias, recognizing that Menelaus was a particularly dangerous element in the Jewish situation, had arranged his execution (2 Macc. 13: 3–8). Such a situation could not last long. ✲

A NEW RÉGIME IN SYRIA

7 In the year 151,[a] Demetrius son of Seleucus left Rome, landed with a handful of men at a town on the coast, and
2 there made himself king. While he was travelling to the

[a] *That is* 161 B.C.

royal seat of his ancestors, the army seized Antiochus and Lysias, intending to hand them over to him. When this 3 was reported to him, he said, 'Do not let me set eyes on them.' The soldiers accordingly put them to death, and 4 Demetrius ascended the throne.

✻ Demetrius, son of Seleucus IV, was born in 186 B.C. In 175 B.C. he had been sent to Rome as a hostage for Seleucid loyalty, while Antiochus IV, the previous hostage in Rome, took the throne. Demetrius, in fact, was the rightful heir, and asked the Roman Senate for permission to take his throne. The Senate refused, though perhaps not without some sympathy for him; an able Antiochus IV might not be entirely to their advantage. In 162 B.C. Roman commissioners investigating Syria's armed resources were murdered, and Antiochus V and Lysias thereby naturally incurred Rome's displeasure. Demetrius seized the opportunity, and, with the help of the historian Polybius, left Rome for Syria.

1. *the year 151* on the Macedonian dating began autumn 162 B.C., on the Babylonian, spring 161 B.C. *with a handful of men:* Polybius says sixteen, which 2 Macc. 14: 1 enlarges to 'a powerful army and fleet'. *a town on the coast:* according to 2 Macc. 14: 1 this was Tripolis, 96 km (60 miles) north of Beirut.

2. *the royal seat* was Antioch, about 270 km (170 miles) north of Tripolis. The army supported Demetrius and removed his rivals.

3. Diplomatically, Demetrius does not actually order their death.

NEW INITIATIVES FROM THE
JERUSALEM GOVERNMENT

All the godless renegades from Israel, led by Alcimus, 5 who aspired to be high priest, came to the king and brought 6 charges against their people. They said to him: 'Judas and his brothers have killed all your supporters, and have

7 driven us from our country. Be pleased now to send a
man whom you trust, to go and see what devastation they
have brought upon us and upon the king's territory, and
8 to punish them and all their supporters.' The king chose
Bacchides, one of the royal Friends, who was governor
beyond the Euphrates, a man of high standing in the
9 empire and loyal to the king. He sent him and the godless
Alcimus, on whom he had conferred the high-priesthood,
with orders to take vengeance on Israel.

10   They set out with a large army and entered Judaea.
Bacchides sent envoys to Judas and his brothers to make
11 false offers of friendship; but when they saw what a large
force he had brought with him, they took no notice of
these offers.

✴ When Demetrius came to the throne, some eight or twelve
months after Antiochus V's letter ratifying the peace terms
(2 Macc. 11: 22–6; see above on 6: 59), there were two major
problems in Judaea to be solved. First, the high-priestly office
was vacant; and second, Judas' supporters appear (verses 6
and 7) to have been attacking the homes and property of pro-
Syrian landlords and aristocracy.

5. *Alcimus* was 'a priest of the family of Aaron' (verse 14),
but high priests, at least until the appointment of Menelaus,
had to be able to claim descent from Zadok, originally the
Canaanite priest of David's Jerusalem but in time legitimized
by incorporation into the family of Aaron (see 1 Chron. 6:
1–15). 2 Macc. 14: 7 records Alcimus' claim to the 'hereditary
dignity' of the high-priesthood, and it is possible that he
belonged to the Aaronite family of Jakim (1 Chron. 24: 12).
He was probably the obvious moderate replacement for
Menelaus. He had 'submitted voluntarily to pollutions at the
time of the secession' (2 Macc. 14: 3), i.e. after Antiochus'
decree. Thus he would be acceptable to Syria as a hellenizer,

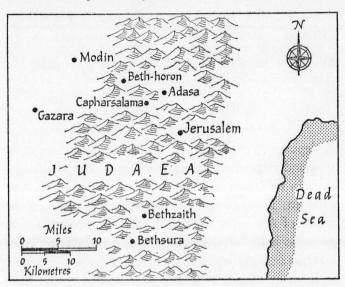

3. The final campaign of Nicanor (1 Macc. 7: 12–50;
2 Macc. 14: 15).

and, with reservations, to the Hasidaeans (for whom see 2: 42)
as belonging to the house of Aaron. But the Maccabaeans and
their historian thought of him as 'godless' (verse 9) like the
renegades. However, Demetrius made Alcimus high priest,
thus putting power back into the hands of the hellenizing
party, for the high priest naturally controlled what went on
in the temple as well as in other affairs.

6. *brought charges against their people:* Judas' supporters are
identified by 1 Maccabees with the people of Israel. It is at
least clear that by now the Maccabees were well supported
by the country people. Alcimus accuses Judas and his supporters of a campaign of terrorism, for which the hellenizers are
apparently seeking 'vengeance' (verse 9).

8. *governor:* see p. 9. The phrase *beyond the Euphrates*
betrays a Mesopotamian or Iranian standpoint, and this

95

description of the western region is inherited from the Babylonian and Persian empires.

10–11. *large army:* again, Syria does not underestimate the Maccabees, who, for their part, have enough strength – or determination – to ignore Bacchides' offers of friendship.

ALCIMUS' POLICY AND ITS RESULTS

12,13 A deputation of doctors of the law came before Alcimus and Bacchides, asking for justice. The Hasidaeans were in fact the first group in Israel to make overtures 14 to them; for they said to themselves, 'A priest of the family of Aaron has come with their forces, and he will 15 do us no harm.' The language of Alcimus was conciliatory; he assured them on oath that no harm was intended 16 to them or their friends. But once he had gained their confidence, he arrested sixty of them and put them to death in a single day; as Scripture says:

17   'The bodies of thy saints were scattered,
                 their blood was shed round Jerusalem,
                 and there was none to bury them.'

18 This put all the people in fear and terror of them, and they said to each other, 'There is neither truth nor justice among them; they have broken their pledge and the oath 19 they swore.' Then Bacchides left Jerusalem and camped in Bethzaith; and he ordered the arrest of many of those who had deserted to him, together with some of the people, and had them slaughtered and thrown into a great 20 pit. He assigned the whole district to Alcimus, detailed some troops to assist him, and returned to the king.

21,22 Alcimus fought hard for his high-priesthood. All the

trouble-makers rallied to him; they gained control over Judaea, and did terrible damage in Israel. When Judas saw 23 all the mischief which Alcimus and his followers had brought upon the Israelites, far worse than anything the Gentiles had done, he marched through all the territory 24 of Judaea and its environs, punishing deserters and debarring them from access to the country districts. When 25 Alcimus saw that Judas and his band had grown powerful, and recognized that he was unable to withstand them, he returned to the king and accused them of atrocities.

* Alcimus and Bacchides ruthlessly purged the Hasidaeans and other past Maccabaean supporters who had showed themselves willing to come to terms with Syria and the Jerusalem government. This hardened attitudes and forced men to take sides, for waverers would suffer from Judas (verse 24) if they had not already suffered from Alcimus or Bacchides. The hellenizers had in theory political control over 'Judaea' (verse 22), but the Maccabaeans had effectual control of the 'country districts' (verse 24), and forced Alcimus to make a second appeal to the king.

12. *doctors of the law:* probably the Hasidaeans of verse 13. What they meant by *asking for justice* is not entirely clear, but it was probably the restoration (in accord with the terms of Antiochus V's peace offer) of the normal legalities of Jewish life. As lawyers (a portrait of the lawyer is given in Ecclus. 39: 1–11) they naturally wanted once again to be 'in demand at public discussions...prominent in the assembly' and to 'sit on the judge's bench' (Ecclus. 38: 33).

13–14. See the commentary on verse 5 above.

15. The Hasidaeans mistook their man and the moment, fatally. Alcimus did not feel secure; opponents once, the Hasidaeans might oppose again. Lawyers can be dangerously critical of a one-sided régime.

17. The verse quotes – very approximately – Ps. 79: 2–3, a psalm which begins with the words

> O God, the heathen have set foot in thy domain,
> defiled thy holy temple
> and laid Jerusalem in ruins.

The psalm probably referred to the Babylonian action in 586 B.C., but could be understood as generally appropriate to the circumstances of the 160s B.C.

18. The execution of the Hasidaeans was Alcimus' mistake; the people lost confidence in him.

19. Bacchides continued Alcimus' policy in the country; *Bethzaith* ('the house of the olive') is perhaps *beit zeita*, 24 km (15 miles) south of Jerusalem towards Bethsura. He disposed of his victims as Ishmael had disposed of pro-Babylonian Jews at Mizpah (Jer. 41: 7). The *pit* was probably an old cistern hewn out of the limestone whose plaster had cracked, rendering it useless for water storage.

20. Alcimus is formally made, under Demetrius and with Syrian support, head of state in Judah and Jerusalem, as Onias, Jason and Menelaus had been.

21–5. Alcimus' and Bacchides' policy provoked violent reprisals from Judas.

24. *deserters:* cp. verse 19; Judas replies in kind. Jerusalem and Judaea, town and country, on the whole are sharply divided, supporting Alcimus and Judas respectively.

25. Alcimus is forced to appeal again to the king. This is the situation described in 2 Macc. 14: 3–14, where Alcimus, apparently temporarily deprived of his office (14: 7) and even of access to the temple (14: 3), appeals to Demetrius, who sends the general Nicanor to his aid (2 Macc. 14: 11 – 15: 37). *

A NEW APPROACH BY NICANOR

Then the king sent Nicanor, one of his distinguished 26
commanders and a bitter enemy of Israel, with orders to
wipe them out. Nicanor arrived at Jerusalem with a large 27
force, and sent envoys to Judas and his brothers to make
false offers of friendship: 'Let there be no quarrel between 28
us,' he said; 'I propose to come with a few men for a
friendly personal meeting.'

He came to Judas and they greeted one another as 29
friends, yet the enemy were preparing to kidnap Judas.
When Judas discovered that Nicanor's visit was a trick, he 30
took alarm and refused to meet him again. Nicanor, realiz- 31
ing that his plan had been detected, marched out to engage
Judas near Capharsalama. About five hundred of Nicanor's 32
army were killed, and the rest escaped to the city of David.

* If Bacchides' campaign had taken place, as seems reasonable, in summer 161 B.C. (see on 7: 1 ff.), Nicanor would have
arrived in autumn 161 B.C. (no date is given). He was killed
on 17 March 160 B.C. (7: 49).

It is worth considering what the policy of the Syrian king
in such a situation should be. He might think first of simply
supporting the hellenizers and crushing the rebels, and this is
what 1 Macc. 7: 26 envisages; Nicanor is to be another Bacchides, with a policy of 'false...friendship' (cp. verse 10 above).
2 Macc. 14: 13 says that Nicanor is 'to dispose of Judas himself and disperse his forces, and to install Alcimus as high priest',
but shows Nicanor attempting a more subtle policy than 1
Maccabees suggests. Nicanor respects his opponent, attempts
to negotiate a settlement, befriends Judas and encourages him
to settle down. This reconciliatory policy, however, is wrecked
by the hellenizers, who object to the king that Nicanor is more

partial to the rebels than to the loyalists; Alcimus has no desire to share power with Judas. Nicanor reacts by turning against both sides (2 Macc. 14: 31 ff.). 2 Maccabees' account seems politically and psychologically sounder than that in 1 Maccabees. Nicanor is really sent to negotiate a settlement between the two Jewish parties. A bitterly divided Judaea, demanding the presence of troops and generals badly needed in the East, was hardly to Demetrius' liking.

26. *one of his distinguished commanders:* in fact, 'commander of the elephant corps' (2 Macc. 14: 12) before the Romans had the elephants destroyed in 162 B.C. *a bitter enemy:* he had been defeated by Judas in 165 B.C. (see 3: 38 – 4: 27; 2 Macc. 8: 9–36). He had helped Demetrius on his escape from Rome, and is now given command of Judaea (2 Macc. 14: 12).

27. 2 Macc. 8: 34; 15: 3 calls Nicanor a 'double-dyed villain', yet 2 Maccabees shows traces of a better side to him. His attitude to the Jews may not have been so inimical and treacherous as our Jewish sources suggest. 2 Macc. 14: 16 f. speaks of a minor engagement preceding Nicanor's friendly advances.

28–32. These verses make Nicanor sound like another Sanballat of Samaria (cp. Neh. 6: 1–14). Judas, however, met Nicanor at least once, and 2 Maccabees suggests that the friendship was mutual and genuine.

30. There were probably Maccabaeans as well as hellenizers who mistrusted Judas' fraternizing with a Syrian general. The possibility of co-operation had been destroyed by the work of Alcimus and Bacchides.

31. *Capharsalama*, 'village of Salem', was perhaps *khirbet selma* 11 km (7 miles) north-west of Jerusalem, from which Nicanor's men could retreat easily (verse 32) to the safety of the Syrian garrison in Jerusalem. 2 Maccabees, however, does not mention this battle (unless it is one of the engagements of 2 Macc. 14: 16–17, both of which appear to be Jewish defeats). Josephus (*Antiquities* XII. 10. 4) describes it as a victory for Nicanor (though some scholars emend Josephus' text to make it agree with the verdict of 1 Maccabees). ✳

NICANOR THREATENS THE TEMPLE

After these events, Nicanor went up to Mount Zion, 33
and some of the priests and members of the senate came
out from the temple to give him a friendly welcome, and
to show him the burnt-offering which was being sacrificed for the king. But he mocked them, jeered at them, 34
and spat on them,[a] boasting and swearing angrily: 'Un- 35
less Judas and his army are surrendered to me at once, when
I return victorious I will burn down this house.' And he
went off in a rage. Thereupon the priests went in, and 36
stood facing the altar and the temple. They wept and
said: 'Thou didst choose this house to bear thy name, to 37
be a house of prayer and supplication for thy people;
take vengeance on this man and his army, and make them 38
fall by the sword. Remember all their blasphemy, and
grant them no reprieve.'

* After the failure of negotiations and perhaps a minor
defeat, Nicanor's attitude to both sides of the civil war has,
understandably, hardened.

33. *went up:* the traditional Jewish phrase. In fact he would
have descended from the citadel to the temple. Sacrifices *for
the king* were offered twice daily; prayers had been said in the
temple for the king in Persian times (Ezra 6: 10). The *priests
and members of the senate* (the ruling body of Jerusalem; cp.
1: 26; 2 Macc. 4: 44), serving under Alcimus, would mostly be
loyal to Syria, but they would resent high-handed Syrian
interference, particuarly in the temple, which at this moment
was particularly tactless.

34. *spat on them:* this was offensive, but worse; it made the
priests unclean. See the N.E.B. footnote, which gives the
literal translation, 'and polluted them'.

[a] *Literally* and polluted them.

35. The demand was an impossible one; it was an expression of impatience from a frustrated army officer. According to 2 Macc. 14: 33 Nicanor added a threat to build a temple to Dionysus in place of the present one.

36. The *altar* of burnt-offering stood in the court before the temple porch. Compare Joel 2: 17,

> Let the priests, the ministers of the LORD,
> stand weeping between the porch and the altar
> and say, 'Spare thy people, O LORD.'

37. The prayer recalls the words put into Solomon's mouth at the dedication of the temple: 'this place of which thou didst say, "My Name shall be there"... When thy people Israel are defeated by an enemy... and they turn back to thee, confessing thy name and making their prayer and supplication to thee in this house, do thou hear in heaven' (1 Kings 8: 29, 33 f.). ✶

THE BATTLE OF ADASA AND DEATH OF NICANOR

39 Nicanor moved from Jerusalem and encamped at Beth-horon, where he was joined by an army from Syria.
40 Judas encamped at Adasa with three thousand men; there
41 he prayed in these words: 'There was a king whose followers blasphemed, and thy angel came forth and struck
42 down one hundred and eighty-five thousand of them. So do thou crush this army before us today, and let all men know that Nicanor has reviled thy holy place; judge him as his wickedness deserves.'

43 The armies joined battle on the thirteenth of the month Adar, and the army of Nicanor suffered a crushing defeat,
44 he himself being the first to fall in the battle. When his army saw that Nicanor had fallen, they threw away their
45 arms and took to flight. The Jews, sounding the signal trumpets in the enemy's rear, pursued them as far as

Gazara, a day's journey from Adasa. From all the villages 46
of Judaea round about, the inhabitants came out and
attacked their flanks, forcing them back upon their pursuers. They all fell by the sword; there were no survivors.
The Jews seized spoil and booty; they cut off Nicanor's 47
head and that right hand which he had stretched out so
arrogantly, and brought them to be displayed at Jerusalem. There was great public rejoicing and that day was 48
kept as a special day of jubilation. It was ordained that 49
the day should be observed annually, on the thirteenth of
Adar. Thus Judaea entered upon a short period of peace. 50

* Nicanor's mission ends in his defeat and death.

39. Jerusalem was no longer a secure place for Nicanor,
now unpopular with both Jewish parties. In any case, he
needed reinforcements, which he went north to meet at the
pass of *Beth-horon* (cp. 3: 16 ff.). 2 Macc. 15: 1 f. says that
Nicanor had news of Judas' activity in Samaria, which could
also be true.

40. *Adasa*, perhaps the Hadashah of Josh. 15: 37, 8 km (5
miles) from Jerusalem towards Beth-horon. 2 Macc. 15 does
not name the site of Nicanor's final defeat, though 2 Macc.
14: 16 places an earlier action at the village of Dessaou for
which the N.E.B. conjectures 'Adasa'. *three thousand men:* a
smaller army than in 164 B.C., perhaps partly because of the
losses described in verses 16–20.

41. The historical reference (which 2 Macc. 15: 22, cp. 8:
19, makes explicit) is to the disaster which struck the Assyrian
Sennacherib in 701 B.C. (see 2 Kings 19: 35, Isa. 37: 36).
blasphemed: i.e. by denying that God could save Jerusalem
(2 Kings 18: 35; 19: 6).

43. *Adar* (cp. Ezra 6: 15, Esther 3: 7) was the last month of
the Babylonian calendar; the date here given is 17 March
160 B.C. The size of Nicanor's army is not certain; 2 Macc. 15:

20–1, 27 says that it contained elephants (perhaps captured in the east to replace those destroyed by Rome), cavalry, and that 35,000 men were killed. The reason for Nicanor's defeat is also uncertain, but he may have been simply out-generalled.

44–7. The country Judaeans between the hills and *Gazara*, 32 km (20 miles) to the west, clearly made the enemy's flight towards the friendly coastal towns a disaster. The victory resembles other famous Jewish victories, with the enemy's flight westward (as in Saul's defeat of the Philistines, 1 Sam. 14: 31), the enemy's complete annihilation (verse 46; cp. the capture of Ai, Josh. 8: 22), and the display of cut-off limbs (e.g. the heads of Goliath and Holofernes, 1 Sam. 17: 54, Judith 13: 15; 14: 1).

48–9. The *Megillath Ta'anith* (see pp. 7 f.) describes the feast commemorating this victory, but it was dropped from the calendar after A.D. 70. It was held the day before the feast of Purim, the origin of which is explained in the book of Esther (cp. Esther 9).

50. 2 Maccabees regards the defeat and death of Nicanor as the climax of the history of these years, but 1 Maccabees regards it in a wider context as merely introducing *a short period of peace*. It was in fact a period of less than two months, and the importance of the victory needs careful assessment. It was not (as 2 Maccabees appears to suggest) Judas' last battle against the Syrians; two months later Judas was killed in battle with Bacchides, and the hellenizing party appeared to have the upper hand (cp. 9: 23 ff.). Judas' successor Jonathan was forced to retreat to the hills with a small band of men. Another two years passed before the Maccabaeans were politically strong again, and this was perhaps as much a consequence of the death of Alcimus as of Jonathan's successes. In spring 160, however, when the opposition between the two parties in Judaea had been sharpened by the brutality of Alcimus and Bacchides, Judas' victory temporarily raised the morale and enhanced the status of the Maccabees. They are no longer mere rebels; their self-identification with the people of Israel is on

the way to becoming a reality. At all events, they are perhaps important enough for the Romans to find it worthwhile to treat with them. ✳

THE ROMANS

Now Judas had heard about the Romans: they were re- **8** nowned for their military power and for the welcome they gave to those who became their allies; any who joined them could be sure of their firm friendship. He was told 2 about the wars they had fought, and the valour they had shown in their conquest of the Gauls, whom they had laid under tribute. He heard of their successes in Spain, where 3 they had seized silver-mines and gold-mines, maintaining 4 their hold on the entire country—distant as it was from their own land—by their patience and good judgement. There were kings from far and near who had marched against them, but they had been beaten off after crushing defeats; others paid them annual tribute.

They had crushed in battle and conquered Philip, and 5 Perseus king of Kittim, and all who had attacked them. Antiochus the Great, king of Asia, had marched against 6 them with one hundred and twenty elephants, with cavalry and chariots and an immense force, but they had totally defeated him. They had taken the king alive, and 7 had required that he and his successors should pay them a large annual tribute, give hostages, and cede the territories 8 of India, Media, and Lydia, together with some of their finest provinces. These they had taken from him and given to King Eumenes.

When the Greeks planned to attack and destroy them, 9 they heard of it and sent a single general against them. 10

Battle was joined, and many of the Greeks fell; the Romans took their women and children prisoner, plundered their territory and annexed it, razed their fortifica-
11 tions, and made them slaves, as they are to this day. The remaining kingdoms, the islands, and all who had ever opposed them, they destroyed or reduced to slavery.
12 With their friends, however, and all who put themselves under their protection, they maintained firm friendship. They thus conquered kings near and far, and all who heard
13 their fame went in fear of them. Those whom they wished to help and to appoint as kings, became kings, and those they wished to depose, they deposed; and thus they rose
14 to great heights of power. For all this, not one of them made any personal claim to greatness by wearing the
15 crown or donning the purple. They had established a senate where three hundred and twenty senators met daily to deliberate, giving constant thought to the proper
16 ordering of the affairs of the common people. They entrusted their government and the ruling of all their territory to one of their number every year, all obeying this one man without envy or jealousy among themselves.

* This passage gives a general picture of Rome's successes and acquisitions in the second century B.C. and contrasts the Romans favourably with the other powers of the hellenistic world, especially those who oppressed the Jews. This attitude changed; in 63 B.C. Roman Pompey entered Jerusalem, and a first-century B.C. psalm calls him a dragon (Psalms of Solomon 2:29). The gospels show Rome as the major Jewish enemy. After the Jewish revolt of A.D. 66–70, the Roman eagle became a symbol for apocalyptic disaster (2 Esdras 11). But there were many moderate Jews who approved of Rome, for

Rome, like Antiochus III or the Persian kings, was prepared to allow the Jews to live according to their own laws.

2. Rome conquered *the Gauls* of the Po valley south of the Alps in 222 B.C. and 190 B.C.

3–4. *Spain*, whose mineral wealth (verse 4) had aided Hannibal in the Carthaginian war of 218–202 B.C., was conquered between 206–195 B.C. and 154–133 B.C.

5. *Philip* V of Macedon was defeated in 197 B.C., and *Perseus, king of Kittim* (Macedon), in 168 B.C.

6–7. *Antiochus* III was defeated at Magnesia in Asia Minor (where he had 50, not 120, elephants) by Scipio Africanus in 189 B.C., but he was not *taken alive*. He had become *king of Asia* (2 Macc. 3: 3 gives the title to his successor Seleucus as well) by his conquest of the western seaboard of Turkey in 197 B.C., but by the Treaty of Apamea in 188 B.C. he had to *cede* this area and pay an indemnity of 12,000 talents in *annual* instalments. For one effect of this financial burden, see 2 Macc. 3.

8. *India* was not in fact Antiochus' possession, though he campaigned to its borders. The Romans had no interest in *Media* at this time, but gave *Lydia* in western Asia Minor to *Eumenes* king of Pergamum for his aid against Antiochus in 190–189 B.C.

9–10. In 147–146 B.C. the Achaean League of the Peloponnese in Greece resisted Rome and was defeated by Lucius Mummius. Mummius occupied Corinth and, though it had not resisted, treated it like Carthage; the men were killed, the women and children sold, the city destroyed. It was a deliberate warning to Greece, which was now governed for Rome from Macedonia. The author of 1 Maccabees appears to approve of this inhuman behaviour – but then, a Maccabaean supporter cannot be expected to have much love for the Greeks and their civilization. *to this day* probably means until some time in the reign of John Hyrcanus (134–104 B.C.).

11. This verse refers to the Roman capture of such places as Carthage (146 B.C.), Sicily (made a province, 227 B.C.),

large parts of Spain (154–133 B.C.) and the Balearic Islands (123 B.C.).

13. From Jewish sources alone we learn that the Romans protected or helped establish Eumenes of Pergamum (verse 8), Ptolemy VI of Egypt against Antiochus IV (cp. Dan. 11: 29–30), and Antiochus V against Demetrius I (cp. 1 Macc. 7: 1–2, and the commentary there).

14. The final verses of this passage describe the Roman constitution and the Roman virtues. *wearing the crown:* the title 'king' and its trappings were forbidden to any Roman.

15. The *senate* had 300, not 320, members, though perhaps the figure given includes officers such as tribunes, quaestors, praetors and consuls. The Senate did not meet *daily*.

16. *one of their number every year:* presumably this refers to the consuls, of which there were two, not one. The mistake is difficult to explain except by the author's ignorance.

The whole picture given by this section is idealized – for example, the Romans were faithful allies (cp. verses 1, 12) and spoke scornfully of *Punica fides* (Carthaginian faith) by which they meant treachery, but they were not averse to opportunism. Some details here are mistaken – see verses 6–8, 15–16 – and verses 9 and 10 describe events and their consequences which Judas in 161–160 B.C. could not have known. The overall picture is coloured by the author's appreciation of the part played by Rome in the Jewish struggle against the Seleucids and of Judas' political astuteness. ✳

NEGOTIATIONS WITH ROME

17 Judas accordingly chose Eupolemus son of John son of Accos, and Jason son of Eleazar, and sent them to Rome
18 to conclude a treaty of friendship and alliance, so that the Romans might rid them of tyranny, for it was clear that
19 the Greek empire was reducing Israel to slavery. They made the long journey to Rome and entered the Senate,

where they spoke as follows: 'Judas, known as Macca- 20
baeus, his brothers, and the Jewish people have sent us to
you to conclude a treaty of friendly alliance with you,
so that we may be enrolled as your allies and friends.'
The Romans found the proposal acceptable, and the fol- 21, 22
lowing is a copy of the reply which they inscribed on
tablets of bronze and sent to Jerusalem, so that the Jews
there might have a record of the treaty of alliance:

Success to the Romans and the Jewish nation by sea 23
and land for ever! May sword and foe be far from them!
But if war breaks out first against Rome or any of her 24
allies throughout her dominion, then the Jewish nation 25
shall support them whole-heartedly as occasion may
require. To the enemies of Rome or of her allies the 26
Jews shall neither give nor supply provisions, arms,
money, or ships; so Rome has decided; and they shall
observe their commitments, without compensation.

Similarly, if war breaks out first against the Jewish 27
nation, then the Romans shall give them hearty support
as occasion may require. To their enemies there shall 28
be given neither provisions, arms, money, nor ships;
so Rome has decided. These commitments shall be
kept without breach of faith.

These are the terms of the agreement which the 29
Romans have made with the Jewish people. But if,
hereafter, both parties shall agree to add or to rescind 30
anything, then they shall do as they decide; any such
addition or rescindment shall be valid.   31

To this the Romans added: As for the misdeeds which
King Demetrius is perpetrating against the Jews, we have

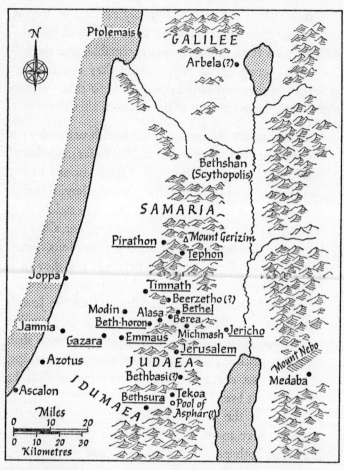

4. Judas' last campaign and the work of Bacchides
(1 Macc. 9). Places fortified by Bacchides are underlined.

written to him as follows: 'Why have you oppressed our
friends and allies the Jews so harshly? If they make any 32
further complaint against you, then we will see that justice
is done them, and will make war upon you by sea and by
land.'

* There had already been some correspondence between the
Romans and the Jewish people (see 2 Macc. 11: 34–8), perhaps
early in the year 164 B.C., though the letter may have been
addressed to the Jewish government rather than to Judas. But
Judas chose a good time to open negotiations, for Rome needed
a stick with which to beat Demetrius, who had taken the
Syrian throne against the Senate's express wish. See verses 31–2.

17. *accordingly:* i.e. in view of Rome's virtues just described, especially those of verse 12, and her readiness to oppose
the Greeks. *Eupolemus* and *Jason* are Greek names, but the
fathers' names are Hebrew. Eupolemus, grandson of Accos,
may belong to a priestly family (cp. 'the family of Hakkoz',
Ezra 2: 61) and Jason to a legal family (2 Macc. 6: 18). Eupolemus' father John also appears to have been a diplomat, responsible for mediating to the Jews the privileges granted by
Antiochus III (2 Macc. 4: 11). The use of Greek names in such
orthodox families is perhaps an indication of how far assimi-
lation had gone. But Judas, seeking diplomatic relations
abroad, could not ignore the use of the Greek language, and
Eupolemus, perhaps the Jewish writer of that name who wrote
a history of the Jewish kings (about 158–157 B.C.), would have
been a useful representative. Later, Jason's son Antipater (cp.
12: 16; 14: 22) serves on Jonathan's and Simon's diplomatic
mission to Rome. *a treaty of friendship and alliance:* Judas aims
high; at this stage, after all, he does not even represent all
Judaea, which in any case was not an independent nation.

19. *long journey:* at least a month. If the ambassadors set out
after Nicanor's defeat, it is unlikely that they returned before
Judas' death in May 160 B.C. But Josephus (*Antiquities* XIV. 10.

15) quotes a letter from the Roman official Gaius Fannius, perhaps datable to 161 B.C., to the magistrates of the island of Cos (cp. 15: 23) requesting the safe passage of some Jewish envoys. Possibly Judas sent his ambassadors on news of Demetrius' arrival in Syria and lived to hear of their success.

20. The ambassadors speak in the name of *Judas…his brothers, and the Jewish people*, but they cannot speak in the name of the Jerusalem senate.

22. It was the original copy only which would be inscribed on bronze tablets and kept in the Capitol (the temple of Jupiter) at Rome. In 1 Maccabees we have only a Greek translation of a Hebrew version of the original.

23. *Success…!:* an approximation to the usual formula, 'Whatever is good, propitious and favourable to the Roman people…'. We know of similarly worded treaties between Rome and other allies, and some of the phrases are standard and formal. But like all treaties, this treaty needs reading carefully.

24–6 and 27–8 are parallel clauses. Each side must come to the aid of the other if war breaks out, but only *as occasion may require* (verses 25, 27), and it is probably Rome in each case who will decide what the occasion may require.

24. *throughout her dominion:* Rome had possessions or political control in many areas from Spain to western Turkey by the mid-second century B.C.

26. *provisions, arms, money or ships* was probably a standard formula: the Jews had no ships. *without compensation* may be the result of a misreading (Latin *sine dote* for *sine dolo*) of the regular phrase found in verse 28, *without breach of faith*.

30. The treaty ends with a clause allowing alterations by common consent; either side can thus re-open negotiations if circumstances change.

31–2. That Rome made a treaty with Judas has been doubted, but needlessly, in view of Rome's contemporary interest in the eastern Mediterranean. That the Romans wrote to Demetrius threatening intervention is rather more doubtful.

The language here is Jewish (e.g. *oppressed* conceals 'laid your heavy yoke upon' in the original, cp. 2 Chron. 10: 11) and it is at least unlikely that we have the Senate's wording. If the letter existed, Demetrius does not seem to have taken its threat very seriously. ✳

BACCHIDES RETURNS TO JUDAEA

When Demetrius heard that Nicanor and his forces had **9** fallen in battle, he sent Bacchides and Alcimus a second time into Judaea, with the right wing of his army. They **2** marched along the Gilgal road, laid siege to Messaloth in Arbela, and captured it, inflicting heavy loss of life.

In the first month of the year 152,[a] they moved camp **3** to Jerusalem. From there they marched to Berea with **4** twenty thousand infantry and two thousand cavalry. Now **5** Judas was in camp at Alasa, with three thousand picked men. But when they saw the size of the enemy forces, their **6** courage failed, and many deserted, leaving a mere eight hundred men in the field.

When Judas saw that with the campaign going against **7** him his army had melted away, his heart sank, for there was no time to rally them. Though much discouraged, he **8** said to those who were left, 'Let us move to the attack and see if we can defeat them.' But his men tried to dis- **9** suade him: 'Impossible!' they said. 'No; let us save our lives now and come back later with our comrades to fight them. Now we are too few.' But Judas replied: **10** 'Heaven forbid that I should do such a thing as run away! If our time is come, let us die bravely for our fellow-countrymen, and leave no stain on our honour.'

[a] *That is* 160 B.C.

✻ From the Syrian point of view, Nicanor's work, both political and military, had been a failure. Demetrius therefore sent the more able (and perhaps more ruthless, cp. 7: 19) Bacchides to re-instal Alcimus and put down Judas.

1. *a second time:* for the first, cp. 7: 8–20. The *right wing* of an army belongs to the context of a battle, not a march, and the phrase is perhaps accidentally intruded here from verse 12.

2. *Messaloth* may mean 'raised banks', 'ascents' and refer to the steep hillside caves in which Josephus says many refugees were besieged by Bacchides (*Antiquities* XII. 11. 1). *Arbela* may be *khirbet 'irbid* west of the Sea of Galilee and nowhere near the Old Testament Gilgal, which was near Jericho. Some scholars follow Josephus in reading 'Galilee' for *Gilgal*; others read 'Gilead'. But Gilgal may be a place otherwise unknown to us and so correct here.

3. The *first month of the year 152* is Nisan (April–May) 160 B.C. *to Jerusalem:* presumably to reinstate Alcimus.

4. *Berea:* possibly *el-bireh* 16 km (10 miles) north of Jerusalem. Bacchides seems to have moved towards the hills near Modin where Maccabaean sympathies were strong.

5. *Alasa* is perhaps *el-'isa* near Beth-horon, though this is too far from Berea for the Syrian army to be seen (verse 6). Josephus says that Judas camped at Berzetho, perhaps *bir ez-zeit* 8 km (5 miles) north of *el-bireh*. For further evidence of the area, see verse 15.

6–7. Once again (cp. Lysias' campaign in 164 B.C., 6: 28–63) a full-scale Syrian expedition is too strong for Judas. In favourable circumstances Judas might gain support from the villagers (cp. 7: 46), but now, in spite of Nicanor's death and in spite, perhaps, of a treaty with Rome, morale is low.

9. Characteristically Judas proposes to gain the initiative by attacking first.

10. For the style of the prayer '*Heaven forbid that I should...*', cp. Gen. 44: 7. ✻

THE LAST BATTLE OF JUDAS

The Syrian army left its camp and took up position to 11
meet the Jews. The cavalry[a] was divided into two detach-
ments; the slingers and the archers went ahead of the main
force, and the picked troops were in the front line. 12
Bacchides was on the right. The phalanx came on in two
divisions with trumpets sounding; Judas's men also 13
sounded their trumpets. The earth shook at the din of the
armies as battle was joined, and they fought from dawn
until evening.

When Judas saw that Bacchides and the main strength 14
of his army was on the right flank, all his stout-hearted
men rallied to him, and they broke the Syrian right; then 15
he pursued them as far as Mount Azotus. When the 16
Syrians on the left wing saw that their right had been
broken, they turned about and followed on the heels of
Judas and his men, attacking them in the rear. The fighting 17
became very heavy, and many fell on both sides. Judas 18
himself fell, and the rest of the Jews took to flight.
Jonathan and Simon carried off Judas their brother; they 19
buried him in the family tomb at Modin, and wept over 20
him. Great was the grief in Israel, and they mourned him
for many days, saying,

> 'How is our champion fallen,   21
> the saviour of Israel!'

The rest of the history of Judas, his wars, exploits, and 22
achievements – all these were so numerous that they have
not been written down.

[a] The Syrian army... cavalry: *or* The Jewish army left its camp and
stood to meet the enemy. The Syrian cavalry...

✳ The battle is clearly described, and the author concludes his account of Judas briefly and simply, with a poetic allusion to Saul and Jonathan and a prose formula which reminds us of the ancient kings of Israel.

11. The movements are uncertain, for the subjects of the verbs are not clear. A possibility not given by the N.E.B. is 'The Syrian army left its camp and the Jews took up position against them'. See also the N.E.B. footnote. The *cavalry* was presumably on the two wings (cp. 6: 38), and the infantry formed right and left flanks or wings in the centre (cp. verses 14 ff.).

15. *Azotus* was the Greek name for Ashdod (cp. 5: 68), but there is no mountain there; an old suggestion is that the original Hebrew phrase meant 'to the foothills of the mountain', the pursuit thus being, as often before, westward from the hill country towards the coastal plain (cp. 7: 43 ff.).

19. As the spoils and corpses of battle belonged to the victor, Josephus (*Antiquities* XII. 11. 2) may be right in saying that Simon and Jonathan obtained Judas' body under a truce.

20. Mattathias (2: 70), Judas and Jonathan (13: 25) were all buried in the *family tomb*. After Jonathan's death Simon built a monument above it (see 13: 25–30).

21. The lament recalls David's lament over Saul and Jonathan, who died fighting the Philistines (2 Sam. 1: 17–27), and *saviour of Israel* recalls the language used of the judges (cp. Judg. 3: 9).

22. Compare the final remarks passed by 1 and 2 Kings on the kings of Israel and Judah (see, e.g., 1 Kings 11: 41). Compare also the final sentence of 1 Maccabees and two sentences at the end of the Fourth Gospel (John 20: 30; 21: 25). Probably the author of 1 Maccabees knows more than he tells; some hint of the kind of event which might have been recorded for us may be found in the poem of 1 Macc. 3: 3–9 or the summary of 2 Macc. 8: 5–7. ✳

JONATHAN BECOMES LEADER

After the death of Judas the renegades raised their heads 23
in every part of Israel, and all the evil-doers reappeared.
In those days a terrible famine broke out, and the country 24
went over to their side. Bacchides chose apostates to be in 25
control of the country. These men set inquiries on foot, 26
and tracked down the friends of Judas and brought them
before Bacchides, who took vengeance on them, loading
them with indignities. It was a time of great affliction for 27
Israel, worse than any since the day when prophets ceased
to appear among them. Then all the friends of Judas 28
assembled and said to Jonathan: 'Since your brother Judas 29
died, there has not been a man like him to take the lead
against our enemies, Bacchides and those of our own
nation who are hostile to us. Today, therefore, we choose 30
you to succeed him as our ruler and leader and to fight
our battles.' So Jonathan took over the leadership at that 31
time in place of his brother Judas.

* It is now summer 160 B.C., and with the victory over
Nicanor so soon outweighed by the defeat and death of Judas,
Maccabaean fortunes were at low ebb. The country farmers
who had supported the Maccabaeans had suffered considerable
hardship from the sabbatical year 164–163 B.C. onwards. Campaigns in Judaea were a drain on the country more than on
Jerusalem, and Alcimus, Bacchides and Judas had killed those
they suspected of favouring the other side (cp. 7: 19, 21–4).
Now comes famine, and the searching out of Maccabaean
supporters, and in these desperate circumstances the Maccabaean resistance begins again, under the leadership of Jonathan.

24. The *famine* was at least in part the result of mismanage-
ment over the past few years, but it was in any case a frequent

problem in Palestine, occurring more than once in the Maccabaean period alone (cp. 6: 54; 13: 49). Food would doubtless
be subject to government control, *and the country went over to
their side*, not surprisingly.

26. The *friends of Judas* would be given away, doubtless,
by the informers which such a situation breeds.

27. *the day when the prophets ceased to appear:* the last
prophetic book included in the Hebrew scriptures, apart from
Daniel, was probably Malachi, dating from the early fifth
century B.C. In 9: 54 *the prophets* mentioned are perhaps the
post-exilic prophets Haggai and Zechariah (dating from about
520–516 B.C.). In 4: 46 and 14: 41 there is hope of a period
when a new prophet might arise. Clearly the author of 1
Maccabees thinks that the presence of prophets is a mark of the
well-being of Israel, and that the present period was the lowest
ebb of the post-prophetic age.

30. If Israel had no prophet, she could still have a *ruler and
leader* to fight her battles (cp. 2: 66; 13: 8, 42) – a judge, in fact,
not unlike Jephthah (cp. Judg. 11: 4–11) who is made 'lord
and commander' against the Ammonites.

31. Why *Jonathan*, the younger brother, is chosen instead
of the older Simon is not clear; perhaps a recent minor 'reverse'
(see 2 Macc. 14: 17) told against him. But as the author of
1 Maccabees rates Simon the greatest of the Maccabees, he
may have remained silent about the less successful side of
Simon's career. *

RAID AND REVENGE IN TRANSJORDAN

32 The news reached Bacchides, and he set himself to kill
33 Jonathan. When Jonathan and his brother Simon and all
their men learnt of this, they took refuge in the desert of
34 Tekoa, encamping by the pool of Asphar. Bacchides discovered this on the sabbath, and crossed the Jordan with
35 his whole army. So Jonathan sent his brother John to take

the camp followers and appeal to his friends the Nabataeans to look after their baggage train, which was of
some size. But the Jambrites appeared from Medaba and 36
kidnapped John; they seized the baggage and made off
with it. Some time afterwards, news was brought to 37
Jonathan and his brother Simon that the Jambrites were
celebrating an important wedding, and bringing the
bride, the daughter of one of the great nobles of Canaan,
from Nadabath with a large retinue. Remembering how 38
their brother John had been killed, Jonathan and his men
set out and hid themselves under cover of a hill. They 39
looked out and there they saw the bridegroom, in the
middle of a bustling crowd and a train of baggage, coming
to meet the bridal party, escorted by his friends and kinsmen fully armed, to the sound of drums and instruments
of music. Emerging from ambush, Jonathan attacked and 40
cut them down; many fell, while others made off into the
hills and the Jews took all their goods as spoil. So the 41
wedding was turned into mourning, and the sound of
music to lamentation. The blood of their brother was fully 42
avenged, and Jonathan returned to the marshes of Jordan.

* This episode, with its theme of revenge and its local colour,
has all the marks of truth about it. It is undated, but 1 Maccabees sets it between the first month of the year 152 and the
second of 153, i.e. between April 160 and May 159 B.C. The
incident itself allows for a time-lag of several months (cp.
verse 37).

33. The Maccabaeans are forced by Syrian and government
pressure, and by lack of support from the country peasants,
who are busy trying to keep themselves and their families
alive, to retire from the hills north-west of Jerusalem to the

wilderness south-east of the city. Similarly David withdrew to this region to escape from Saul (see 1 Sam. 21–9). *Tekoa*, the home of Amos, is about 24 km (15 miles) south of Jerusalem, high on the eastern slopes of the mountains, looking down towards the Dead Sea. The *pool of Asphar* could be one of the cisterns dug in the wilderness by Uzziah in the eighth century B.C. (cp. 2 Chron. 26: 10), and its remains are perhaps to be seen about 2 miles south of Tekoa.

35. Similarly, David sent his family to Moab for safety (1 Sam. 22: 3–4). In the wilderness, as fugitives, it is better to travel light. For the Nabataeans see above on 5: 25. They would favour the Maccabaeans because the Syrian government was an obstacle to their own growth. But then as always the central government of that area could not control all the doings of its wilful member tribes.

36. *Jambrites:* a tribe like the Baeanites (5: 4) or the Zabadaeans (12: 31), whose name is perhaps to be connected with that of a Nabataean chief called Iamru, known to us from an inscription found near Eilat. *Medaba*, now famous for its mosaic map (dating from about A.D. 560) on the floor of the local church, existed from early times (cp. Num. 21: 30). It lay in ancient Moab on the 'king's highway' (Num. 20: 17), which in Maccabaean times was becoming an important Nabataean trade-route.

37. *Canaan:* the author is importing overtones of Jewish opposition to Canaanite paganism into his story. Canaan no longer existed, but as one commentator neatly puts it, 'the old name excuses the massacre'. Similarly, in mentioning the Jambrites the author of 1 Maccabees may have in mind the Amorites, defeated long ago at Medaba by Israel (Num. 21: 30). *Nadabath* is unknown; it could be a local village, or it could conceal a name such as Medaba, Nebo, or the Nabataeans.

38. *John* (verse 35) is the brother called 'Gaddis' (2: 2). The name (cp. Num. 13: 11) may mean 'fortunate'.

39. The groom's party is vividly pictured, and reminds us

of Samson's wedding party and the thirty young men of his
escort (Judg. 14: 10–11) or of the bridegroom's friends of
Jesus' parable (Mark 2: 19).

41. Compare Amos 8: 10,

> I will turn your pilgrim-feasts into mourning
> and all your songs into lamentation.

42. This incident in itself had nothing to do with the power-
struggle west of the Jordan, but it occurred because the Maccabaeans were looking for some support in their troubles from
the Nabataeans. It led to a skirmish with Bacchides at the
Jordan on Jonathan's return from his vengeful excursion. The
reference to Bacchides' movement in verse 34 is misplaced;
it belongs with verse 43, where the original movement is
described. Had Bacchides been waiting for Jonathan at or
across the Jordan, as verse 34 suggests, it is unlikely that the
Maccabaean force would have reached Medaba unchecked.
It makes better sense to suppose that news of Jonathan's exploit
reached Bacchides, who thereupon moved down to the Jordan
to block Jonathan's retreat at *the marshes of Jordan*, near the
river's entry into the Dead Sea. ✳

A BATTLE AT THE RIVER JORDAN

Bacchides heard this and came to the banks of Jordan 43
on the sabbath with a powerful force. Jonathan said to his 44
men: 'Now is the time to fight for our lives; we are today
in worse plight than ever: the enemy in front, the water 45
of Jordan behind, to right and left marsh and thicket;
there is no escape. Cry to Heaven to save you from the 46
hands of the enemy.' Battle was joined, and Jonathan had 47
raised his hand to strike down Bacchides, when he fell
back and evaded him. Then Jonathan and his men leapt 48
into the Jordan and swam over to the other side; but the

49 enemy did not cross the river in pursuit. The army of Bacchides lost about a thousand men that day.

✻ Seizing the fords of the Jordan in the enemy's rear was a fairly standard and obvious piece of strategy (see Judg. 12: 1–6). The course of the battle and its outcome are not clearly stated. The main difficulty is the exact position of Jonathan and Bacchides: on which side of the river do they fight?

43. Bacchides probably came from the region of Jerusalem or the central mountains. Verse 34 (probably out of place) says that he actually crossed the Jordan. If he crossed to the east bank, he could conceal his troops and ambush Jonathan's rear as he approached the river. But verses 48, 50 might suggest that after the battle Bacchides returned to Jerusalem without crossing the river, and thus that he was on the west bank throughout.

45. If Bacchides was on the west bank, then Jonathan crossed the river from the east and found Bacchides waiting for him, trapping him with the river *behind, to right and left marsh and thicket*. But some repunctuate this sentence and translate, 'we shall have to fight on our front and to our rear, with the waters of the Jordan on one side and the marsh and scrub on the other.'

48. *swam over to the other side:* i.e. probably to the east (with the danger of meeting tribesmen from Medaba anxious for revenge).

49. Bacchides' losses may be exaggerated; Jonathan's are not mentioned. Jonathan was clearly defeated, but the signs of this are carefully glossed over. ✻

SYRIAN CONTROL OF JUDAEA: THE DEATH OF ALCIMUS

50 Bacchides returned to Jerusalem and fortified with high walls, gates, and bars a number of places in Judaea: the fortress at Jericho, Emmaus and Beth-horon, Bethel,

Timnath-pharathon, and Tephon; in all of these he placed 51
garrisons to harass Israel. He fortified the towns of Beth- 52
sura and Gazara and the citadel, placing forces and stores
of provisions there. He took the sons of the leading men of 53
the country as hostages and put them under guard in the
citadel at Jerusalem.

In the second month of the year 153,[a] Alcimus gave 54
orders for the wall of the inner court of the temple to be
demolished, thereby destroying the work of the prophets.
But at the moment when he began demolition, Alcimus 55
had a stroke, which put a stop to his activities. Paralysed
and with his speech impaired, he could not utter a word
or give final instructions about his property. Thus he died 56
in great torment. On learning that Alcimus was dead, 57
Bacchides returned to the king, and for two years Judaea
had peace.

---

* Bacchides now consolidates his victories – to him it must
have looked like the final dispersal of the rebel army – by
settling garrisons in strategic towns. Alcimus, before his sudden death, begins to reassert the hellenizing policy in the
temple.

50. *Jericho* – a fortress there, perhaps not the town itself –
controlled the Jordan fords. *Emmaus* and *Beth-horon* (cp. 3: 16,
40) controlled the home territory of the Maccabees and the
north-west approaches to Jerusalem. *Bethel* controlled the
main road to Jerusalem from the north. *Timnath-pharathon*
perhaps combines two places: Timnath was the site of
Joshua's burial about 16 km (10 miles) north-west of Bethel
(Josh. 19: 50), and Pirathon (cp. Judg. 12: 15) was about 13 km
(8 miles) south-west of modern Nablus. These two garrisons,
with *Tephon* (Tappuah, Josh. 12: 17), lay in Samaria rather

[a] *That is* 159 B.C.

than in Judaea, and perhaps controlled an area where the Maccabaeans had been particularly vigorous in their guerrilla activities.

51–2. *Bethsura* had been fortified by Judas (4: 61) and later occupied and garrisoned by Lysias and Antiochus V (6: 50). We do not hear what happened to that garrison between 164 B.C. and Bacchides' work there. Excavations in 1931 showed that Bacchides had started again from the bedrock to build a fortress 20 by 30 metres in area; 10: 12–14 reveals that Bacchides installed mercenary troops and hellenizing citizens there. *Gazara* (cp. 7: 45) was a hellenistic town about 32 km (20 miles) west-north-west of Jerusalem, not far beyond Emmaus. It was to be captured by Simon in 142 B.C. Until then it was a town like Azotus and Joppa which would support the Syrians against the Jews. The *citadel* in Jerusalem is strengthened and used as a prison for sons of leading men taken as hostages for their parents' good behaviour. Bacchides thus did everything a conscientious and successful soldier could do to guarantee the stable government of the country.

54. *the second month of the year 153*: i.e. May 159 B.C. Alcimus, securely in office, acts as drastically as his hellenizing predecessors. The *wall* he demolished was that separating the outer gentile court from the inner courts of the women and men of Israel. This would make the temple one court in which all citizens of the city could worship, just as in any hellenistic city. He wanted to remove the division so vital to orthodox Jews between Jew and Gentile – a division which in Herod's temple was made clear by warning notices which read 'Let no foreigner enter inside the barrier and the fence around the sanctuary. Whosoever is caught will be the cause of death following as a penalty.' (See *New Testament Illustrations* in this series, p. 54.) Two courts are mentioned in 2 Kings 21: 5 and Ezek. 44: 17, 19, but they may have existed in Solomon's temple (cp. 1 Kings 7: 12).

thereby destroying the work of the prophets may refer to the fact that the second temple with its two courts was built under the leadership of Haggai and Zechariah 'and the prophets of God' (Ezra 5: 2) between 520 and 516 B.C.

55–6. Alcimus' death is clearly seen as a punishment for his sacrilegious activity.

57. *returned to the king:* very likely, for further orders. Alcimus' death left the hellenizing party leaderless and the high-priesthood vacant, needing the king's appointment to fill it. Perhaps in part because no attempt seems to have been made to fill it, *for two years Judaea had peace.* Further, as the next verse describes 'Jonathan and his people' as 'living in peace and security', it seems that it was not Jonathan's policy to go on campaigning. The country people were still recovering from the famine, and their leaders did not care to provoke the Syrians into killing men held as hostages. The Syrians were only too thankful for peace and did not care to provoke the nationalists. The last hellenizing attack on the temple failed because Alcimus died before he could put his plans into effect, and the traditional law and its statutes prevailed. In short, it was a peace of exhaustion, which allowed the Maccabaeans, who had won a theological victory by demonstrating that the people as a whole would not allow a blatant hellenization of their religion and culture, to regroup and become over the next two years the real political power in the land. ✳

THE END OF THE WAR

Then the renegades put their heads together: 'Look!' 58 they said, 'Jonathan and his people are living in peace and security. Let us bring Bacchides here; he will capture them all in a single night.' They went and conferred with 59 Bacchides, and he set out with a large force, sending 60 letters secretly to all his supporters in Judaea, with instructions to seize Jonathan and his men. But they were unable to do so, because their plan leaked out. About fifty of the 61 ringleaders of this villainy in Judaea were seized and put

62 to death. Jonathan, Simon, and their men then made their
way out to Bethbasi in the desert, built up its ruined
63 fortifications and strengthened it. When Bacchides learnt
of this, he gathered together all his army and sent word
64 to those in Judaea. He came and took up position against
Bethbasi, and attacked it for a long time, erecting siege-
65 engines. Jonathan left his brother Simon in the town and
66 slipped out into the country with a few men. He attacked
Odomera and his people and the Phasirites in their en-
67 campment; he began to get the better of them and to
advance towards Bethbasi with his forces.

Simon and his men made a sally out of the town and set
68 fire to the siege-engines. They fought Bacchides and
defeated him. They kept up heavy pressure upon him,
69 and so his plan and his expedition proved fruitless. There
was great anger against the renegades at whose instance
he had invaded the land, and many of them were put
to death. Bacchides then decided to return to his own
country.

70 When Jonathan learnt of this, he sent envoys to Bacchides to arrange terms of peace with him and a return of
71 the Jewish prisoners. Bacchides agreed and did as Jonathan
proposed, swearing to do him no harm for the rest of his
72 life. He sent him back the prisoners he had taken previously
from Judaea, and returned to his own country; never
73 again did he enter their territory. So the war came to an
end in Israel. Jonathan took up residence in Michmash
and began to govern the people, rooting the godless out
of Israel.

✳ After suppressing a conspiracy against him and beating off Bacchides' siege of a Maccabaean fort, Jonathan made peace with Syria and began to govern Judah himself.

58. The date is presumably 157 B.C. (cp. verse 57).

60. *their plan leaked out:* perhaps because there were too many conspirators for security (cp. verse 61).

62. *Bethbasi* was possibly one of the forts built by Uzziah (2 Chron. 26: 10). It may have been in the hills near Bethlehem.

63–4. Siege warfare suited the Syrians better than guerrilla warfare, but in the end Jonathan's courage and audacity combined to defeat Bacchides' Syrian *army* and supporters *in Judaea.*

66. *Odomera and his people and the Phasirites* are unknown to us; they were probably tribesmen of the area who did not welcome newcomers and were prepared to side with the Syrians against the Maccabaeans.

69. *There was great anger against the renegades:* the text and translation leave vague who was angry and who put many of the renegades to death. It may have been the Maccabaeans, or the Jewish populace (who would not enjoy the presence of Syrian troops once again on the land, with all that that entailed), or even Bacchides (who would resent fighting the hellenizers' battles for them, and being defeated). Bacchides' defeat meant the further weakening of the hellenizing party.

70. Jonathan was the only figure of importance left in the field with whom the Syrians could treat.

71. Jonathan got favourable terms, though the *hostages* (verse 53) were not returned (cp. 10: 9).

73. With Syrian acquiescence if not support *Jonathan took up residence* – the phrase suggests something formal – *and began to govern the people.* The Greek word here translated *to govern* means 'to judge', and perhaps the ancient judges of Israel are in the author's mind. *the people,* the inhabitants of Judaea are seen as the people of God, Israel, from whom Jonathan like a judge of old roots out the *godless. Michmash,* 14 km (9 miles) north of Jerusalem, was a garrison from which a

previous Jonathan had ejected the Philistines (1 Sam. 14), and this, too, may have been in the author's mind.

This verse gives an idealized picture of Jonathan in these years. One wonders how much official power Jonathan had. His judgeship was not a formal office to which the Syrians had appointed him, and he held no authority from them that we know of until 152 B.C. (see 10: 6). He did not reside in Jerusalem, where the Syrian garrison still had military control of the city and where the only rightful head of state would be the Jewish high priest. In these years the office was vacant. This posed a problem which had to be resolved. 1 Maccabees passes lightly over the years 157–152 B.C., during which Jonathan informally cultivated and exercised some sort of authority by prestige over the people, and moves directly to the change of events in the Seleucid empire which altered the status of the Maccabees and the people of Judaea. ✻

Jonathan rules the nation

JONATHAN'S NEW OFFICIAL STATUS

10 IN THE YEAR 160,[a] Alexander Epiphanes son of Antiochus came and took possession of Ptolemais, where he
2 was welcomed and proclaimed king. When King Demetrius heard of this, he raised a huge army and marched
3 out to meet him in battle. At the same time Demetrius
4 sent Jonathan a letter in friendly and flattering terms; for he said to himself, 'Let us forestall Alexander by making peace with the Jews before Jonathan comes to terms with
5 him against us, for he will remember all the harm we have

[a] *That is* 152 B.C.

done him by our treatment of his brothers and of his
nation.' He gave Jonathan authority to collect and equip 6
an army, conferred on him the title of ally, and ordered
the hostages in the citadel to be handed over to him.
Jonathan came to Jerusalem and read the letter aloud 7
before all the people and the garrison of the citadel, who 8
were filled with apprehension when they heard that the
king had given Jonathan authority to raise an army. They 9
surrendered the hostages to him, and he restored them to
their parents.

Jonathan took up his quarters in Jerusalem and began 10
to repair and rebuild the city. He gave orders to those 11
engaged on the work to build the walls and surround
Mount Zion with a fortification of squared stones, and
this was done. The foreigners in the strongholds which 12
Bacchides had built made their escape, each man leaving 13
his post and returning to his own country; however, in 14
Bethsura there were still left some of those who had
abandoned the law and ordinances, and had found asylum
there.

* Demetrius, under pressure from a rival for his throne, makes
considerable concessions to Jonathan in the hope of gaining
his support.

1. *The year 160* began either autumn 153 B.C. or spring 152
B.C.; *Alexander* probably took Ptolemais in spring 152 B.C.
Since 159 B.C. he had been supported, as an alleged and
possibly genuine *son of Antiochus* IV, by King Eumenes of
Pergamum (cp. 8: 8) as a rival to Demetrius; in 153 B.C. the
Roman Senate was also persuaded to support Alexander, who
was now waiting over the border from Syria in Cilicia, ready
to move if Demetrius gave him chance. He *was welcomed and*

proclaimed king because Demetrius had made himself unpopular at home by his imperious remoteness ('for', says Josephus (*Antiquities* XIII. 2. 1), 'he had shut himself in a palace with four towers which he had built not far from Antioch, and admitted no one, but was lazy and careless about public affairs') and abroad by his scheming (for example, he tried to bribe the Egyptian governor of Cyprus to betray the island to him).

3–4. Both sides began to compete for Jewish support; cp. verses 15 ff.

5. *all the harm*...: compare the Roman accusation of 8: 31. The words reflect the Jewish standpoint.

6. Demetrius recognizes where the power lay in Judaea, and gives official recognition to forces raised by Jonathan. The title of *ally* formally improved upon the existing peace-treaty (cp. 9: 70). The release of the *hostages* (cp. 9: 53) was a real concession.

8. The garrison's *apprehension* was justified enough; they might well feel themselves betrayed by the throne they had supported against the Maccabaean rebels.

10–11. Jonathan's move into Jerusalem and his building of walls and fortifications (dismantled by Lysias in 163 B.C., cp. 6: 62) are highly significant. Jonathan is now in full political control, and the hellenizing party has lost all influence with Syria (cp. verse 61).

12. The return to Syria of Bacchides' garrison troops (cp. 9: 50–1) left the control of Judaea open to the Maccabaeans, and in due course the major garrisons also were taken by Jonathan's successor Simon (Bethsura, 11: 66, Gazara, 13: 43, the Jerusalem citadel, 13: 49–53). *

JONATHAN BECOMES HIGH PRIEST

15 King Alexander heard of the promises which Demetrius had sent to Jonathan, and was told of the battles and heroic deeds of Jonathan and his brothers, and the hard-

ships they had endured. 'Where shall we ever find another 16
man like this?' he exclaimed. 'Let us make him our friend
and ally.' He therefore wrote a letter to Jonathan to this 17
effect:

> King Alexander to his brother Jonathan, greeting.   18
> We have heard about you, what a valiant man you 19
> are and how fit to be our friend. Now therefore we 20
> do appoint you this day to be High Priest of your
> nation with the title of King's Friend, to support our
> cause and to keep friendship with us.

He sent him a purple robe and a gold crown.

Jonathan assumed the vestments of the high priest in 21
the seventh month of the year 160[a] at the Feast of Tabernacles, and he gathered an army together and prepared a
large supply of arms.

---

* Jonathan took advantage of Demetrius' offers, but perhaps
also made sure by diplomatic means that Alexander would hear
both of what Demetrius had promised and of what he had not
promised. At all events, Alexander, who wished to avoid
having an ally of Demetrius in his rear as he moved against
Syria, was shrewd enough to offer Jonathan a position he
would not be able to resist – the high-priesthood, coupled
with a place in Alexander's council.

18. The letter's opening phrase is conventional, though the
address *brother* is diplomatic and flattering.

20. The price of the honours conferred is loyalty to Alexander and his *cause*. *a purple robe and a gold crown:* purple
clothing was the mark of high rank (cp. Mark 15: 17, Luke
16: 19). A *King's Friend* (see pp. 9 f.) would wear purple, and
a high priest's clothing was made of 'gold; violet, purple, and

[a] *That is* 152 B.C.

scarlet yarn; and fine linen' (Exod. 28: 5). According to Exod.
28: 36–8, the high priest wore on his head a turban with a
gold rosette inscribed 'Holy to the LORD'; the Hebrew word
nezer (crown) was sometimes used for this head-dress and
implied separation (cp. the Nazirite, for whom see the note
on 3: 49). Alexander is thus providing the clothing appropriate to Jonathan's new offices, though it seems unlikely that
a high priest could wear vestments made by Gentiles.

21. The date is October 152 B.C. *Tabernacles* in post-exilic
times commemorated the Israelites' wandering in the wilderness (see Lev. 23: 39–43) but derived from the old harvest
feast of Ingathering 'at the end of the year, when you bring
in the fruits of all your work on the land' (Exod. 23: 16). It
had come to be regarded as 'a most holy and most eminent
feast' (Josephus, *Antiquities* VIII. 4. 1). I Maccabees is silent on
the reception Jonathan got from the Jewish people on entering
his new office, but it may not have been entirely enthusiastic.
A later royal high priest, Jannaeus (103–76 B.C.), was pelted by
the people at Tabernacles with ethrogs (the citrus fruit carried
at the feast, cp. Lev. 23: 40), and the reason may have been
in part popular mistrust of the combination of the offices of
king and high-priest in one person. Jonathan in any case was
of a priestly but not of a high-priestly family; the legitimate
high priest, Onias IV, was in Egypt at Leontopolis. Some
scholars have suggested that it was Jonathan whom the
Qumran community described in their literature as the
'Wicked Priest'. The hellenizers, however, would be unlikely
to complain of Jonathan on that score, for they had been
ready enough in the past to accept a non-Zadokite appointed
by the Syrian king, such as Menelaus, as high priest. Jonathan
the Maccabee, however, is not compromising Maccabaean
principles in accepting office from the alleged son of Antiochus
IV. It is Syria that has thus admitted defeat. ✳

DEMETRIUS INCREASES HIS OFFER

When this news reached Demetrius he was mortified. 22
'How did we come to let Alexander forestall us', he 23
asked, 'in gaining the friendship and support of the Jews?
I too will send them cordial messages and offer honours 24
and gifts to keep them on my side.' So he sent a message 25
to the Jews to this effect:

King Demetrius to the Jewish nation, greeting.

We have heard with great pleasure that you have 26
kept your agreements and remained in friendship with
us and have not gone over to our enemies. Continue, 27
then, to keep faith with us, and we shall reward you
well for all that you do in our cause, both by granting 28
you numerous exemptions and making you gifts.

I hereby release and exempt you and all Jews what- 29
soever from tribute, from the tax on salt, and from the
crown-money. From today and hereafter I release you 30
from the one-third of the grain-harvest and the half of
the fruit-harvest due to me. From today and for all
time, I will no longer exact them from Judaea or from
the three administrative districts, formerly part of
Samaria and Galilee, which I now attach to Judaea.
Jerusalem and its environs, with its tithes and tolls, shall 31
be sacred and tax free. I also surrender authority over 32
the citadel in Jerusalem and grant the High Priest the
right to garrison it with men of his own choice. All 33
Jewish prisoners of war taken from Judaea into any part
of my kingdom, I set at liberty without ransom. No
man shall exact any levy whatsoever on the cattle of

34 the Jews. All their festivals, sabbaths, new moons, and appointed days, and three days preceding and following each festival, shall be days of exemption and release for
35 all the Jews in my kingdom; no one shall have authority to impose any exaction or burden on a Jew in any respect.

36 Jews shall be enlisted in the forces of the King to the number of thirty thousand men; they shall receive
37 the usual army pay. Some of them shall be stationed in the great royal fortresses, others put in positions of trust in the kingdom. Their commanders and officers shall be of their own race, and they shall follow their own customs, just as the King has ordered for Judaea.

38 The three districts added to Judaea from the territory of Samaria shall be attached to Judaea so as to be under one authority, and subject to the High Priest alone.

39 Ptolemais and the lands belonging to it I make over to the temple in Jerusalem, to meet the expenses proper
40 to it. I give fifteen thousand silver shekels annually, charged on my own royal accounts, to be drawn from
41 such places as may prove convenient. And the arrears of the subsidy, in so far as it has not been paid by the revenue officials, as it formerly was, shall henceforth
42 be paid in for the needs of the temple. In addition, the five thousand silver shekels which used to be taken from the annual income of the temple are also released,
43 because they belong to the ministering priests. Whoever shall take sanctuary in the temple at Jerusalem, or in any part of its precincts, because of a debt to the crown or any other debt, shall be free from distraint on his person or on his property within my kingdom.

134

The cost of the rebuilding and repair of the temple shall 44
be borne by the royal revenue; also the repair of the 45
walls of Jerusalem and its surrounding fortification, as
well as of the fortresses in Judaea, shall be at the expense
of the royal revenue.

When Jonathan and the people heard these proposals, 46
they did not believe or accept them, for they recalled the
terrible calamity the king had brought upon Israel, and
his harsh oppression. They favoured Alexander, because 47
it was he who had been the initiator of peaceful overtures;
so they remained his allies to the end.

* Demetrius raises the bid for Jonathan's allegiance, for much
is at stake. He makes no appeal to his earlier offer (verses 4-6),
which Jonathan has acted upon if not formally accepted.
Further, he addresses his new offer 'to the Jewish nation'
(verse 25), not to Jonathan. This is diplomatically subtle and
historically plausible, though, it seems, in practice a failure.
Demetrius appeals to the hellenizing Jews and the Maccabaeans
as a nation, and the nation, under the hellenizing government
in Jerusalem and under Jonathan's rule at Michmash, has
remained at peace with Demetrius (verse 26). Demetrius continues to leave the question of the nomination of the high
priest open; the office alone is referred to (verses 32, 38). In
this, if these offers were in fact made (see below), Demetrius
is either proceeding with caution, having learned from experience that appointments to the high-priestly office needed
great care, or silently acquiescing in a situation he cannot control. Most of his inducements, therefore, are financial, appealing
to the people's purse ('exemptions' and 'gifts', verse 28).

29. *tribute* was normally due annually from a subject to his
imperial master. The Greek word here is plural, and refers
either to the portions collected from individual areas or to the

following salt- and crown-taxes. The *tax on salt* was perhaps levied on salt recovered from the Dead Sea (cp. 11: 35). *crown-money* was levied to pay for the expensive 'voluntary' state gift of a crown to the king on occasions such as his birthday; Alcimus presented one to Demetrius (2 Macc. 14: 4).

30. The *grain-harvest* came before the *fruit-harvest*, and the division between the two was traditional (cp. Lev. 27: 30). The proportions demanded seem high, but the Egyptian king's tenants and farmers paid much the same under Roman rule, and these may have been the accustomed levels of payment taken over by the Syrian administration from the Egyptian in 198 B.C. Jonathan later offers the king 300 talents for the commuting of this levy (11: 28–37), which indicates the value of Demetrius' present promise to abolish it for Judaea and Jerusalem and for *the three administrative districts, formerly part of Samaria and Galilee, which I now attach to Judaea*. The addition of *Galilee* is an error (cp. verse 38; 11: 28, 34), and the areas of Apherema (Old Testament 'Ephraim'), Lydda and Ramathaim (11: 34) are meant. See the map on p. 154.

31. *tithes and tolls:* if these are internal taxes levied by the priests on worshippers for the temple's revenue, these levies themselves may have been subject to Syrian taxation (cp. 11: 35). *sacred and tax-free:* the Greek is difficult grammatically, but the phrase may be built on the technical phrase found, e.g. on the coins of Ptolemais under Demetrius I, 'holy and inviolate'; that is, the sanctuary, like other sanctuaries, enjoyed some privileges of immunity. (A higher privilege enjoyed by some coastal trading cities was the right to mint their own silver coinage.)

32. This offer was over-generous and probably mistrusted by the Jews. Throughout these years the question of the presence of the Syrian garrison in Jerusalem remained a central one (cp. 11: 41; 12: 36), and it was the last sign of Syrian control to disappear (13: 49–53).

33–5. Prisoners of war were usually enslaved, or ransomed; Demetrius thus offers to forgo a source of income. The *cattle* were perhaps subject to some form of transit duty; the reference is obscure and the sentence perhaps out of place, unless it refers to sacrificial animals at festival time, when the Jews were to be exempt from certain government demands (verse 34); just what *any exaction or burden* (verse 35) refers to is not clear. *three days preceding and following each festival* allows for time spent in travel to and from Jerusalem.

36. Demetrius encourages the enlistment of paid mercenaries (in a subject state he might normally conscript) on favourable terms of service.

38. See above on verse 30. If Demetrius knew of the historic differences between Jerusalem and Samaria he was being remarkably tactless in this arrangement.

39. *Ptolemais* was in fact at the time occupied by Alexander (10: 1) and was hostile to the Jews (2 Macc. 6: 8; 13: 25), and would not easily be made to contribute to the Jerusalem temple.

40. Cyrus (Ezra 6: 3–5), Darius (Ezra 6: 8), Artaxerxes I (Neh. 2: 7–8), Artaxerxes II (Ezra 7: 15, 21), Antiochus III (Josephus, *Antiquities* XII. 3. 3), Seleucus IV (2 Macc. 3: 3) and even the dying Antiochus IV (so 2 Macc. 9: 16) had all contributed gifts to the Jerusalem temple, but the *fifteen thousand shekels annually* was a 'subsidy' (verse 41).

41. The *arrears* dated from, perhaps, 167 B.C.

42. The payment here described was perhaps that demanded by Lysias in 164 B.C.; according to 2 Macc. 11: 3, he planned to subject 'the temple to taxation like all gentile shrines'.

43. See verse 31. This promise to respect the persons and property of those with *a debt to the crown or any other debt* reflected Greek, not Jewish, law; the Jews allowed only unintentional homicides to seek sanctuary at the altar (Exod. 21: 13–14) or in the cities of refuge (Josh. 20: 1–9).

44–5. Demetrius offered to defray the cost of temple-repairs, as had (within limits) Cyrus (Ezra 6: 3–5) and Antiochus III (Josephus, *Antiquities* XII. 3. 3). But the offer of help in reconstructing military fortifications is without precedent, and somewhat surprising, even for a man in Demetrius' situation.

46. *Jonathan and the people*: the hellenizing party is ignored. *terrible calamity... and his harsh oppression*: see chapters 7 and 9.

47. In fact Demetrius, not Alexander, had been *the initiator of peaceful overtures* (verses 3–6, 15). Perhaps the Hebrew word behind the Greek of *peaceful overtures* meant rather 'gifts'; the sentence then means that Alexander was the Jews' 'leading benefactor'.

Much of this letter deals with concessions also made in the letter of Demetrius II to Jonathan and the Jewish nation in 145 B.C. (11: 30–7) and in Demetrius' answer to Jonathan's request (11: 41–3). The exemption from poll-tax, crown-tax and salt-tax and the return of prisoners of war had been granted by Antiochus III at the beginning of the century (Josephus, *Antiquities* XII. 3. 3). In view of this, and of the somewhat clumsy arrangement (e.g. verses 30, 38), difficult sentences (e.g. verse 31), and errors (e.g. Galilee, verse 30) some have thought that this letter is a compilation based on the other similar letters. If the present letter is an original document, it has certainly suffered in the process of translation and editing. But in general the offers are consistent with Demetrius' situation, and many are later repeated by Demetrius II. ✷

THE SUCCESS OF ALEXANDER

48 King Alexander mustered powerful forces and took up
49 position against Demetrius, and the two kings joined
battle. The army of Alexander took to flight, and Deme-
50 trius pursued him and got the better of them. He fought
hard till sunset, but on that day Demetrius fell.

51   Thereupon Alexander sent ambassadors to Ptolemy king
52 of Egypt, with a message to this effect: 'I have returned
to my kingdom and sit on the throne of my ancestors. I
have assumed the government, defeated Demetrius, and
53 made myself master of our country; for I gave him battle,

and he and his army were crushed by us, and we sit on
the throne of his kingdom. Let us now form an alliance; 54
make me your son-in-law by giving me your daughter
in marriage, and I will give presents to you and her
worthy of your royal state.'

King Ptolemy replied: 'It was a happy day when you 55
returned to the land of your ancestors and ascended the
throne of their realm. I will now do as you ask; only come 56
to Ptolemais so that we may meet, and I will become your
father-in-law as you propose.'

In the year 162,[a] Ptolemy set out from Egypt, with his 57
daughter Cleopatra, and arrived at Ptolemais, where King 58
Alexander met him, and Ptolemy gave him his daughter
in marriage. The wedding was celebrated in royal style,
with great pomp.

✲ The narrative, resumed from verse 2 after the lengthy
description of negotiations (verses 3–47), continues with the
defeat of Demetrius and Alexander's political marriage with
the daughter of Ptolemy VI of Egypt.

48–50. According to Josephus (*Antiquities* XIII. 2. 4), Demetrius' army was victorious on the left wing but defeated on
the right, where Demetrius himself was stationed. His horse
got bogged down in a swamp, and he was surrounded and
killed by spearmen. Where the battle took place is unknown.

51–4. Alexander announces to Ptolemy VI that he now,
as the legitimate heir (see the note on verse 1), has taken the
throne and stresses the complete control he has gained of the
kingdom. He then proposes an *alliance*, strengthened by a
diplomatic marriage; he did not want Egypt free to join any
opposition that might arise to him from Demetrius' family.

55. Ptolemy VI had been defeated by his uncle Antiochus

[a] *That is* 150 B.C.

IV in late 170 B.C., and in 169–168 B.C. Antiochus seems to have tried to control Egypt by using Ptolemy as his puppet king. Rome prevented this; but later Demetrius I tried to seduce Cyprus from Egyptian to Syrian control. Ptolemy VI might wish to support rivals to Demetrius, but was clearly cautious in his approach to any Seleucid king. Once Alexander was in power, however, an alliance which might give Ptolemy a foothold in Palestine once again was very tempting. But Ptolemy was quite prepared to be treacherous (cp. 11: 1–2). Like other Egyptian rulers before him he gave asylum to Jews who opposed Syria, and in his reign a Jewish colony and temple under Onias IV, son of the high priest Onias III, were established at an obscure place called Leontopolis at the base of the Nile delta. The colony was primarily military; in 145 B.C. it supported Ptolemy VI's legitimate successor Cleopatra (cp. verse 57) with a small force at Alexandria, and in Julius Caesar's time it guarded the route from Palestine to Egypt. The colony was probably composed of priests and supporters of Onias III and his dynasty. Ptolemy was doubtless happy to have some Jewish supporters and a rival high priest to use, if need be, in the power-game against Syria over Judaea.

56. Ptolemy's reply (verse 55) was diplomatically phrased, but his insistence on Ptolemais as the *rendez-vous* for the kings' meeting and the royal marriage reminds us that the city was named after an Egyptian king and symbolized Egyptian presence and power on the Palestinian coast. Alexander is thus made to appear as an Egyptian protégé. In 193 B.C. Antiochus III had married his daughter Cleopatra to the king of Egypt at Raphia on the Egyptian coast; the present ceremony at Ptolemais reflects the changed balance of power since 193 B.C.

57. The *year 162* began in autumn 151 B.C. The battle between Alexander and Demetrius (verses 48–50) was probably fought in summer 151 B.C.; Jonathan became high priest in October 152 B.C., and the negotiations with Demetrius (verses 22–47) took place in the winter and spring of 152–151 B.C.

THE SUCCESS OF JONATHAN

King Alexander wrote to Jonathan to come and meet 59
him. Jonathan went in state to Ptolemais, where he met 60
the two kings; he gave them silver and gold, and also made
many gifts to their Friends; and so he won their favour.

There were some scoundrelly Jewish renegades who 61
conspired to lodge complaints against Jonathan. The king,
however, paid no attention to them, but gave orders for 62
Jonathan to be divested of the garment he wore and robed
in purple, and this was done. The king made him sit at his 63
side, and told his officers to go with Jonathan into the
centre of the city and proclaim that no one should bring
any complaint against him or make trouble for him for
any reason whatsoever. When this proclamation was 64
made and those who planned to lodge complaints saw
Jonathan's splendour, and the purple robe he wore, they
all made off. Thus the king honoured him, enrolling him 65
in the first class of the order of King's Friends, and making
him a general and a provincial governor. Jonathan re- 66
turned to Jerusalem well pleased with his success.

* Jonathan had supported Alexander, at least by inactivity,
and Jonathan's support was equally valuable to Ptolemy, who
was doubtless looking ahead to the next step in regaining
Palestine. Consequently Jonathan is courted by both kings.

60. *gifts:* not merely bribes, but acts of courtesy made from
a position of some strength. Jonathan could afford to be
gracious, and it was politic to be so.

61. The *scoundrelly Jewish renegades* were members of the
hellenizing party who naturally considered that Syria had
betrayed her loyal supporters.

62–4. The ceremonial and public demonstration of Jonathan's elevation to the purple – already a *King's Friend* (verse 20) he was now (verse 65) enrolled in the order's 'first class' – silenced his political enemies, who may have included some of the more orthodox Hasidaeans and others who disliked Jonathan's assumption of the high-priesthood.

65. *a general and a provincial governor:* i.e. military and civil governor of Judaea under the Syrian empire.

66. Jonathan was rightly *well pleased.* His party had won the civil war, and had gained the Syrian support hitherto given to the hellenizing party. Yet the Syrian garrisons remained at the Jerusalem citadel, Bethsura and Gazara. Judaea was not yet independent. *

THE ARRIVAL OF DEMETRIUS II

67 In the year 165,[a] Demetrius, the son of King Demetrius,
68 arrived in the land of his fathers from Crete. King Alexander was greatly upset by this news, and returned to
69 Antioch. Demetrius appointed as his commander Apollonius the governor of Coele-syria, who raised a powerful force and encamped at Jamnia. From there he sent this
70 message to Jonathan the high priest: 'You are all alone in resisting us, and you are making me look ridiculous
71 and absurd. Why do you defy us up there in the hills? If you have confidence in your forces, come down to meet us on the plain, and let us try conclusions with each other
72 there, for I have the power of cities behind me. Make inquiries; find out who I am and who are our allies; you will be told that you cannot stand your ground against us, for your predecessors have twice been routed in their own
73 territory, and now you will not be able to resist my cavalry,

[a] *That is* 147 B.C.

and such a force as mine, on the plain, where there is not so much as a stone or a pebble to give you cover, or any place to which you can escape.'

* 1 Maccabees says nothing about the next three or four years, in which Judaea was probably settling down under Jonathan's control. The arrival of the son of Demetrius to claim the Syrian throne brought new political difficulties to Jonathan.

67. The date is the year beginning autumn 148 B.C., and Demetrius probably *arrived* in spring or summer 147 B.C. He was a younger son, now fourteen years old, of Demetrius I (Alexander had killed the eldest son), and had been sent for safety to Cnidus (cp. 15: 23) on the south-west coast of modern Turkey. After visiting Crete to recruit mercenary troops (for Cretan mercenaries as far back as David's time cp. 'the Kerethite guards' of 2 Sam. 8: 18) he landed (Josephus, *Antiquities* XIII. 4. 3) in Cilicia on Syria's north-west border. This would explain why Alexander *returned* from Ptolemais north *to Antioch* (verse 68), which he had entrusted to two military governors.

69. The text is difficult; the original meaning may be rather that Demetrius *appointed . . . Apollonius* as *governor of Coele-syria*. (Coele-syria was originally the hollow between the Lebanon and Anti-Lebanon mountain ranges, but the name became used for the whole region of the Levant.) If Demetrius was in Cilicia, and Apollonius at Jamnia in the southern coastal plain, the plan was perhaps to attack Alexander simultaneously from south and north. But first Apollonius must deal with Jonathan in his rear, loyal to Alexander and to Ptolemy.

70–3. Apollonius' message was a taunt to lure Jonathan from his home ground to the plains where the discipline and weight of a large army with cavalry would tell.

72. Jonathan's unsuccessful *predecessors* were either Judas, *twice . . . routed* at Bethzacharia (6: 47) and Alasa (9: 6–19), or the Israelites defeated long ago by the Philistines (1 Sam. 4: 10).

73. An indication that the author of I Maccabees had the stories of I Samuel in mind may be found in the reference to a *pebble*; the Greek word is rare, occurring elsewhere only in the Septuagint of I Sam. 14: 14. The words *to give you cover* are not in the Greek, and may not give the intended meaning. The plain would provide vegetation as cover rather than stones, and Apollonius' point may be that there were no stones or pebbles on the plain for ammunition (which is how they were used in the Greek version of I Sam. 14: 14). ✷

JONATHAN'S CAMPAIGN AGAINST APOLLONIUS

74 Jonathan was provoked by this message from Apollonius. He took ten thousand men and marched out from Jerusalem, and was joined by his brother Simon with 75 reinforcements. He laid siege to Joppa, whose gates the citizens had closed against him because Apollonius had a 76 garrison there. But when fighting started, the citizens took fright and opened the gates, thus Jonathan became master 77 of Joppa. When Apollonius heard of it he took three thousand cavalry and a large force of infantry, and marched to Azotus as if to pass through it, but at the same time, relying on his numerous cavalry, he advanced into 78 the plain. Jonathan went in pursuit as far as Azotus, where 79 the armies joined battle. But Apollonius had left a thou- 80 sand cavalry in hiding in their rear, and Jonathan discovered that there was an ambush behind him. The enemy surrounded his army, showering arrows on our 81 people from dawn till dusk. But they stood fast as Jonathan had ordered them, and the enemy cavalry grew 82 weary. At that point Simon led out his troops and joined battle with the enemy phalanx, now that the cavalry was exhausted. They were routed by him and took to flight.

144

The horsemen scattered across the plain and took refuge 83
in Azotus, where they sought asylum in the temple of
Dagon their idol. But Jonathan set fire to Azotus and its 84
surrounding villages, and plundered them; the temple
of Dagon, and those who had taken refuge there, he
destroyed with fire. The numbers of those who fell by 85
the sword, together with those who lost their lives in the
fire, reached eight thousand. Jonathan marched away 86
from Azotus, and encamped at Ascalon, where the citizens came out to meet him with great pomp. Then he 87
and his men returned to Jerusalem loaded with spoil.

When King Alexander heard of all this, he did Jonathan 88
still greater honour, sending him the gold clasp which it 89
is the custom to give to the King's Kinsmen. He also
presented him with Accaron and all its districts.

* Jonathan's alliance with Ptolemy virtually compelled him
to defend the coastal cities south of Ptolemais from Apollonius,
and his alliance with Alexander obliged him to prevent, if he
could, Apollonius' attack on Alexander from the south. To
follow the strategy of the campaign, see the map on p. 146.

76. In taking *Joppa* (a town once attacked by Judas for its
massacre of Jewish inhabitants, 2 Macc. 12: 3–9) Jonathan had
placed himself between Apollonius and Demetrius and had
gained command of an important harbour, probably Apollonius' supply-port.

77. Apollonius leaves 1,000 cavalry behind (cp. verse 79)
and moves further south down the coast towards *Azotus* (the
old Philistine Ashdod).

78. Jonathan falls into the trap, and follows Apollonius into
the plain.

81–2. According to Josephus (*Antiquities* XIII. 4. 4) Jonathan
drew up his army into a square; later, he divided the troops

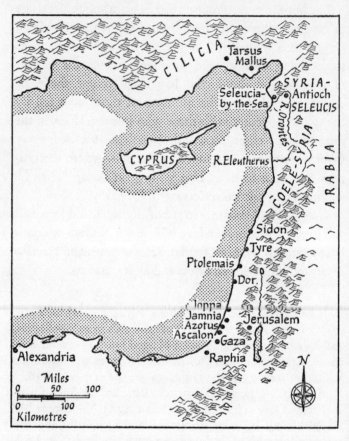

5. The campaign of Ptolemy VI (1 Macc. 11: 1–18).

between himself and Simon, Simon engaging the enemy infantry while Jonathan and his troops made a fence of their
shields and drew the fire of the enemy's javelins. When the
cavalry grew weary (and short of javelins), Simon broke the
infantry and the cavalry joined the flight. The victory seems
to have been gained by sheer courage and determination,

146

though Jonathan's 10,000 infantrymen against Apollonius'
8,000 (so Josephus) may have helped. The cavalry did not have
the effect Apollonius had hoped for (cp. verse 73).

83. There were temples *of Dagon* (the west-Semitic grain-
god of the second millennium B.C.) at Gaza (Judg. 16: 23) and
Azotus (1 Sam. 5: 1–5), and there was a place called Beth-
dagon (house of Dagon) (Josh. 15: 41).

84. For 1 Maccabees' emphasis on the Maccabaean hostility
to paganism, cp. 5: 44, 68.

86. *Ascalon:* a hellenistic harbour, further south, the Philistine Ashkelon (2 Sam. 1: 20). George Adam Smith notes of it
that 'there is a sound of trade, a clinking of shekels, about the
city's very name'.

88–9. Alexander was appropriately grateful to Jonathan,
and gave him court honours (cp. 11: 58), and more usefully,
perhaps, he gave him *Accaron*, the Philistine Ekron, on the
route from Jerusalem to Joppa (Josh. 13: 3). Judaea has begun
to extend her territories. The continued process is described
in 11: 28–37; 12: 33–4; 13: 43–8, and the later Syrian protest
and Jewish reply are recorded in 15: 28–36. ✻

PTOLEMY INVADES SYRIA

The king of Egypt collected a huge army, countless as **11**
the sand on the sea-shore, and a great fleet of ships, meaning to make himself master of Alexander's kingdom by
treachery and add it to his own. He set out for Syria with 2
professions of peace, and the people of the towns proceeded
to open their gates to him and went to meet him; King
Alexander had ordered them to do this, because Ptolemy
was his father-in-law.

As he went on his progress from town to town, Ptolemy 3
left a detachment of troops in each of them as a garrison.
When he reached Azotus, he was shown the burnt-out 4

temple of Dagon, the city itself and its ruined suburbs strewn with corpses, and, piled up along his way, the bodies of those who had been burned in the course of the
5 fighting. They told the king that it was Jonathan's doing, hoping that he would reprimand him; but the king said
6 nothing. Jonathan met him in state at Joppa, where they
7 exchanged greetings and passed the night. Jonathan accompanied the king as far as the river Eleutherus and then
8 returned to Jerusalem. King Ptolemy made himself master of the coast towns as far as Seleucia-by-the-sea. He was harbouring malicious designs against Alexander.

9   He sent ambassadors to King Demetrius with the following message: 'I propose that you and I should make a pact: I will give you my daughter, now Alexander's wife,
10 and you shall reign over the kingdom of your father. I now regret having given my daughter to him, for he has tried to kill me.'

11   He maligned Alexander in this way because he coveted
12 his kingdom, and he took his daughter away and gave her to Demetrius. This led to a breach between him and Alexander, and to open enmity.

13   Ptolemy now entered Antioch, where he assumed the crown of Asia; thus he wore two crowns, that of Egypt and that of Asia.

* Ptolemy VI Philometor of Egypt had been cautious in recognizing Alexander Balas (see the note on 10: 55), and he was equally cautious in turning against him. But this was Syria's weakest moment for half a century. Alexander himself was ineffective, and the rightful heir to the throne, Demetrius, had suffered a serious military reverse (10: 67–87). Ptolemy also knew that Judaea, now an ally worth courting, was hardly a

devoted vassal of Syria. Ptolemy therefore proceeded to take possession of the coastal cities and then Antioch itself.

1. Ptolemy's motive is seen as the acquisition of the Syrian *kingdom*, i.e. the empire of Asia (see verse 13), but Josephus (*Antiquities* XIII. 4. 7) says that Ptolemy disclaimed this with the quip that the throne of Egypt was enough, and Diodorus says that Ptolemy wanted only Coele-syria. Diodorus here may be nearer the truth.

2. *professions of peace:* Ptolemy probably pretended that he was marching to Alexander's aid. On the whole the coastal towns – Raphia, Gaza, Ascalon, Azotus, Jamnia, Joppa, Dor, Ptolemais – would oppose an Egyptian take-over, to judge from verse 18 below, for Syria treated them well. *father-in-law:* see 10: 57.

3. *garrison:* see verse 18.

4. See 10: 84.

5. *the king said nothing*, for he needed Jonathan's support.

6–7. *Jonathan met him* (the verb may imply Jonathan's deference)... *at Joppa* (which Jonathan had recently captured, 10: 76) and marched 200 miles north with him to the river Eleutherus north of modern Tripolis, the southern border of the Syrian territory of the Seleucid king. Jonathan tactfully withdrew at this point to Jerusalem; Alexander was his ally, and in any case it was better policy for him to play off one king against the other than to join one king and defeat the other.

8. *Seleucia-by-the-sea* was Antioch's port, founded by Seleucus I as his capital, captured by the Egyptians under Ptolemy II, and recaptured by Antiochus III for Syria in 219 B.C.

9. Ptolemy now openly withdraws his support from Alexander by allying with Demetrius, son of Demetrius I (cp. 10: 67). Ptolemy was not supporting Demetrius so much as weakening Alexander.

10. *tried to kill me:* Josephus (*Antiquities* XIII. 4. 6) says that Ptolemy was nearly killed at Ptolemais, the plot being formed, with Alexander's connivance, by his chief minister Ammonius.

13. Josephus says (*Antiquities* XIII. 4. 7) that Antioch expelled Alexander; 1 Maccabees, perhaps favourably inclined towards Alexander as Jonathan's patron, says (verse 14) that Alexander was suppressing rebellion in Cilicia, which is probably where Demetrius was (see note on 10: 67). If so, there was nothing to stop Ptolemy entering Antioch where (according to Diodorus) he was offered the crown by Alexander's ministers. For the *crown*, see the note on 6: 15. The two empires of *Egypt* and *Asia* would have been impossible to control against the militant opposition of Demetrius and the political opposition of the Romans, who had already prevented Antiochus IV from joining the two empires (168 B.C.). *

DEMETRIUS II BECOMES KING

14 King Alexander was at this time in Cilicia, because the
15 inhabitants of that region were in revolt. But when he heard the news he marched against Ptolemy, who came to meet him with a powerful army and routed him.
16 Alexander fled to Arabia for protection, and King Ptolemy
17 was triumphant. Zabdiel the Arab chieftain cut off
18 Alexander's head and sent it to Ptolemy. But two days later King Ptolemy died, and his garrisons in the fortresses
19 were killed by the inhabitants. So in the year 167[a] Demetrius became king.

* The inevitable battle between Alexander and Ptolemy led to their deaths and Demetrius' easy and immediate access to the throne.

14. Alexander was probably attempting to defeat Demetrius in Cilicia (see the notes on 11: 13).

15. The Greek geographer Strabo (who lived about 64 B.C.–A.D. 24) says the battle was fought at the river Oenoparus not

[a] *That is* 145 B.C.

far from Antioch. Alexander had returned from Ptolemais to Antioch (10: 68) in 147 B.C., moved into Cilicia in 146 B.C., and in his absence had lost Antioch to Ptolemy. Alexander probably counter-attacked in summer 145 B.C.

16. *Arabia* is perhaps the Arabia of Paul's retirement (Gal. 1: 17), somewhere between Antioch and the Euphrates.

17. *Zabdiel:* Diodorus gives him his Greek name, Diocles, and says that Alexander was murdered by his own generals, who in this way sought the favour of Demetrius and Diocles. 1 Maccabees shows Zabdiel ingratiating himself with Ptolemy.

18. Ptolemy was badly wounded in the battle, but did not die until he had heard news of Alexander's death and seen his severed head – 'most pleasant things to hear and to see', says Josephus (*Antiquities* XIII. 4. 8). The Egyptian garrisons in the coastal towns were promptly killed, and Ptolemy's army fled back to Alexandria, leaving the elephants in Demetrius' hands. ✵

JONATHAN'S DIPLOMACY

At this time Jonathan gathered together the Judaeans to 20 assault the citadel in Jerusalem, and they brought up many siege-engines against it. But a number of renegades, 21 enemies of their own people, went to the king and reported that Jonathan was besieging the citadel. The king 22 was furious at the news and immediately moved his quarters to Ptolemais. He wrote to Jonathan ordering him to raise the siege, and to meet him for conference at Ptolemais with all speed.

When Jonathan received this letter, he gave orders for 23 the siege to be continued. Then, selecting elders of Israel and priests to accompany him, he set out on his dangerous mission. He took with him silver and gold, and robes, and 24 many other gifts, and went to meet the king at Ptolemais.

25   He won the favour of Demetrius, although some rene-
26 gade Jews tried to lodge complaints against him. But the
king treated him just as his predecessors had done, honour-
27 ing him in the presence of all his Friends. He confirmed
him in the high-priesthood and in all his former dignities,
and appointed him head of the first class of the King's
Friends.

* Jonathan had returned to Jerusalem (verse 7) probably in
summer 146 B.C. He had once been Demetrius' opponent
(10: 67–87), but now that Demetrius was king, the situation
had changed. Demetrius wanted Jonathan's support against
Egypt and against dissidents inside his kingdom, while Jonathan wanted Demetrius' support for his own rule against the
hellenizers (cp. verses 21, 25). The problem was one of getting
the best possible terms.

20. To attack the citadel in Jerusalem before negotiations
were opened would give Jonathan a stronger position from
which to bargain with Demetrius. The *renegades*, loyal to
Syria, are probably now in a minority, but they naturally
protested to the king.

22. The king reacted sharply – but while he wished to
placate his supporters in Judaea he also needed to gain the
support of Jonathan whose previous loyalty had been rather
ambiguously divided between Ptolemy and Alexander. So,
moving south in slightly threatening fashion to *Ptolemais*, he
summoned Jonathan to a *conference*.

23. Jonathan knew the strength of his position, and leaving
the siege in progress he took not soldiers but diplomatic representatives and gifts to Ptolemais.

25. *He won the favour of Demetrius* as five years previously
he had won the favour of Ptolemy and Alexander, and in the
face of similar representations from the hellenizing Jews (cp.
10: 59–66).

26. *as his predecessors had done:* cp. 10: 3–6, 15–20, 59–66.

27. *the high-priesthood* had been conferred by Alexander, cp. 10: 20–1. *all his former dignities* presumably included his position as *general and provincial governor* (10: 65). *head of the first class*...: perhaps Jonathan is made one of the King's Kinsmen (cp. 10: 89), but the Greek may mean only that Jonathan was included among the first class of the Friends as before, cp. 10: 65. A Seleucid king did not necessarily adopt the Friends of his predecessor, but Jonathan, on the borders of Egypt, is too important to ignore. ✳

JONATHAN'S REQUESTS

Jonathan requested the king to exempt Judaea and the 28 three Samaritan districts*a* from tribute, promising him in return three hundred talents. King Demetrius consented, 29 writing to Jonathan on all these affairs as follows:

King Demetrius to his brother Jonathan, and to the 30 Jewish nation, greeting.

This is a copy of our letter written to our kinsman 31 Lasthenes about you, which we have had made for your information:

'King Demetrius to his respected kinsman Lasthenes, 32 greeting.

'Because our friends the Jewish nation show us good- 33 will, and observe their obligations to us, we are resolved to become their benefactor. We have therefore settled 34 on them the lands of Judaea and the three districts, Apherema, Lydda, and Ramathaim, which are now transferred from Samaria to Judaea, together with all the lands adjacent thereto, for the benefit of the priesthood at Jerusalem. This is a transfer of the annual dues

[a] three...districts: *probable reading; Gk.* three districts and Samaria.

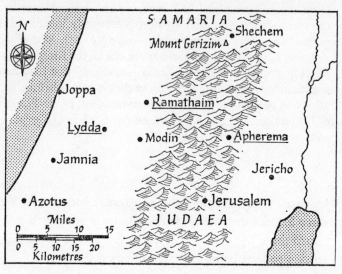

6. The 'three districts' transferred to Judaea (I Macc. II: 34). The 'districts' are underlined.

which the King formerly received from these territories,
35   from the produce of the soil and of the orchards. Other
of our revenues, the tithes and tolls now pertaining to
us, the salt-pans, and the crown-money, all these we
36   shall cede to them. These provisions are irrevocable
37   from now for all future time. See to it then that you
make a copy of them to be given to Jonathan and set by
him in a conspicuous position on the holy mountain.'

* Demetrius probably demanded that Jonathan withdraw his
attack on the citadel, and Jonathan's request was a counter-
demand. In 152 B.C. Demetrius I had offered what Jonathan
now requests (cp. 10: 30, 38: though it has been suggested
that Jonathan wrote these clauses into Demetrius I's original

offer in order to deceive Demetrius II). The area in question is the *meris* of Judaea and Samaria, which was part of the *eparchy* of Coele-syria. Since Jonathan already controlled the coastal plain as far north as Joppa and Galilee, and Gilead across the Jordan, the control of Samaria to his immediate north was an obvious target. Demetrius granted it, but he did not make the offer Jonathan was really looking for of the withdrawal of the garrison in Jerusalem.

28. *the three Samaritan districts* (10: 30, 38; 11: 34) did not legally belong to Jonathan, though Jonathan's request tacitly assumes his ownership. The Greek reading 'three districts and Samaria' (N.E.B. footnote) may be the Greek translator's mistranslation of a phrase meaning 'three districts of Samaria'. There seems to have been some ancient confusion in the interpretation of this verse between these three districts (the Seleucid term was 'toparchies') and other areas – thus Josephus names the districts as Samaria, Joppa and Galilee (*Antiquities* XIII. 4. 9), while 1 Macc. 10: 30 rather oddly mentions Galilee. *three hundred talents:* perhaps Samaria's annual tribute to Syria (the historian Sulpicius Severus, A.D. 363–420, says this sum was paid to Antiochus IV annually), or a once-for-all payment.

30. *to his brother* (cp. 10: 18) *Jonathan and to the Jewish nation:* Demetrius I ignored Jonathan in his address (10: 25–45); Alexander ignored the nation (10: 18–20). Demetrius II wants support from both.

31. *kinsman* (cp. 10: 89), the closest of all the King's Friends. *Lasthenes* was in fact the general of Demetrius' Cretan mercenaries (cp. the note on 10: 67), and now Demetrius' right-hand man (in the Greek of verse 32 he is called 'father').

34. *settled . . . for the benefit of the priesthood at Jerusalem:* the proposal of 10: 38 was to make Apherema, Lydda and Ramathaim 'subject to the High Priest alone'. Demetrius is allowing taxes formerly received from the grain and fruit of Judaea and the three Samaritan districts to go to the support of the Jerusalem cult and temple.

35. The *tithes and tolls* (see 10: 31), salt- and crown-taxes (see 10: 29) are repealed. Whether the basic annual tribute was repealed is not clear. But Judaea is clearly still technically under Syrian control, and the garrison is not removed from Jerusalem. Some of the concessions offered by Demetrius I in 152 B.C. are not mentioned (cp. 10: 33–7, 39–45). Demetrius has not yielded as much as he might have done; he was in fact a strong ruler, though capable of serious political mistakes.

37. For the idea of a publicly displayed copy of a treaty, see 8: 22. *the holy mountain* (cp. 'Jerusalem, thy city, thy holy hill', Dan. 9: 16, 20) perhaps suggests a Jewish hand at work on the letter's phraseology; but not necessarily, for the concept of a holy mountain would be known in Syria. ✻

DEMETRIUS' DIFFICULTIES

38 When King Demetrius saw that the country was quiet under his rule and resistance was at an end, he disbanded all his forces, sending every man home, with the exception of the foreign mercenaries he had hired from the islands of the Gentiles. Then all the troops enlisted under 39 his predecessors turned against the king. A certain Trypho, formerly of the party of Alexander, aware of the disaffection of all the forces towards Demetrius, went to Imalcue, the Arab chieftain, who had charge of the child 40 Antiochus, Alexander's son, and kept pressing him to hand the boy over to him to be made king in succession to his father. He also informed Imalcue of all the measures Demetrius was taking and of his unpopularity with his troops. There he remained for some time.

41 Meanwhile Jonathan sent to King Demetrius requesting him to withdraw, from the citadel in Jerusalem and from the fortresses, the garrisons which were constantly haras-

sing Israel. Demetrius sent Jonathan this reply: 'I will not 42
only meet your request, but when opportunity arises I
will do you and your people the highest honour. And 43
now be so good as to send men to support me, for all my
troops are in revolt.'

Jonathan dispatched three thousand fighting men to 44
Antioch, and the king was much relieved at their arrival.
The citizens poured into the centre of the city, a hundred 45
and twenty thousand strong, bent on killing the king. He 46
took refuge in the palace, while the citizens seized control
of the streets and fighting broke out. King Demetrius 47
called the Jews to his assistance, and they rallied to him at
once. They then dispersed all over the city and slaughtered
that day as many as a hundred thousand, setting the city 48
on fire and taking much booty. And thus they saved the
king's life.

When the citizens saw that the Jews had the city com- 49
pletely at their mercy, their courage failed them and they
clamoured to the king to accept their surrender and to 50
stop the Jews fighting against them and the city. They 51
threw down their arms and made peace; and the Jews,
now in high repute with the king and all his subjects,
returned to Jerusalem loaded with booty. But when King 52
Demetrius was secure upon his throne, with the country
quiet under him, he went back on all his promises and 53
broke off relations with Jonathan; instead of repaying the
benefits he had received, he put severe pressure upon him.

* The strength of Jonathan's position is now made clear by
the fact that Demetrius, facing internal revolt, appeals to
Jonathan for help.

38. In fact it was Lasthenes (cp. verse 31), 'a man without religion, without conscience, who pushed his master to the most shameful actions' (Diodorus), who *disbanded* all the forces except the *mercenaries* under his own command. He perhaps intended to take the power into his own hands. But the demobilization of local, regular troops led to disaster for Demetrius and his supporters.

39. *Trypho*, once a soldier of Demetrius I, then a governor of Antioch for Alexander, was now one of Demetrius II's Friends. *Imalcue* was perhaps the son and successor of Zabdiel (cp. verse 17). *Antiochus* was born in 150 or 149 B.C., and so was 'a mere lad' (verse 54) at this time.

40. Antiochus' father Alexander died in autumn 145 B.C. (verse 16), and Trypho shortly crowned the boy as Antiochus VI (verse 55). Later, having gained his own ends, he murdered him (13: 31–2).

41. Demetrius I had promised to remove the citadel garrison (cp. 10: 32), but neither he nor his successors had done so. Jonathan had recently besieged it (11: 21), apparently unsuccessfully. For the fortresses, see 9: 50–1.

42–3. Jonathan's *request* is well timed; Demetrius needed troops in Antioch. But even so he did not withdraw the garrison (cp. verse 52–3; 12: 36), instead persuading Jonathan to send Jewish troops to Antioch.

45. The *citizens* included, presumably, large numbers of Demetrius' ex-soldiers.

47–51. Josephus (*Antiquities* XIII. 5. 3) says that the Jewish troops hurled missiles on the crowds from the palace roof, and set fire to the city, while the king's mercenary troops confronted the crowds in the narrow streets. Diodorus (XXXIII. 4) says that executions and confiscations followed and that Demetrius 'even outdid his father in harshness and thirst for blood'.

52–3. Demetrius' treachery is perhaps not surprising, but there may have been some factor, tactfully omitted by I Maccabees, to account for his new attitude towards Jonathan.

Josephus (*Antiquities* XIII. 5. 3) says that Demetrius now threatened Jonathan with war 'unless he paid him all the kinds of tribute which the Jewish nation was required to pay from the time of the first kings'. This would revoke the provisions of the letter of 11: 29-37 above. ✳

TRYPHO SEIZES POWER

After this, Trypho returned, and with him Antiochus, a 54 mere lad. Antiochus was crowned, and all the forces 55 Demetrius had so contemptuously discharged rallied to the king. These fought against Demetrius, and he was utterly routed. Trypho brought up his elephants and made 56 himself master of Antioch. The young Antiochus wrote 57 to Jonathan confirming him in the high-priesthood, with authority over the four districts, and making him one of the King's Friends. He also sent him a service of gold plate, 58 and gave him the right to drink from a gold cup, to be robed in purple, and to wear the gold clasp. He appointed 59 Jonathan's brother Simon as officer commanding the area from the Ladder of Tyre to the borders of Egypt.

✳ Demetrius is now in a precarious position, and Trypho, having gained Imalcue's support (see verses 39-40), returns to take advantage of it. Jonathan's estrangement from Demetrius is an obvious advantage to Trypho.

54. The date is probably late 145 B.C. *a mere lad:* see on verse 39.

55. The *forces Demetrius had so contemptuously discharged* (literally, 'sent to the crows', a strong expression) accepted Trypho, perhaps for Antiochus' sake as much as for his own. Diodorus (XXXIII. 4) comments that as a result of Demetrius II's behaviour, the kings of his family 'were hated for their

transgressions and those of the other house were loved for their equity'.

56. *elephants:* probably those left behind by Ptolemy VI's army when retreating earlier that year (see the note on verse 18). Trypho took over Antioch; Demetrius fled to Seleucia on the coast where he tried to continue rule with the support of Cilicia, the Phoenician coast (cp. 12: 24–34), Gaza (11: 61), and Media (cp. 14: 1).

57–8. Once again Jonathan's allegiance is courted. For the *high-priesthood,* cp. 10: 20; for the *four districts* cp. verses 28, 'Judaea and the three Samaritan districts' (though perhaps the fourth was not Judaea but Accaron, cp. 10: 89), 34. *one of the King's friends:* cp. 10: 20, 65, 89; 11: 27. Gold vessels and purple robes were the courtiers' privilege, cp. 10: 20 and 1 Esdras 3: 5; for the *gold clasp,* cp. 10: 89. Jonathan did in fact support Trypho against Demetrius (see verses 63–74; 12: 24–32). But Trypho never trusted the Jews, and eventually killed Jonathan (13: 23). Simon then reopened negotiations with Demetrius (13: 34–40).

59. The important new offer was the appointment of Simon as *officer* (Greek *strategos*) of the coastal area (in which Simon had already held Jewish command, cp. 5: 20–3; 10: 74, 82). Alexander had made Jonathan a general (*strategos*) (10: 65), probably of the inland area, and Demetrius had perhaps confirmed him in this office (11: 27). But now the coastal towns, not all pro-Jewish and not all ready to accept Trypho, were under Jewish military administration. Clearly, Trypho wanted at least to deny the advantage of these towns to Demetrius. The *Ladder of Tyre* was a stepped road between the sea and the cliffs of *ras en-nakurah,* a headland which cut off the region of Ptolemais from the region of Tyre and which today marks the border between the coasts of Israel and Lebanon. The *borders of Egypt* then as now fluctuated with political fortunes; perhaps the *wadi el-arish,* reaching the coast half-way between Gaza and the Nile, is in mind. ✳

CAMPAIGNS OF JONATHAN AND SIMON

Jonathan made a tour through the country on the far 60
side of the river and the towns there; and all the forces of
Syria gathered to his support.

He went to Ascalon, where he was received with great
honour by the citizens. From there he went on to Gaza, 61
but the inhabitants closed the gates against him; so he
blockaded the city, set fire to its suburbs, and plundered
them. The citizens of Gaza then sought peace, and he 62
made terms with them, taking the sons of their magistrates as hostages and sending them off to Jerusalem; he
himself continued his progress through the country in the
direction of Damascus.

Jonathan heard that Demetrius's officers had arrived at 63
Kedesh-in-Galilee with a large force to prevent him from
reaching his objective. He went to meet them, leaving his 64
brother Simon in Judaea. Simon took up position against 65
Bethsura and, after prolonged fighting, blockaded it.
Finally the citizens sued for terms of peace and Simon 66
consented; he evicted them, took over the town, and
installed a garrison there.

Jonathan, who had encamped with his army by the 67
Lake of Gennesaret, marched out early in the morning
into the plain of Asor. There in the plain the gentile army 68
was advancing to meet him; they had set an ambush for
him in the hills, while they themselves confronted him.
When the men from the ambush emerged and joined in 69
the fighting, all Jonathan's men took to flight; not one 70
remained except Mattathias son of Absalom, and Judas
son of Chalphi, officers in the army. Jonathan tore his 71

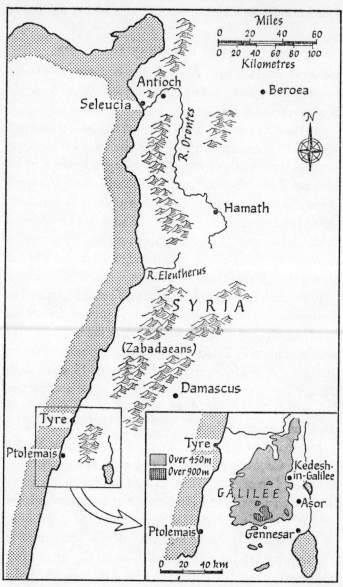

7. Jonathan in Galilee and Syria (1 Macc. 11: 63–74; 12: 24–32).

clothes, put dust upon his head, and prayed. Then he 72
turned upon the enemy and routed them in headlong
flight. When the fugitives of Jonathan's army saw this, 73
they rallied to him and joined in the pursuit as far as the
enemy base at Kedesh; there they encamped. That day 74
about three thousand of the Gentiles fell. Jonathan then
returned to Jerusalem.

* Jonathan tours 'the country on the far side of the river and
the towns there' (verse 60) – that is, probably, the province
west of the Euphrates (cp. 7: 8, where a similar phrase describes Bacchides' sphere of command). The verse is a general
introduction to the passage following (though some take it
as referring to a campaign in Transjordan such as that of
5: 24–54). Jonathan's purpose was ostensibly to encourage
support for the new régime and to gather troops for
Trypho (Josephus says he failed in this), but in fact to extend
his own influence.

60. *Ascalon* (cp. 10: 86) welcomed Jonathan, wanting no
trouble.

61. *Gaza* opposed him: with Egypt so close, Gaza was
never pro-Jewish or pro-Syrian. Gaza had even held out for
two months against Alexander the Great. In ancient times
Gaza had been a slave-trade port through which Edomites,
Phoenicians and Philistines passed Israelite slaves (cp. Amos
1: 6, 9). The port, however, was separate from the city, and
thus blockading the city could be effective.

62. Jonathan did not send the hostages to Trypho but kept
them under his own guard. He then marched north towards
Damascus, perhaps to meet Trypho for an attack on Demetrius.

63. Demetrius, based at Seleucia, sent *officers* (named Sar-
pedon and Palamedes) *with a large force* (probably mercenaries
raised in Cilicia) south to prevent Jonathan joining Trypho
(just as once before he had sent Apollonius south, 10: 67–73).

Kedesh-in-Galilee is *tell qades*, once the home of Barak (Judg. 4: 6), on the western edge of the upper Jordan valley.

65–6. *Bethsura* had been fortified and garrisoned by Bacchides (9: 51), and refugee hellenists had settled there (10: 14). Simon captured Bethsura in summer 144 B.C.; the day was celebrated annually by the Jews on 23 June (17 Sivan) until A.D. 70 (see p. 8). The Jewish *garrison* now protected Judaea's southern flank against Syrian or Idumaean attacks (cp. 13: 21, note).

67. *Lake of Gennesaret:* the Sea of Galilee, so named from the plain Gennesar ('prince's garden') on its west (cp. Luke 5: 1). *Asor*, the Hazor captured by Joshua (Josh. 11: 10–11), excavated by Yigael Yadin in 1955–9, was an important town controlling the road to the north that ran west of the marshy Huleh basin. West of Asor the hills of Galilee rose fairly steeply, reaching at this point up to about 2,000 ft above sea-level.

68. Troops were placed in *ambush, in the hills* rising steeply to the west of the road, ready to fall on the rear or flank of Jonathan's army which Demetrius' main force confronted on the road.

70. *Mattathias son of Absalom:* perhaps the Absalom of 2 Macc. 11: 17. *Judas* is otherwise unknown. The name *Chalphi* appears as Clopas (John 19: 25) or in a Greek form as Alphaeus (Mark 3: 18).

71. Tearing clothes and putting dust in one's hair (cp. Job 1: 20) were normal ways of expressing grief; such behaviour was forbidden to the high priest (Lev. 10: 6; 21: 10) except, it seems, in extreme circumstances (cp. Matt. 26: 25).

72–4. The battle probably ended in complete confusion, each side thinking it had won. 1 Maccabees presents the battle as a defeat turned into victory by Jonathan's own prayer and single-handed valour, but the result is that Jonathan returns to Jerusalem and Demetrius has at least prevented him from joining Trypho. ✶

JONATHAN'S DIPLOMATIC RELATIONS

Jonathan now saw his opportunity and sent picked men **12** on a mission to Rome to confirm and renew the treaty of friendship with that city. He sent letters to the same effect 2 to Sparta and to other places. The envoys travelled to 3 Rome and went to the Senate House to deliver their message: 'Jonathan the High Priest and the Jewish people have sent us to renew their former pact of friendship and alliance.' The Romans gave them letters requiring the 4 authorities in each place to give them safe conduct to Judaea.

Here follows a transcript of the letter which Jonathan 5 wrote to the Spartans:

Jonathan the High Priest, the Senate of the Jews, the 6 priests, and the rest of the Jewish people, to our brothers of Sparta, greeting.

On a previous occasion a letter was sent to Onias the 7 High Priest from Arius your king, acknowledging our kinship; a copy is given below. Onias welcomed your 8 envoy with full honours and received the letter in which the terms of the alliance and friendship were set forth. We do not regard ourselves as needing such 9 alliances, since our support is the holy books in our possession. Nevertheless, we now venture to send and 10 renew our pact of brotherhood and friendship with you, so that we may not become estranged, for it is many years since you wrote to us. We never lose any 11 opportunity, on festal and other appropriate days, of remembering you at our sacrifices and in our prayers,

12 as it is right and proper to remember kinsmen; and we
13 rejoice at your fame. We ourselves have been under the
pressure of hostile attacks on every side; all the sur-
14 rounding kings have made war upon us. In the course
of these wars we had no wish to trouble you or the rest
15 of our allies and friends: we have the aid of Heaven to
support us, and so we have been saved from our
16 enemies, and they have been humbled. Accordingly,
we chose Numenius son of Antiochus, and Antipater
son of Jason, and have sent them to the Romans to
renew our former friendship and alliance with them.
17 We instructed them to go to you also with our greetings, and to deliver this letter about the renewal of our
18 pact of brotherhood. And now we pray you to send us
a reply to this letter.

19 This is a copy of the letter sent by the Spartans to Onias:

20   Arius, King of Sparta, to Onias the High Priest,
greeting.

21   A document has come to light which shows that
Spartans and Jews are kinsmen, descended alike from
22 Abraham. Now that we have learnt this, we beg you
23 to write and tell us how your affairs prosper. The message we return to you is, 'What is yours, your cattle
and every kind of property, is ours, and what is ours is
yours', and we have therefore instructed our envoys to
report to you in these terms.

* There had been diplomatic activity between the Jews
(perhaps the hellenizing party) and the Romans in 163 B.C.
(cp. 2 Macc. 11: 34–8), and between Judas and the Romans in
161 B.C. (cp. 1 Macc. 8: 17–32). Demetrius I had ignored the

resulting threat from Rome (8: 31-2). In 146 B.C., after the destruction of both Carthage and Corinth, Rome's power was much more visible; and in Greece, Sparta alone had any semblance of power. But neither Rome nor Sparta was willing to embroil herself seriously on the Jewish side in the present struggle. Jonathan in any case was seeking prestige and recognition abroad as much as physical aid.

1. *picked men:* cp. verse 16. *to renew the treaty:* see 8: 17-32.

2. *Sparta:* her independent power at this time, just after the Roman conquest of Greece, was slight, though the destruction of Corinth and the Achaean League in 146 B.C. had removed her local rivals. Traditionally, her constitution was based on a law-giver, Lycurgus, and this may have appealed to the Jews. *other places:* unknown, but Rhodes and some of the other places in the list of 15: 23 seem likely candidates.

3. The formula *Jonathan the High Priest and the Jewish people* implies an independence Demetrius might have questioned. *people* (Greek *demos*, cp. 8: 29) refers to the Jews as a political body; the Syrians would call them an *ethnos*, a racial group under Syrian rule.

4. It is not said that the Romans did renew the treaty, nor is their letter quoted, but the treaty probably was renewed. *safe conduct:* Josephus (*Antiquities* XIV. 10. 15) preserves a letter from one Gaius Fannius to the magistrates of the island of Cos (cp. 15: 23) about the safe conduct of Jewish envoys. This may refer to the embassage of 161 B.C. (8: 17-32).

5. The letter to Sparta should probably be taken as representing what the author of 1 Maccabees thought appropriate to the occasion.

6. If the letter's heading represents accurately the constitution of Judaea in 144 B.C., Jonathan rules with the help of the *Senate* and *priests* (cp. 7: 33; 11: 23). The 'elders' of the Senate would be the heads of the leading non-priestly families, whose power as leaders went back at least as far as the exile (cp. Ezek. 8: 1). The Senate, or Sanhedrin, also contained representatives of the leading priestly families, and, by New Testament

times but not in Maccabaean times, Pharisaic scribes as well. In the reign of Antiochus IV the Senate and priests would have been largely hellenizers, but by 144 B.C. they were probably much more nationalistic at heart. *brothers:* the word was of ancient use in eastern diplomacy, and was used of treaty-partners (cp. 1 Kings 9: 13; 1 Macc. 10: 18; 11: 30). Probably the kinship described below is also in mind.

7. *Onias I* (in office about 300 B.C.) and *Arius I* of Sparta (309–265 B.C.) could have corresponded, but why the Spartans should then look to a small and distant people ruled by Egypt is hard to see. Josephus (*Antiquities* XII. 4. 10) set the correspondence in the time of Onias III (about 200–175 B.C.), which seems a more likely time for Sparta to make contact, threatened as she then was by the advancing powers of Rome and Syria. Perhaps the Jews, knowing little of Sparta's history, have ascribed the letter anachronistically to Arius, a name they knew.

8. *envoy:* Josephus names him as Demoteles. *letter:* see verses 19–23.

9. The sentiment is hardly tactful, and with verse 10 sounds patronizing. *holy books in our possession:* these are 'the law, the prophets, and the other writings of our ancestors' which about 180 B.C. Jesus son of Sirach had studied (see the *Preface* to Ecclesiasticus). The second century B.C. saw the virtual acceptance of a canon of sacred writings, and a growing dependence on them.

11. *remembering you:* cp. 7: 33, where sacrifices are offered for the Syrian king. But the last words of verse 10 make this claim sound a little insincere.

12 ff. These verses perhaps reflect phrases from the psalms (see, e.g., Ps. 2: 1 ff.; 118: 10 ff.), which were important among 'the other writings of our ancestors' (cp. verse 9, note, and Luke 24: 44). In describing the various campaigns, 1 Maccabees has made clear *the aid of Heaven*: cp. 3: 18–22; 3: 42–4: 25.

16. For the envoys, see 14: 22; 15: 15, and the note on 8: 17.

17. Probably Sparta was visited by the envoys as they returned from Rome.

19–20. See on verse 7 above.

21. We need not doubt that the Spartans and the Jews were prepared to ally with one another as brothers and to find genealogical justification for this. Similar cases were known elsewhere in the hellenistic world, and both Spartans and Jews appear to have accepted the diplomatic fiction (cp. 14: 19–23; 2 Macc. 5: 9).

23. The style is Hebraic: compare 1 Kings 22: 4; 2 Kings 3: 7, 'What is mine is yours: myself, my people, and my horses.' The letter was perhaps composed by the author of 1 Maccabees to fill out the story of the diplomatic mission, or by Jonathan himself, as a piece of recognizable diplomatic fiction, to support the claim of kinship. ✳

CAMPAIGNS OF JONATHAN AND SIMON
(CONTINUED)

24 Jonathan heard that Demetrius's generals had returned 25 to attack him with larger forces than before. He marched from Jerusalem and met them in the region of Hamath, 26 giving them no chance to set foot in his territory. He sent spies to their camp, who on their return reported that 27 preparations were being made for a night attack. At sunset Jonathan gave orders to his men to stay awake and stand to arms all night, ready for battle; and he stationed 28 outposts all round the camp. When the enemy heard that Jonathan and his men were ready for battle, they were alarmed; their courage failed, and they withdrew, first 29 lighting watch-fires in their camp. Jonathan and his men, seeing the watch-fires burning, did not realize what had happened until morning. Then Jonathan set out in pur- 30 suit, but failed to overtake them, for they had crossed the river Eleutherus. So Jonathan turned aside against the 31

Arabs called Zabadaeans, and he dealt them a severe blow
32 and plundered them. He struck camp and came to Damascus, and then made a march through the whole country.
33,34   Simon set out and marched as far as Ascalon and the neighbouring fortresses. He then turned towards Joppa; he had heard that the citizens intended to hand it over to the supporters of Demetrius, but before they could do so, he occupied the town and placed a garrison there to defend it.
35   When Jonathan returned he convened the senate. With their agreement he decided to build fortresses in Judaea,
36 to heighten the walls of Jerusalem, and to erect a high barrier to separate the citadel from the city and so to
37 isolate it that the garrison could not buy or sell. They assembled to rebuild the city, for the wall along the ravine to the east had partly collapsed, and he repaired the section
38 of the wall called Chaphenatha. Simon also rebuilt and fortified Adida in the Shephelah, erecting gates and bars.

* These verses continue the military story from 11: 74, though we are now probably in the year 143 B.C.; two campaigns from Jerusalem to the north in one season are unlikely. As in the previous campaign (11: 63–74) Jonathan leaves Simon in the south, to protect Jerusalem and continue the work of extending Jewish control over the coast.

24. Demetrius is not satisfied with the results achieved earlier (see 11: 63–74). It is surprising that he does not attempt to restore diplomatic relations with Jonathan, to separate him from Trypho; but in fact it is Jonathan who is really in control of the situation and who derives most advantage from it.

25. Jonathan crossed into Syrian territory; *Hamath* (renamed Epiphaneia by Antiochus IV) lay on the river Orontes, well beyond the river Eleutherus (cp. 11:7), the frontier of the

region over which Alexander had appointed Jonathan general
(10: 65).

26–9. In view of their intelligence reports (verses 26, 28,
29), both sides seem to have been unwilling to make the first
move during the night; a better Syrian general might have
turned the Jewish vigil to his own advantage. Josephus (*Antiquities* XIII. 5. 10) says that when Demetrius' generals 'discovered that Jonathan knew their plan, they were no longer
able to use sound judgement', and 'did not consider themselves
a match for Jonathan's men, if they were to fight in the open'.
Syrian morale seems to have been low.

30. The enemy fled west across the northern arm of the
river Eleutherus into the coastal area which Demetrius controlled.

31. *Zabadaeans:* they lived 46 km (29 miles) north-west of
Damascus. To reach them, Jonathan *turned aside* eastwards.
There may be a connection with the Arab Zabdiel (11: 17),
in which case Jonathan's motive may be revenge for the
murder of Alexander, who of all the Seleucids had been most
friendly towards the Jews. The *Megillath Ta'anith* (see pp. 7 f.)
mentions persecution of Jews settled at a place called Beth
Zabdai; if this is connected, Jonathan's motive was the rescue
of Jews. *plundered:* Josephus says the plunder was sold in
Damascus.

32. *through the whole country:* this refers either to Jonathan's
march home, or to a tour of Syria, which in the present state
of civil war between Trypho and Demetrius lay open to him.
Jonathan may have dreamed of restoring the empire of David,
which included Damascus (cp. 2 Sam. 8: 5–7).

33–4. Simon marched to the coast to prevent active support
for Demetrius. *Ascalon* (cp. 11: 60) would not oppose the
Maccabees, but *Joppa* would. Jonathan had taken Joppa in
147 B.C. (cp. 10: 75); it probably passed into Egyptian control
in 146 B.C. (cp. 11: 6), but back to Jewish control under Simon
as Trypho's officer late in 145 B.C. or in 144 B.C. (11: 59).
Now, perhaps 143 B.C., Simon garrisons the town. Its strategic

importance is underlined still further by Simon's action a little later in ejecting the civilian population (13: 11).

35–6. Jonathan apparently controls the Senate and can get their *agreement* to measures needed to make Judaea militarily more secure against Syria. No renegade representations to Trypho are mentioned as there had been on Demetrius' accession (11: 25; contrast 11: 54–9). The hellenizers no longer exist as an influential party.

fortresses: perhaps those built sixteen years previously by Bacchides (9: 50) and later deserted (10: 12) were used. The *walls of Jerusalem* had been pulled down in 168 B.C. (1: 32), and partly rebuilt in 152 B.C. (10: 11). Demetrius I's offer to rebuild the walls (10: 45) had not been accepted. *to separate the citadel from the city:* Jonathan's blockade was the beginning of the end for the Syrian garrison (cp. 13: 49–52).

37. *the ravine to the east* is the Kidron valley. *Chaphenatha* is possibly a corruption of the Aramaic translation of 'the second quarter' of Jerusalem (see Neh. 11: 9, footnote; cp. 2 Kings 22: 14), which some scholars place north-west of the temple area, and others immediately to its south.

38. The fortification of *Adida* (Hadid of Ezra 2: 33, Neh. 7: 37), part of the district of Lydda (11: 34), would help isolate Gazara a few miles to its south (cp. 13: 43–8). *gates and bars:* cp. Judg. 16: 3; Samson removed Gaza's gate with the two posts, 'bar and all'. *

TRYPHO SEIZES JONATHAN

39 Trypho now aspired to be king of Asia; he meant to rebel against King Antiochus and assume the crown him-
40 self. But he was afraid that Jonathan would fight to prevent this, so he cast about for some means of capturing
41 and killing him. He set off and reached Bethshan. Jonathan marched out to meet him with forty thousand picked
42 troops, and he also reached Bethshan. Trypho, seeing that

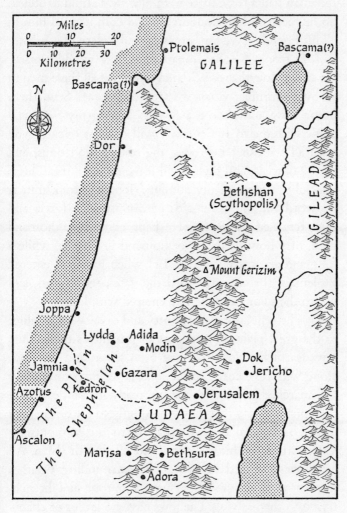

8. The campaigns of Trypho and Kendebaeus
(1 Macc. 12: 39 – 13: 53; 15: 10 – 16: 10).

173

Jonathan had a large force with him, was afraid to attack.
43 So he received him honourably and commended him to
all his Friends, gave him presents, and ordered his Friends
and his troops to obey Jonathan as they would himself.
44 He said to Jonathan: 'Why have you put all these men to
45 so much trouble, when we are not at war? Send them
home now and choose a few to accompany you, and
come with me to Ptolemais. I will hand it over to you
with all the other fortresses, the rest of the troops, and
all the officials, and then I will leave the country. This is
46 the only purpose of my coming.' Jonathan took him at
his word and did as he said: he dismissed his forces and
47 they returned to Judaea. He kept back three thousand
men, of whom he left two thousand in Galilee, while a
48 thousand accompanied him. But when Jonathan entered
Ptolemais, the citizens closed the gates, seized him, and
put to the sword all who had entered with him.

49   Trypho sent a force of infantry and cavalry into Galilee
50 to the great plain, to wipe out all Jonathan's men. They
now learnt that Jonathan had been seized and was lost,
along with his escort, but they put heart into one another
51 and marched in close formation, ready for battle. When
their pursuers saw that they would fight to the death, they
52 turned back. So all came safely home to Judaea, mourning
for Jonathan and his followers, and filled with alarm. All
53 Israel was plunged in grief. The surrounding Gentiles
were now bent on destroying them root and branch,
saying to themselves, 'The Jews have no leader or champion, so now is the time to attack, and we shall blot out
all memory of them among men.'

✲ The date is probably 143 B.C. Trypho controlled Antioch (11: 56), but Demetrius still controlled the Phoenician coast, Cilicia and Mesopotamia, and the Maccabees controlled the coast and hinterland south of the river Eleutherus. But neither Demetrius, who had suffered defeat from Jonathan and was unpopular in Antioch, nor the young Antiochus, was a serious obstacle to Trypho's ambition; Jonathan was a different matter.

39. *king of Asia:* cp. 11: 13. Trypho wanted the whole empire, not just Syria. *Antiochus:* cp. 11: 54; 13: 31–2.

40. *Bethshan* (its Greek name was Scythopolis, 2 Macc. 12: 29–30) lay at a strategic point in the Jordan valley. It was friendly towards the Jews. Trypho's appearance here threatened the Samaritan toparchies recently given to Judaea (11: 57), and was perhaps meant to pressurize Jonathan into raising the blockade of the Jerusalem citadel (cp. verse 36).

41. *forty thousand picked troops:* perhaps an exaggerated figure. The largest Jewish force mentioned so far is Jonathan's 10,000 with Simon's reinforcements at Joppa (10: 74).

42–3. Trypho changed his tactics and played on Jonathan's readiness to accept flattery and gifts (cp. 10: 59–66; 11: 6, 23–7).

45. Jonathan is given to understand that Trypho would hand over *all the other fortresses* (Gazara, the citadel in Jerusalem), and the troops and administrative officials that went with them.

47–8. Jonathan was perhaps not so deceived as 1 Maccabees suggests. In 145 B.C. he had met Demetrius at Ptolemais accompanied only by priests and elders (11: 23); this time he took *a thousand* men, with *two thousand* more stationed *in Galilee* to secure his retreat if necessary. But what Jonathan had not bargained for was the treachery of Ptolemais' citizens (hostile though they were to the Jews, cp. 5: 15). Nor had Jonathan on this occasion the added protection of the king of Egypt, or of a Syrian king who needed his help.

49–51. Trypho's attack on the forces in Galilee was an obvious sequel, but their mood was too dangerous to challenge.

52–3. The author of 1 Maccabees comments sadly on the situation, stressing the contrast between *All Israel* and *The surrounding Gentiles* so prominent earlier in the book (cp. 1: 11–15; 2: 25, 45–8, etc.). The latter would include the coastal towns (except perhaps Ascalon), but we hear of no attack apart from Trypho's. The Gentiles' threat (verse 53) is reminiscent of 3: 35 and 5: 1. The word *champion* was used of Judas at his death (9: 20). ✳

The high-priesthood of Simon

SIMON BECOMES LEADER

13 THE NEWS REACHED Simon that Trypho had mustered a large force for the invasion and destruction of 2 Judaea, and it threw the people into a state of panic. When Simon saw this, he went up to Jerusalem, called an 3 assembly, and encouraged them in these words: 'I need not remind you of all that my brothers and I and my father's house have done for the laws and the holy place, what battles we have fought, what hardships we have 4 endured. My brothers have all fallen in this cause, fighting 5 for Israel, and I am the only one left. Now Heaven forbid that I should grudge my own life in any moment of 6 danger, for I am not worth more than my brothers. No! I will take up the cause of my nation and the holy place, of your wives and children, since all the Gentiles in their 7 hatred have gathered to destroy us.' At these words the 8 people plucked up courage, and they shouted in answer: 'You shall be our leader in place of Judas and your 9 brother Jonathan. Fight our battles, and we will do what-

ever you tell us.' So Simon mustered all the fighting men 10
and hurried on the completion of the walls of Jerusalem
until it was fortified on all sides. He sent Jonathan son of 11
Absalom with a considerable force to Joppa; he expelled
its inhabitants and remained in possession of the town.

* Simon 'called Thassis' (2: 3), 'wise in counsel' (2: 65),
experienced in battle, especially in the coastal district over
which he held command from Antiochus VI (11: 59), was
the obvious person to assume leadership.

2. *went up to Jerusalem:* presumably from the coast (cp. 12:
33–4). *called an assembly:* literally, 'gathered the people',
probably from the whole of Judaea.

3–6. Simon's speech suits the occasion, and underlines the
familiar themes of 1 Maccabees – devotion to the *laws*, the
holy place, and the *nation* of Israel. *My brothers have all fallen:*
Eleazar (6: 46) and Judas (9: 18) had died; Jonathan had not
yet died (see verse 23), but in such a speech his death might be
assumed. Simon himself was to be murdered, though not by
the Seleucids (16: 16). *I am the only one left* reminds us of the
words of Elijah (1 Kings 18: 22); did Simon make this comparison himself, or did the author of 1 Maccabees? When we
compare this speech with that of Mattathias in chapter 2, we
may see in the reference to Simon's care for *wives and children*
a hint of a more settled situation than that of 167 B.C.

7–8. The people's response echoes the dying commendation
of Mattathias (2: 65 ff.) and the appointment of Jonathan (9:
29–31), though while Jonathan was appointed leader by 'the
friends of Judas' Simon is appointed by *the people* – an indication of the changed state of affairs between 159 B.C. and 143
B.C.

10. *walls of Jerusalem:* cp. 12: 36–7.

11. Simon makes Joppa a purely military base. According to
14: 5 this was among his 'notable achievements' and was
designed 'to secure his communications overseas'. G. A. Smith

remarks that 'the exultation of this statement – the glad "at last!" that is audible in it – was very natural' (*The Historical Geography of the Holy Land*, 1966 ed., p. 107). Israel now had a port. Simon had garrisoned the town, perhaps earlier that year (12: 33–4); now he expelled the civilian population to preserve the garrison from internal attack, as he had earlier done in the case of Bethsura (11: 66). *Jonathan son of Absalom* was possibly a brother of Mattathias (11: 70). ✳

TRYPHO ATTACKS SIMON

12 Trypho marched out from Ptolemais with a large force to invade Judaea, taking Jonathan with him as a prisoner.
13 Simon encamped at Adida on the edge of the plain.
14 When Trypho learnt that Simon had come forward to take the place of his brother Jonathan, and that he was about to join battle with him, he sent envoys to Simon with
15 the following message: ' We are detaining your brother Jonathan because of certain monies which he owed to the
16 royal treasury in connection with the offices he held. To ensure that he will not again revolt if we release him, send one hundred talents of silver and two of his sons as
17 hostages, and we will let him go.' Simon himself realized that this was a trick, but he had the money and the children brought to him, fearing that otherwise he might
18 arouse deep animosity among the people, who would say, 'It was because you did not send the money and the
19 children that Jonathan lost his life.' So he sent the children and the hundred talents, but Trypho broke his word and did not release Jonathan.
20 After this, Trypho set out to invade the country and ravage it, taking a roundabout way through Adora.

Simon and his army marched parallel with him everywhere he went. Meanwhile the garrison of the citadel 21
were sending emissaries to Trypho, urging him to come
to them by way of the desert, and to send them provisions.
Trypho prepared to send all his cavalry, but that night 22
there was a severe snow-storm, which prevented their
arrival; so he withdrew into Gilead. When he reached 23
Bascama, he had Jonathan put to death, and there he
was buried. Trypho then turned and went back to his 24
own country.

* Trypho attempts, first by bargaining and then by invasion,
to regain Syrian control of Judaea. He has already forced
Jonathan's rearguard in Galilee to return to Jerusalem (12: 52),
and the possession of Jonathan gives him an advantage which
he now tries to exploit.

13. *Adida*, recently fortified (12: 38), guarded the road from
Ptolemais to Jerusalem.

15. What *monies* Jonathan *owed* we do not know; possibly
Trypho had tribute money in mind. But any excuse would be
sufficient.

16. Trypho accuses Jonathan of having revolted; perhaps he
has the rebuilding of Jerusalem's walls, the blockade of the
citadel, and Jonathan's march to Bethshan (12: 36–7, 41) in
mind. The charge was not without substance, for Jonathan
was clearly using the opportunity of a divided Syria to prepare
for an independent Judaea.

17–18. Simon's dilemma is clear: if he refused Trypho's
demands he would be held responsible for Jonathan's death;
if he acceded, he would be making a free gift of the money
and the children to an unscrupulous Trypho. As Trypho would
kill Jonathan in either case, the second course of action would
at least leave Simon's leadership intact.

20. Trypho marched south down the coast, presumably

between Simon's garrisons at Joppa and Adida, and perhaps *via* Gazara, where there was still a Syrian garrison (cp. 9: 51; 13: 43–8), inland to *Adora* south-west of Jerusalem and Hebron. Adora, like nearby Marisa, and like Bethsura until recently, was a hellenistic town. His route was thus *roundabout*, while Simon *marched parallel with him*, keeping between Trypho and Jerusalem and blocking his access up the valleys of the western hills.

21. The citadel garrison, which Trypho was perhaps trying to relieve from its blockade, advised him to attack Jerusalem *by way of the desert*, i.e. from the south or south-east, by-passing Bethsura where Simon had a garrison (11: 66).

22. *snow storm:* not uncommon at Jerusalem in December. This was probably winter of 143–142 B.C. Trypho *withdrew into Gilead*, perhaps by completing his circle round Jerusalem and crossing the Jordan near Jericho.

23. *Bascama* was either somewhere north-east of the Sea of Galilee, or perhaps near modern Haifa. If the latter suggestion is right, we should perhaps read 'Galilee' for 'Gilead' in verse 22, to ease the geographical difficulties. Jonathan was no longer any use to Trypho, who had got little value out of holding him hostage, so he was put to death. ✶

THE MACCABEES' TOMB AND MONUMENT

25 Simon had the body of his brother Jonathan brought to
26 Modin, and buried in the town of their fathers; and all Israel made a great lamentation and mourned him for
27 many days. Simon built a high monument over the tomb of his father and his brothers, visible at a great distance,
28 faced back and front with polished stone. He erected seven pyramids, those for his father and mother and his
29 four brothers arranged in pairs. For the pyramids he contrived an elaborate setting: he surrounded them with

great columns surmounted with trophies of armour for a perpetual memorial, and between the trophies carved ships, plainly visible to all at sea. This mausoleum which 30 he made at Modin stands to this day.

* Jonathan is buried, and Simon builds a monument over the family tomb.

25-6. Jonathan does not receive the eulogies bestowed on Judas or Simon (cp. 3: 1-9; 14: 28-47). Mattathias' death-bed speech singles out Judas and Simon, but does not mention Jonathan (2: 65-8). Jonathan's contribution to the Maccabaean cause was more diplomatic than military. He skilfully used the internal troubles of the Seleucid kingdom to gain independence for Judaea, and when he died it was almost within his grasp. He had been courted by both sides of the Seleucid monarchy and by Ptolemy of Egypt. He had gained some territory for Judaea and had restored the high-priesthood. It may have been this last, along with his comparatively poor military showing, which damaged his reputation, for he was not of the high-priestly family. It is sometimes suggested that Jonathan was regarded by the Qumran community as the 'Wicked Priest'. In the commentary on Hab. 2: 5-6 and 2: 8 the Qumran author refers the texts to the Wicked Priest 'who was called by the name of truth when he first arose. But when he ruled over Israel his heart became proud, and he forsook God and betrayed the precepts for the sake of riches', and 'whom God delivered into the hands of his enemies because of the iniquity committed against the Teacher of Righteousness and the men of his Council'. Jonathan, with his readiness to accept honours from the Syrian and Egyptian courts, may not have been altogether popular with the more extreme nationalist sectarians of the period, among whom were probably the brethren of Qumran. See p. 12.

27. *tomb of his father:* Mattathias' family seems to have been sufficiently well off to have had its own family grave (the

poor were buried in communal graves or in some convenient cave). Such a grave would consist of a rock chamber with small recesses for bodies, hewn out of the limestone. Isaiah criticizes one Shebna for 'carving yourself a resting-place in the rock' (Isa. 22: 16).

28. *pyramids* on a large scale had been used by the Egyptians nearly 3,000 years earlier, but similar, if smaller, monuments were known in Israel, cp. Absalom's pillar (2 Sam. 18: 18). Simon's seventh pyramid, standing by itself, would be intended for himself.

29. *trophies of armour:* it was Greek practice for the victor to set up such trophies on the battlefield. The idea here is similar; they are to be *for a perpetual memorial* of the Maccabaean victories. *carved ships, plainly visible to all at sea* (19 km (12 miles) away), perhaps celebrated the Jewish capture of Joppa and symbolized the dream of a restored Jewish navy comparable with Solomon's (1 Kings 9: 26-8; 10: 11-12, 22).

30. *mausoleum* (the Greek is *taphos*, 'tomb') recalls the monument erected in the fourth century B.C. at Halicarnassus by Artemisia, widow of Mausolus, king of Caria in southwestern Asia Minor, to his memory. Simon's monument may have inherited something of this tradition, but the N.E.B. translation probably uses the word simply in the sense of 'splendid tomb'. ✶

JUDAEA GAINS INDEPENDENCE

31 Trypho now plotted against the young King Antiochus
32 and murdered him. He usurped his throne and assumed the crown of Asia. This was a disaster for the country.

33   Simon rebuilt the fortresses of Judaea, furnishing them with high towers and great walls with gates and bars; he
34 also provisioned the fortresses. He sent representatives to King Demetrius to negotiate a remission of taxes for the country, on the ground that all Trypho's exactions had

been exorbitant. Demetrius replied favourably to this 35
request and wrote him a letter in the following terms:

> King Demetrius to Simon the High Priest and friend of 36
> kings, and to the Senate and nation of the Jews, greeting.

> We have received the golden crown and the palm 37
> branch which you sent, and we are ready to make a
> lasting peace with you and to instruct the revenue
> officers to grant you immunities. All our agreements 38
> with you stand, and the strongholds which you built
> shall remain yours. We give a free pardon for any errors 39
> of omission or commission, to take effect from the date
> of this letter. We remit the crown-money which you
> owed us, and every other tax formerly exacted in Jeru-
> salem is henceforth cancelled. All those of you who are 40
> suitable for enrolment in our retinue shall be so enrolled.
> Let there be peace between us.

In the year 170,[a] Israel was released from the gentile 41
yoke. The people began to write on their contracts and 42
agreements, 'In the first year of Simon, the great high
priest, general and leader of the Jews'.

✻ Trypho at last seizes the Syrian throne for himself, but
the failure of his campaign in Judaea (verses 12–24) has demonstrated his weakness and left Simon all but independent. Simon
is now free to drive a bargain with the other Seleucid ruler,
Demetrius, which results in the abolishing of tribute payments
to Syria.

31. *murdered him*: by the context, 1 Maccabees suggests that
the date is 142 B.C., perhaps early spring. Coins of Antiochus
VI cease with the Seleucid year 171 (autumn 142–141 B.C.),
however, and Josephus (*Antiquities* XIII. 7. 1) places the murder

[a] *That is* 142 B.C.

of Antiochus after Demetrius' campaign in the east (14: 1). The Roman historian Livy (59 B.C.–A.D. 17) says that Antiochus was ten years old at his death; he was born in the year beginning autumn 150 B.C. Possibly, then, in 142 B.C. Trypho merely deposed Antiochus, actually murdering him three or four years later. In any case, Trypho, who dated his coins by his regnal years and not by the Seleucid era, reigned four years and was succeeded in Seleucid year 174 (autumn 139–138 B.C.) by Antiochus VII, so he counted the years of his reign from the year 142–141 B.C.

32. *a disaster:* the original Greek may refer (more generally than N.E.B. suggests) to Trypho's various despotic acts. He called himself *autocrator* ('sole ruler'), alienated the Jews by the murder of Jonathan and by 'exorbitant exactions' (verse 34), and alienated his own populace by the murder of Antiochus VI, and his army by his dictatorial ways. The army went over to Cleopatra, Demetrius' wife, who invited Demetrius' brother Antiochus to marry her and take the throne. For Antiochus VII's reign, see 15: 1 ff.

33. Simon continues his policy of fortifying Jewish possessions (cp. 11: 66; 12: 33–4, 38) and of removing Syrian garrisons (see verses 43–53 below).

34. Presumably Trypho, on coming to power (cp. 11: 54–9), had not made any tax concessions; the concessions made by Demetrius (11: 30–7) had perhaps been cancelled by Demetrius at the end of his reign (11: 52–3) or by Trypho himself. *all Trypho's exactions... exorbitant:* literally, 'all Trypho's actions were violent robberies', the original Hebrew word behind 'violent robberies' perhaps being *terephoth*, a pun on Trypho.

35. *replied favourably:* Simon was in a strong position.

36. The address does not imply the independence of Simon and the Jewish *nation* (Greek *ethnos*, for which see the note on 12: 3). *friend of kings* is an unusual phrase, inaccurate of Simon if meant in the technical sense of a King's Friend, and perhaps an addition to the text here.

37. *golden crown and palm* (the palm was perhaps a gold sceptre in the form of a palm branch; the palm became a symbol of Judaea) had been the gifts of Alcimus to Demetrius I (2 Macc. 14: 4) and they implied allegiance.

38. *all our agreements:* cp. 11: 25–37. *the strongholds which you built:* cp. verse 33. The garrisons at Bethsura, Joppa and Adida are probably also meant. Demetrius was in no position to recapture them.

39. The pardoned *errors* refer to recent support for Trypho and the defeats inflicted on Demetrius (11: 63–74; 12: 24–32). *crown-money:* an annual tax (distinct from the occasional gift of a 'crown') 'irrevocably' ceded to the Jews by Demetrius earlier (11: 35); see the note on verse 34 above. *every other tax:* see the notes on 10: 29–31.

40. *enrolment in our retinue:* perhaps the enlisting of Jews in Demetrius' royal guard. Demetrius had profited earlier from Jewish soldiers (11: 47–8).

41–2. *the year 170* is probably spring 142–141 B.C. The *Megillath Ta'anith* (see p. 8) says that the crown-tax was abolished on Iyyar 27 (20 May). Events were often dated in the ancient Near East by the regnal year of the king (Trypho at this time was dating his reign this way) and Simon's *first year* would have run either from Jonathan's capture late in 143 B.C. or from his death early in 142 B.C. (The Seleucid year 172 (14: 27) thus corresponds with, or overlaps, 'the third year of Simon's high-priesthood'.)

Israel was released from the gentile yoke: we should note, however, that Syria still had garrisons at Gazara and Jerusalem, that Demetrius had not declared Judaea's political independence, and that Antiochus VII assumes Judaea's political dependence (cp. 15: 2–9). However, Judaea's practical gains were sufficient ground for rejoicing. Whether the people realized at this stage that a new era of independence was dawning is doubtful, though the author of 1 Maccabees puts this interpretation on the agreement with Demetrius. ✳

SIMON CAPTURES GAZARA AND THE JERUSALEM
CITADEL

43 Then Simon invested Gazara,[a] and surrounded it with his forces. He constructed a siege-engine and brought it up to the town, made a breach in one of the towers and 44 captured it. The men on the siege-engine leapt out of it 45 into the town, and there was a great commotion. The townspeople and their wives and children climbed up on to the city wall with their garments torn, clamouring 46 to Simon to offer them terms. 'Do not treat us as our wickedness deserves,' they cried, 'but as your mercy 47 prompts you.' Simon came to terms with them, and brought the war to an end. But he expelled them from the town, and after purifying the houses in which the idols stood, he made his entry with songs of thanksgiving and praise. He removed every pollution from it and settled 48 men in it who would keep the law. He strengthened its fortifications and built a residence there for himself.

49 The men in the citadel in Jerusalem were prevented from going in and out to buy and sell in the country; 50 famine set in and many of them died of starvation. They clamoured to Simon to accept their surrender, and he agreed: he expelled them from the citadel and cleansed 51 it from its pollutions. It was on the twenty-third day of the second month in the year 171[b] that he made his entry, with a chorus of praise and the waving of palm branches, with lutes, cymbals, and zithers, with hymns and songs, to celebrate Israel's final riddance of a formidable enemy. 52 Simon decreed that this day should be observed as an

[a] *Probable reading; Gk.* Gaza.   [b] *That is* 141 B.C.

annual festival. He fortified the temple hill opposite the citadel, and he and his men took up residence there. When 53 Simon saw that his son John had become a man, he made him commander of all the forces, with Gazara as his headquarters.

✻ Simon gains complete military control of Judaea and the coast by the capture of the last Syrian garrisons in the area.

43. *Gazara:* the Greek text has 'Gaza', but Gaza had already been captured (11: 62), and in the subsequent narrative Gazara features prominently as a Jewish military centre (cp. verse 53; 14: 7, 34; 15: 28, 35). Gazara was 'one of the few remarkable bastions which the Shephelah flings out to the west... high and isolated, but fertile and well watered, a very strong post and a striking landmark' (G. A. Smith). On the road between Joppa and Jerusalem, it was important to Simon for his control of the pro-Syrian coastal cities (cp. 12: 33–4). Its population was non-Jewish, though perhaps a few hellenizing Jews lived there. *siege-engine:* see the note on 6: 31.

47. Simon *expelled* the population, as he had at Bethsura and Joppa (11: 66; 13: 11), and removed traces of pagan idolatry (cp. the action of Judas and Jonathan at Azotus, 5: 68; 10: 84).

48. The installation of law-keeping Jews probably served the double purpose of ensuring that Simon's own *residence* had a loyal population round it and of giving property to Jewish veteran soldiers or the poorer peasantry. *fortifications:* traces of Simon's breach of the walls (verse 43) and rebuilding were discovered by R. A. S. Macalister's excavations (1902–9), and a piece of limestone was found on which an unwilling workman – perhaps a prisoner – had scratched 'Says Pamprias, may fire descend on Simon's palace'.

49. The blockade of the citadel had been started by Jonathan, probably in 143 B.C. (12: 36).

50. It surrendered in spring 141 B.C. Simon treated it as

he had the garrisons at Bethsura and Gazara, expelling the soldiers, purifying the buildings, and making a festal entry (cp. verses 47, 51).

51-2. The date is 28 May 141 B.C. For the festivities, compare those of the rededication of the temple (4: 54).

52. The citadel itself was re-garrisoned with Jewish troops (14: 37); Simon and his close supporters established themselves on the fortified *temple hill opposite the citadel* (perhaps the site of the Roman Antonia, Acts 21: 30 ff.).

53. *his son John*, later John Hyrcanus, Simon's successor (134–104 B.C.). See chapter 16.

THE PARTHIANS CAPTURE DEMETRIUS

14 In the year 172,[a] King Demetrius mustered his army and went into Media to recruit additional forces for his 2 war against Trypho. When Arsakes king of Persia and Media heard that Demetrius had entered his territories, 3 he sent one of his generals to capture him alive. The general marched out and defeated Demetrius, captured him and brought him to Arsakes, who put him in prison.

* The presence of this short note at this point of the narrative shows clearly how Simon's era of peace (cp. verse 4 below) was built on the weakness of the Syrian throne. Trypho controlled Antioch, and Demetrius the rest of the Syrian empire, though in the east the Parthians (who lived south-east of the Caspian Sea) had gained virtual control of Media to their west and Persia to their south (cp. verse 2) and in 141 B.C. attacked Babylonia.

1. *the year 172*: autumn 141–140 B.C. Josephus (*Antiquities* XIII. 5. 11) says that Demetrius wished to make the Mesopotamian region 'his base for an attempt to control the entire

[a] That is 140 B.C.

kingdom', and that Greeks and Mesopotamians living there invited him to join them in fighting the Parthians.

2. *Arsakes* was the dynastic name; this king is more commonly known by his personal name, Mithridates I. Demetrius was at first successful.

3. Arsakes treated Demetrius well, giving him his daughter as wife; it suited him to have a possible future Syrian king dependent on his support. *

'JUDAEA WAS AT PEACE'

As long as Simon lived, Judaea was at peace. He pro- 4 moted his people's welfare, and they lived happily all through the glorious days of his reign. Among other 5 notable achievements he captured the port of Joppa to secure his communications overseas. He extended his 6 nation's territories and made himself master of the whole land. He repatriated a large number of prisoners of war. 7 Without meeting any resistance he gained control over Gazara and Bethsura and over the citadel, and removed their pollution.

They farmed their land in peace, and the land produced 8 its crops, and the trees in the plains their fruit. Old men 9 sat in the streets, talking together of their blessings; and the young men dressed themselves in splendid military style. Simon supplied the towns with food in plenty and 10 equipped them with weapons for defence. His renown reached the ends of the earth. He restored peace to the 11 land, and there were great rejoicings throughout Israel. Each man sat under his own vine and fig-tree, and they 12 had no one to fear. Those were days when every enemy 13 vanished from the land and every hostile king was crushed.

14 Simon gave his protection to the poor among the people;
he paid close attention to the law and rid the country of
15 lawless and wicked men. He gave new splendour to the
temple and furnished it with a wealth of sacred vessels.

* These verses are printed by several modern versions as
poetry and are similar in content to the ode in praise of Judas
(3: 3–9). Verses 4–7 summarize Simon's military successes;
verses 8–15 are more idyllic, and are coloured by traditional
Jewish pictures of the new age to come.

5. *captured...Joppa:* see 13: 11 and the note there. *communications overseas:* it is ironic that the Maccabees should have
secured and prized a means of communication with the Greek
world whose influence they had so urgently resisted.

6. *extended his nation's territories:* by settling Jews in Joppa,
Bethsura and Gazara; but Jonathan had gained more by
diplomacy (cp. 11: 28–37).

7. *prisoners of war:* perhaps taken from Bethsura, Joppa,
Gazara, and the Jerusalem citadel.

8. The verse echoes Lev. 26: 4, 'the land shall yield its
produce and the trees of the countryside their fruit'. Farms no
longer suffered from the owners' absence on campaign or the
enemy's spoliation.

9. The verse echoes Zech. 8: 4, 'Once again shall old men
and old women sit in the streets of Jerusalem, each leaning
on a stick because of their great age'.

10. *food in plenty:* the result of the revival of agriculture.
Defence measures for the towns are referred to in 12: 34;
13: 33; 14: 33.

12. For this picture of the expected era of peace, compare
1 Kings 4: 25, Mic. 4: 4.

14. *the poor among the people* are the class among whom the
Maccabees found much support, the country peasantry, traditionally faithful to the old religious ways and the opponents
of the *lawless and wicked men*, the hellenizing aristocracy. The

word *poor* may carry other overtones; they are the people for whom formerly the Jewish king and later the Messiah were to have special regard; cp. 2 Sam. 22: 28, or the New Testament beatitude 'How blest are you who are in need; the kingdom of God is yours' (Luke 6: 20).

15. Simon's high-priestly care for the temple is praised; but in this as in other parts of this passage the author may be hinting that Simon is to be compared with the great King Solomon. Simon is portrayed as the leader of a community living in a near-golden age. Yet in fact Judaea was not at peace 'as long as Simon lived' (verse 4) nor were they days 'when every enemy vanished from the land and every hostile king was crushed' (verse 13), as we shall see from chapters 15 and 16. ✶

DIPLOMACY WITH ROME AND SPARTA

The report of Jonathan's death reached Rome, and Sparta 16 too, and they were deeply grieved. When they heard, 17 however, that his brother Simon had become high priest in his place, and was in firm control of the country and the towns in it, they inscribed on bronze tablets a renewal 18 of the treaty of friendship and alliance which they had established with his brothers Judas and Jonathan. This 19 was read before the assembly in Jerusalem. The following 20 is a copy of the letter from Sparta:

The rulers and city of Sparta to the High Priest Simon, to the Senate, the priests, and the rest of the Jewish people, our brothers, greeting.

The envoys you sent to our people have told us about 21 your fame and honour; their visit has given us great pleasure. We have entered a transcript of the message 22 they brought in the minutes of the public assembly:

'Numenius son of Antiochus, and Antipater son of Jason, envoys of the Jews, visited us to renew their
23 treaty of friendship with us. It was resolved by the public assembly to receive these men with honour and to place a copy of their address in the public archives, so that the Spartans might have it on permanent record. A copy of this document has been made for Simon the High Priest.'

24 After this, Simon sent Numenius to Rome with a large gold shield, worth a thousand minas, to confirm the alliance with the Romans.

✻ The author continues his chapter in praise of Simon with evidence that both Rome and Sparta recognized Simon's achievements. The material, with which belongs 15: 15-24, has perhaps suffered slight disarrangement, verse 24 making better sense if placed before verse 16, so that the sending to Rome of Numenius to confirm the alliance comes before the Romans renew it (verse 18).

16. *and Sparta too:* the words are possibly an addition to the text. The reference to 'bronze tablets' (verse 18, cp. 8: 22) suggests that the Romans, not the Spartans, are the subject of the verbs in verses 16–18.

17. *When they heard...:* probably from Numenius (verse 24), whose mission took place between Jonathan's death (early 142 B.C.) and the date of the Jewish decree about Simon, September 140 B.C. (cp. 14: 25-49), as 14: 40 makes clear. If Simon's *firm control of the country and the towns* implies the capture of the Syrian garrisons, then the embassy perhaps took place between summer 141 and summer 140 B.C. But perhaps a date at the beginning of Simon's rule in 142 B.C. is more likely.

18. For the treaty established between Rome and Judas and Jonathan, see 8: 17-32; 12: 1-4.

19–20. For Jonathan's embassy to Sparta, see 12: 2, 5–23. For the address, cp. 12: 6. *our brothers* picks up the address and 'pact of brotherhood' in Jonathan's letter (12: 6, 17).

22–3. Simon uses the same envoys as Jonathan (cp. 12: 16). *to renew their treaty of friendship with us* seems more appropriate in connection with Rome than with Sparta (cp. 12: 1, 3; 14: 18), with whom the Jews made a 'pact of brotherhood'. It has been suggested that the letter of verses 20–3 was originally the Roman letter to the Jews in answer to their approaches. In this case, *receive these men with honour* may be reflected in verse 40, 'had gone in state to meet'.

24. *After this*: possibly Numenius is being sent back again to Rome with the gift but then we are left without knowledge of how 'the report of Jonathan's death reached Rome' in the first place. It seems more likely that verse 24 records Simon's initiative and that it has become misplaced. *large gold shield*: cp. the golden crown of 13: 37. *a thousand minas*: if this refers to the gold's actual weight, as some think, the shield might be worth something over £100,000 today. But the real value might have been much less. *

AN INSCRIPTION IN HONOUR OF SIMON

When the people heard of these events they asked 25 themselves how they could show their gratitude to Simon and his sons. For he, with his brothers and his father's 26 family, had stood firm, fought off the enemies of Israel, and ensured his nation's freedom. So an inscription was 27 engraved on tablets of bronze and placed on a monument on Mount Zion. A copy of the inscription follows:

On the eighteenth day of the month Elul, in the year 172[a], the third year of Simon's high-priesthood, at 28 Asaramel, in a large assembly of priests, people, rulers

[a] *That is* 140 B.C.

193

of the nation, and elders of the land, the following facts
29 were placed on record. Whereas our land had been
subject to frequent wars, Simon son of Mattathias, a
priest of the Joarib family, and his brothers, risked their
lives in resisting the enemies of their people, in order
that the temple and law might be preserved, and they
30 brought great glory to their nation. Jonathan rallied
the nation, became their high priest, and then was
31 gathered to his fathers. Their enemies resolved to invade
32 their land and destroy it, and to attack the temple. Then
Simon came forward and fought for his nation. He
spent large sums of his own money to arm the soldiers
33 of his nation and to provide their pay. He fortified the
towns of Judaea, and Bethsura on the boundaries of
Judaea, formerly an enemy arsenal, and stationed a
34 garrison of Jews there. He fortified Joppa by the sea,
and Gazara near Azotus, formerly occupied by the
enemy. There he settled Jews, and provided these towns
35 with everything needful for their welfare. When the
people saw Simon's patriotism and his resolution to
win fame for his nation, they made him their leader
and high priest, in recognition of all that he had done,
of his just conduct, his loyalty to his nation, and his
36 constant efforts to enhance its renown. His leadership
was crowned with success, and the Gentiles were expelled from the land, as were also the troops in Jerusalem who had built themselves a citadel in the city of
David, from which they sallied forth to bring defilement upon the whole precinct of the temple and do
37 violence to its purity. He settled Jews in it and fortified
it for the security of the land and of the city, and he

raised the height of the walls of Jerusalem. King Deme- 38
trius confirmed him in the office of high priest, made 39
him one of his Friends, and granted him the highest
honours; for he had heard that the Romans were 40
naming the Jews friends, allies, and brothers, and had
gone in state to meet Simon's envoys.

The Jews and their priests confirmed Simon as their 41
leader and high priest in perpetuity until a true prophet
should appear. He was to be their general, and to have 42
full charge of the temple; and in addition to this the
supervision of their labour, of the country, and of the
arms and fortifications was to be entrusted to him.
He was to be obeyed by all; all contracts in the country 43
were to be drawn up in his name. He was to wear the
purple robe and the gold clasp.

None of the people or the priests shall have authority 44
to abrogate any of these decrees, to oppose commands
issued by Simon or convene any assembly in the land
without his consent, to be robed in purple, or to wear
the gold clasp. Whoever shall contravene these provi- 45
sions or neglect any of them shall be liable to punishment. It is the unanimous decision of the people that 46
Simon shall officiate in the ways here laid down. Simon 47
has agreed and consented to be high priest, general and
ethnarch of the Jews and the priests, and to be the
protector of them all.

This inscription, it was declared, should be engraved on 48
bronze tablets and set up within the precincts of the temple
in a conspicuous position, and copies should be placed in 49
the treasury, in the keeping of Simon and his sons.

* The eulogy of Simon ends with the quotation of a long public inscription commemorating Simon and his deeds. Memorial inscriptions describing votes of thanks to public servants were common in the hellenistic world, and we see again how far Maccabaean Judaea had accepted hellenistic practices.

27. *Elul* (cp. Neh. 6: 15) is the Babylonian name for the sixth month (see p. 7); the date is September 140 B.C. Simon's high-priesthood perhaps began officially in spring 142 B.C.

28. *Asaramel* is a conundrum. It may be a corruption of 'the Water Gate' (Neh. 8: 1, 3), or of 'the assembly of the people of God', or perhaps of a title 'prince of the people of God'.

29. If this is an accurate record of a public inscription dated as early as 140 B.C., the following evaluation of the movement is of great interest. Compare this verse with Simon's speech, 13: 3–6.

30. Judas is not mentioned by name; Jonathan's part is curtly described.

31. *their enemies:* in particular, Trypho.

32. Here begins the list of Simon's deeds. Simon's use of his *own money* is not otherwise mentioned, but it is one mark of a typical benefactor in a hellenistic city.

33. See 11: 65; 13: 33.

34. See 12: 33–4; 13: 43–8.

35. *patriotism:* an interpretation of the Greek word *pistis* which usually means 'faith'. *they made him their leader* (13: 8) *and high priest:* if this is accurate, it is significant; Jonathan had been made high priest by Alexander. *all that he had done:* when made leader, Simon had not yet, in fact, taken Gazara (verse 34), though the present order implies it.

36. *the Gentiles were expelled* from Bethsura (11: 66), Joppa (13: 11), and Gazara (13: 47), and from the citadel (13: 50). *from which they sallied forth to bring defilement:* see 1: 33–6; 4: 41.

37. *raised the height of the walls:* continuing Jonathan's work, 12: 36.

38-40. Demetrius' letter in 13: 36-40 addresses Simon as 'High Priest', but does not confirm him in that office or make him a Friend, and these points, together with the reference of verse 40, suggest that there was further correspondence. Verses 38-9 also suggest that Demetrius still thought of Judaea as his subject province. For verse 40 see the commentary on 14: 16-24, especially verse 23.

41-3. These verses state the authority given to Simon by the Jews. (The Greek text reports these verses as the continuation of the news that had come to Demetrius' ears, but the N.E.B. with most scholars omits the words 'and that' before verse 41.)

41. *leader* (cp. 13: 8, 42) appears to be another word for 'ethnarch', i.e. civil governor (cp. 14: 47; 15: 1). *high priest in perpetuity* is generally taken to imply that a new high-priestly dynasty was now formally established (the Maccabees were not of the traditional high-priestly family). But a saving clause was added, *until a true prophet should appear*, leaving open the possibility that in the future another priestly line might be divinely revealed. When 300 years earlier a family's claim to the priesthood was being examined, the family was disqualified 'until there should be a priest able to consult the Urim and the Thummim' – a similar saving clause (Neh. 7: 65). Compare also 4: 46. The expectation of a prophet to come appears in the New Testament; cp. John 1: 21, 'Are you the prophet we await?'

42. *general:* cp. his commission to 'Fight our battles' (13:9). Simon's high-priestly and military duties are now stated.

43. Simon's power is little short of regal. *contracts... in his name:* cp. 13: 41. *purple robe and the gold clasp:* cp. 10: 20, 89, the insignia of the high priest and King's Friend. Simon, it seems, was not averse to accepting honours from the Seleucid king.

44-7. These verses have a ring of authority about them; perhaps the actual words of the decree are here quoted.

44. *these decrees:* those reported in verses 41-3. Simon's position is carefully safeguarded.

46. The people's position is also protected.

47. Simon has accepted responsibility for these offices of spiritual, military and civil authority. These provisions, even if they leave much scope for interpretation, are important, for they are the basis of a new constitution of Judaea.

48–9. *it was declared:* the author slips back into reported speech. The arrangements for the publication of the inscription may have been engraved on the tablets as the final part of the inscription. *within the precincts of the temple in a conspicuous position:* cp. Demetrius' directions, 11: 37. *copies... placed in the treasury* would be *in the keeping of* (though not in the private possession of) *Simon and his sons,* for the office of the high priest, who was responsible for the treasury (cp. 2 Macc. 3), was hereditary.

This whole document is interesting. It appears in 1 Maccabees as a eulogy of, and memorial inscription to, Simon and his virtues. But the heart of the inscription is the recording of the people's 'decrees' (verse 44) which regularized the position of Simon and his sons and officially altered (subject to future divine revelation) the high-priestly line of succession. The inscription commemorated a new constitution, no less, and the new state of affairs is reflected in the statement of 1 Macc. 13: 42 that 'people began to write on their contracts and agreements, "In the first year of Simon, the great high priest, general and leader of the Jews"' (cp. 14: 43); though as the constitution was not formally altered until Simon's third year (14: 27), the author may in 13: 42 be reading back the new situation to the beginning of Simon's reign. *

ANTIOCHUS VII ATTACKS TRYPHO

15 Antiochus son of King Demetrius sent a letter from overseas to Simon the high priest and ethnarch of the
2 Jews, and to the whole nation. The contents were as follows:

King Antiochus to Simon, High Priest and Ethnarch, and to the Jewish nation, greeting.

Whereas certain traitors have seized my ancestral 3 kingdom, I have now decided to assert my claim to it, so that I may restore it to its former condition. I have raised a large body of mercenaries and fitted out ships of war. I intend to land in my country and to attack 4 those who have ravaged my kingdom and destroyed many of its cities. Now therefore I confirm all the tax 5 remissions which my royal predecessors granted you, and all their other remissions of tribute. I permit you 6 to mint your own coinage as currency for your country. Jerusalem and the temple shall be free. All the arms you 7 have prepared, and the fortifications which you have built and now hold, shall remain yours. All debts now 8 owing to the royal treasury and all future liabilities thereto shall be cancelled from this time on for ever. When we have re-established our kingdom, we shall 9 confer the highest honours upon you, your nation and temple, to make your country's greatness apparent to the whole world.

In the year 174,[a] Antiochus marched into his ancestral 10 domain, and all the armed forces came over to him, leaving very few with Trypho. Antiochus pursued him, and 11 Trypho came as a fugitive to Dor by the sea. He knew 12 that his position was desperate now that all his troops had deserted. Antiochus, at the head of a hundred and 13 twenty thousand trained soldiers and eight thousand horsemen, laid siege to Dor. He encircled the town, and 14

[a] *That is* 138 B.C.

his ships joined in the blockade from the sea. He thus exerted heavy pressure on it from both land and sea, and prevented anyone from leaving or entering.

✶ Antiochus, encouraged by the wife of his captured brother Demetrius (see on 13: 32), in 139 B.C. moved to attack Trypho, first taking the obvious step of canvassing Simon's support.

1. *son of King Demetrius* I (for whom see chapters 7–10); he took as his official title *Euergetes* ('Benefactor') but was popularly called *Sidetes* after his birth at Sidé in Pamphylia about 161 B.C. *from overseas:* perhaps from the island of Rhodes.

2. *High Priest and Ethnarch:* cp. 14: 47. The latter title ('ruler of the nation') was probably the title officially bestowed by the Syrians. The Jews called him 'leader' (13: 8; 14: 35).

3. *traitors:* Trypho, Antiochus VI, and perhaps his father Alexander Balas. *mercenaries* were a prominent feature of hellenistic wars, drawn largely from Asia Minor and Syria. *ships of war:* probably from Rhodes and other maritime cities, including Sidé itself, whose seamen were famous. Antiochus was well prepared.

4. *ravaged... destroyed:* we know no details, and the accusation may be exaggerated, though Josephus pictures Trypho as a hated tyrant.

5. *remissions:* see 10: 26–35; 11: 30–7; 13: 35–40.

6. Permission to *mint... coinage* was a new and important concession, giving to Judaea greater control over its own economy. But Simon did not mint coins, probably having no time to organize a mint before Antiochus withdrew the concession a few months later (verse 27). *Jerusalem and the temple shall be free:* cp. 10: 31, and note there.

7. *arms:* see 14: 32. *fortifications which you have built* (cp. 13: 33): Demetrius II allowed Simon's ownership of them (13: 38). Antiochus does not necessarily include the garrisons of Joppa, Gazara, and the Jerusalem citadel among these (see verses 28–31).

8. *debts* had also been remitted by Demetrius II (13: 39).

9. Demetrius II had similarly promised 'the highest honour' to Jonathan and his people in return for help (11: 42). Antiochus clearly regards Judaea as his dependent province.

10. *the year 174:* autumn 139–138 B.C. Josephus (*Antiquities* XIII. 7. 1 f.) says that Antiochus came to the port of Seleucia, where Demetrius II's wife Cleopatra had been confined by Trypho, that the army, hating Trypho, had largely deserted to her, and that Antiochus defeated Trypho before pursuing him to Dor.

11. *by the sea:* Dor had been a harbour from early times, and a provincial centre from Solomon's time (1 Kings 4: 11). One pass connected the town with the Esdraelon plain, but the steep wall of Mount Carmel to the north-east, the narrow coastal plain to the north, and a swampy river estuary to the south gave the town considerable natural independence. Antiochus III failed to take it by siege, and Josephus calls it 'a fortress difficult to take'. It thrived until Herod the Great built a better harbour at Caesarea, nine miles to the south. ✶

DIPLOMACY (CONTINUED)

Numenius and his party arrived from Rome with a 15 letter to the various kings and countries, which read as follows:

Lucius, Consul of the Romans, to King Ptolemy, 16 greeting.

Envoys have come to us from our friends and allies 17 the Jews, sent by Simon the High Priest and the Jewish people, to renew their original treaty of friendship and alliance. They brought a gold shield worth a thousand 18 minas. We have decided, therefore, to write to the 19 kings and countries, requiring them to do no harm to

the Jews, nor make war on them or their cities or their country, nor ally themselves with those who so make
20 war. And we have decided to accept the shield from
21 them. If therefore any traitors have escaped from their country to you, hand them over to Simon the High Priest to be punished by him according to the law of the Jews.

22 The same message was sent to King Demetrius, to
23 Attalus, Ariarathes, Arsakes, Sampsakes, and the Spartans, and also to the following places: Delos, Myndos, Sicyon, Caria, Samos, Pamphylia, Lycia, Halicarnassus, Rhodes, Phaselis, Cos, Sidé, Aradus, Gortyna, Cnidus, Cyprus,
24 and Cyrene. A copy was sent to Simon the high priest.

* This passage is the sequel to 14: 16–24 and contains a letter from Rome addressed to 'various kings and countries' in the eastern Mediterranean announcing Rome's friendship and alliance with the Jews. (Compare 8: 31–2, where a letter from Rome to Demetrius I is described.) Possibly the letter is set here to bring out the contrast between Roman friendship for the Jews and Syrian ingratitude (cp. verses 26–31).

15. *Numenius and his party:* cp. 14: 22, 24, and 12: 16. *various... countries:* probably there were Jews settled in most of them, and Rome took the opportunity of making her presence felt throughout the eastern Mediterranean.

16. *Lucius:* perhaps Lucius Caecilius Metellus, consul in 142 B.C. Josephus, however, sets a very similar decree of the Roman Senate, naming the Roman Lucius Valerius and the Jewish Alexander son of Jason and Numenius son of Antiochus, amid the events of 47 B.C. (*Antiquities* XIV. 8. 5), but Josephus may have misplaced the decree. *Ptolemy* VIII (known as Euergetes II), 145–116 B.C., was the brother and successor of Ptolemy VI whose death is recorded in 11: 18.

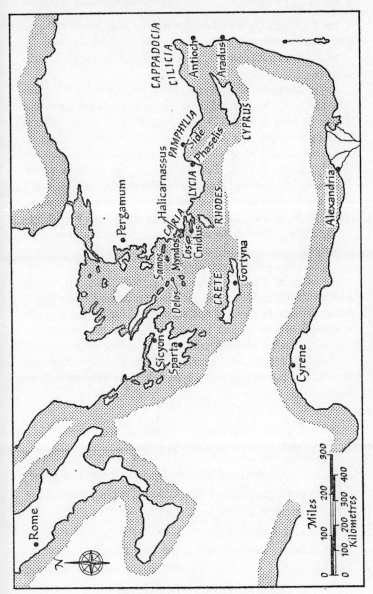

CAPPADOCIA
CILICIA
Antioch
Aradus
PAMPHYLIA
Side
Phaselis
LYCIA
CYPRUS

Halicarnassus
CARIA
Pergamum
Samos
Myndos
Cos
Cnidus
RHODES
Delos
Sicyon
Sparta
CRETE
Gortyna

Rome

Cyrene
Alexandria

Miles
100 200 300
0 100 200 300 400
Kilometres

N

9. To illustrate 1 Macc. 15: 22–4.

203

19. Compare the terms of the treaty made between Rome and Judas (8: 28).

21. The extradition clause is paralleled in other Roman treaties.

22–3. *Demetrius* II of Syria; his capture by the Parthians (cp. 14: 3) had not yet taken place, or was not yet known at Rome. *Attalus* II (159–138 B.C.) was king of the important state of Pergamum in the western half of modern Turkey. *Ariarathes* V was king of Cappadocia (162–131 B.C.) immediately north of Syria. For *Arsakes* see the note on 14: 2. *Sampsakes* is unknown; there is a variant reading 'Sampsames'. The underlying name may be that of a people or place, possibly Amisos on the Black Sea. In the Greek text *Sampsakes, and the Spartans* seem unnaturally placed and may be additional or accidentally misplaced; the N.E.B. smooths out this difficulty by slight rearrangement.

the following places: see the map, p. 203. They are mainly independent states of the eastern Mediterranean. Roman diplomatic interest in them is not surprising, for in 146 B.C. the mainland of Greece had become a Roman protectorate, in 133 B.C. Attalus III bequeathed the kingdom of Pergamum to Rome, in 130 B.C. the Roman province of Asia was founded, and in 129 B.C. Caria and Mysia felt the tramp of Roman legions. ✳

ANTIOCHUS VII THREATENS SIMON

25 King Antiochus laid siege to Dor for the second time,[a] and launched repeated attacks against it; he had siege-engines constructed, and blockaded Trypho, preventing all movement in or out of the town.

26 Simon sent Antiochus two thousand picked men to assist him, with silver and gold and much equipment;
27 but he refused the offer. He repudiated all his previous

[a] *Some witnesses read* on the second day.

agreements with Simon and broke off relations. He sent 28
Athenobius, one of the Friends, to parley with him. This
was his message: 'You are occupying Joppa and Gazara
and the citadel in Jerusalem, cities that belong to my
kingdom. You have laid waste their territories, and done 29
great damage to the country, and have made yourselves
masters of many places in my kingdom. I demand the 30
return of the cities you have captured and the surrender
of the tribute exacted from places beyond the frontiers
of Judaea over which you have assumed control. Other- 31
wise, you must pay five hundred talents of silver on their
account, and another five hundred as compensation for
the destruction you have caused and for the loss of tribute
from the cities. Failing this, we shall go to war with you.'

Athenobius, the King's Friend, came to Jerusalem, and 32
when he saw the splendour of Simon's establishment, the
gold and silver vessels on his sideboard, and his display
of wealth, he was amazed. He delivered the king's message, to which Simon replied: 'We have not occupied 33
other people's land or taken other people's property, but
only the inheritance of our ancestors, unjustly seized for
a time by our enemies. We have grasped our opportunity 34
and have claimed our patrimony. With regard to Joppa 35
and Gazara, which you demand, these towns were doing
a great deal of damage among our people and in our land.
For these we offer one hundred talents.'

Athenobius answered not a word, but went off in a rage 36
to the king; he reported what Simon had said, and described Simon's splendour and all the things he had seen.
The king was furious.

* The narrative is resumed from verse 14. Antiochus, confident now that he has all but ended Trypho's régime, turns to attack Simon.

25. *for the second time:* a puzzling phrase, perhaps an ancient reader's marginal comment on the way the author resumes his subject after the intrusion of the letter from Rome. *siege-engines:* see the note on 6: 31.

26–7. *refused the offer:* Josephus (*Antiquities* XIII. 7. 3) says that Simon's offer made him for a short while one of Antiochus' closest friends, but that after Trypho's death Antiochus 'through covetousness and dishonesty forgot the services which Simon had rendered'. But Josephus ignores the visit to Simon of Athenobius and is perhaps as a result less fair to Antiochus than is 1 Maccabees.

28. Antiochus, knowing Simon's strength, doubtless wished to re-establish some Syrian control over his province. Antiochus had promised Simon that 'the fortifications which you have built and now hold' (15: 7) should remain his, but these, for Antiochus at least, did not include the port of Joppa and the Syrian garrisons of Gazara and the Jerusalem citadel. Antiochus includes the citadel under the designation *cities*, and from the Syrian viewpoint it may have been a fully constituted city (see the note on 1: 33), founded by Antiochus IV.

29. *many places in my kingdom:* perhaps Azotus (10: 84), Gaza (11: 61–2), Bethsura (11: 65–6), Adida (12: 38), and the Samaritan districts (11: 28 ff.) are in mind.

30. *cities you have captured... places beyond the frontiers of Judaea* denote the two groups already mentioned (verses 28–9).

31. The total of a 1,000 talents is a high price, but the offer of an alternative to the return of the disputed cities shows that there is room for negotiation.

32. Simon the Maccabee now appears in full hellenistic *splendour* at his court (cp. the implications of 16: 12; Ptolemaeus 'had great wealth, for he was the high priest's son-in-law'). The *vessels* were perhaps those given by Antiochus VI

(11: 58). But impressing one's opponents with one's wealth and strength does not always have the calculated effect.

33–4. inheritance of our ancestors: 1 Maccabees makes Simon echo Antiochus' own claim (15: 3). The phrase also reflects the Israelite belief that their land was an *inheritance* from God, a *patrimony*; cp. Ps. 105: 11:

> 'I will give you the land of Canaan', he said,
> 'to be your possession, your patrimony.'

The idea of inheritance became vested with religious significance, and later became part of Christian belief; cp. Eph. 1: 11, 14, where the sealing of the Christian with the Holy Spirit is 'the pledge that we shall enter upon our heritage'. The belief in the inheritance of Canaan plays its part in modern politics, and now as in Simon's time a major difficulty lies in drawing the boundaries of the promised land.

35–6. damage among our people and in our land: Simon thus counters Antiochus' charge of 'great damage' (verse 29), but his words do suggest that Simon recognized that Joppa and Gazara were not inalienably Jewish. He was apparently prepared to negotiate about them, but his offer of a mere *one hundred talents* perhaps made further negotiation from Antiochus' side difficult. ✵

WAR WITH ANTIOCHUS

Meanwhile Trypho boarded a ship and made good his escape to Orthosia. The king appointed Kendebaeus as commander-in-chief of the coastal zone, and gave him infantry and cavalry. He instructed him to blockade Judaea, to rebuild Kedron and strengthen its gates, and to make war on our people, while he himself continued the pursuit of Trypho. Kendebaeus arrived in Jamnia and began to harass our people by invading Judaea, and by capturing and killing the inhabitants. He rebuilt Kedron, stationing 37 38 39 40 41 cavalry and troops there to sally out and patrol the roads of Judaea, in accordance with the king's instructions.

16 John came from Gazara and reported to his father Simon
2 the results of Kendebaeus's campaign. Simon summoned his two eldest sons Judas and John, and said to them: 'My brothers and I and my father's family have fought Israel's battles from our youth until this day, and many
3 a time we have been successful in rescuing Israel. Now I am old, but mercifully you are in the prime of life. Take my place and my brother's and go out and fight for our nation. And may help from on high be with you.'

4 He then levied from the country twenty thousand picked warriors and cavalry, and they marched against
5 Kendebaeus. After passing the night at Modin they rose early and proceeded to the plain, where a large force of infantry and cavalry stood ready to meet them on the far
6 side of a gully. When his army had taken up a position opposite, John saw that his men were afraid to cross the gully. So he crossed first himself; his men saw him and
7 followed. John drew up his army with the cavalry in the centre of the infantry, for the enemy cavalry were very
8 numerous. The trumpets were sounded, and Kendebaeus and his army were routed; many of them fell, and the
9 remainder took refuge in the fortress. It was in this engagement that John's brother Judas was wounded. John kept up the pursuit until Kendebaeus reached Kedron,
10 which he had rebuilt. The enemy took refuge in the towers in the open country round Azotus, whereupon John set fire to Azotus. Some two thousand of the enemy fell in the fighting, and John returned to Judaea in safety.

✻ Antiochus and Simon prepare to campaign, and a battle is fought in western Judaea.

37. The sequel to verse 25. *Orthosia* is a port near the mouth of the river Eleutherus (cp. 12: 30). From here Trypho could climb the valley eastwards and cross the watershed into the Orontes valley, and so flee north to Apamea, his home town, where Josephus (*Antiquities* XIII 7. 2) says he was besieged and killed; others say he killed himself. This was in 138 B.C.

38. Antiochus VII replaces Simon, who was 'officer commanding' (Greek *strategos*) of the coastal zone (see 11: 59), by Kendebaeus, whose rank is higher (Greek *epistrategos*). (*Kendebaeus* perhaps derives from the man's home town Candebe in Lycia.) Antiochus is clearly re-asserting Syrian control of the coast.

39. *Kedron:* perhaps *qaṭra* on the lower Kedron valley, about 7 km (4 miles) south-south-east of Jamnia and 16 km (10 miles) south-south-west of Gazara.

40. *Jamnia:* the base of Gorgias (cp. 5: 58). Both Kedron and Jamnia thus threatened Judaea's west, and Simon's son John, stationed at Gazara (cp. 13: 53), might well report Kendebaeus' activities to his father (16: 1).

16: 2. *Judas and John* were presumably named after their uncles (cp. 2: 2–5), and a third son Mattathias (verse 14) after his grandfather. *and said:* for Simon's words compare 13: 3.

3. *old:* as Simon was old enough for command at the beginning of the Maccabaean struggle, he would now be at least over fifty. He reflects (verse 2) on a generation of fighting, in which time his own sons have reached maturity. *my brother's:* perhaps Jonathan is in mind, or perhaps the Greek translator misread the Hebrew plural *'aḥai* as the singular *'aḥi*, an easy mistake when no vowels were written; the original, then, might have read 'my brothers''. The Maccabaean mantle is passed on with words reminiscent of those used to Jonathan and Simon (9: 30; 13: 8–9).

4. *He:* the subject is not named till verse 6. Josephus (*Antiquities* XIII. 7. 3) says that Simon 'took command in the

war like a young man'. 1 Maccabees, having made Simon
hand over the leadership, is perhaps deliberately playing down
Simon's part here. *Modin*, the starting-point of the Maccabaean movement, perhaps once again served as a recruiting
centre, and hence troops were drawn, as of old, *from the
country* (i.e. Judaea, not Jerusalem) – veterans, it seems, and
cavalry. Cavalry was new to Maccabaean armies, and its inclusion helped the growing identification of the Maccabaean
movement with the nation as a whole. Aristocrats and peasants
alike now oppose Syria.

5. *to the plain:* past Gazara towards Jamnia and Kedron. The
gully was perhaps the lower Kedron valley, which flowed
north-west to reach the sea at Jamnia's harbour. Both Jamnia
and Kedron would be *on the far side* of this valley to an army
coming from Modin.

6. The Jewish fear was that of climbing out of the gully to
meet an army drawn up on higher ground, and of having their
retreat impeded by a natural obstacle which in wet weather
could be dangerous.

7. The cavalry were not put on the wings to oppose the
Syrian cavalry (cp. 6: 38), for which they were no match, but
in the centre, where they would oppose the Syrian foot. This
risky tactic seems to have succeeded, for the Syrians were
'routed' (verse 8).

8. *many of them fell:* verse 10 says 'some two thousand'.
the fortress: possibly Kedron, but this is not clear.

9. This might also be translated, 'John kept up the pursuit
until he reached Kedron, which Kendebaeus had rebuilt.'

10. The narrative of the pursuit from verse 8 onwards is
hard to follow. If 'many fell, and the remainder took refuge
in the fortress' (verse 8), it is surprising to read now that *The
enemy took refuge in the towers in the open country round Azotus*,
and perhaps also surprising that John *set fire to Azotus*; perhaps
rather he *set fire to* 'them' (Greek *autous*). Jonathan had burnt
Azotus (10: 84).

This is the last engagement between the Syrians and the

Jews recorded by 1 Maccabees, and it appears to leave Judah intact. But in fact in 134 B.C., after Simon's death, Antiochus VII besieged Jerusalem and forced John's submission; the terms included the payment of tribute for Joppa (cp. 15: 28–31 above), and the walls of Jerusalem were pulled down. But Antiochus was shortly afterwards killed in a campaign against Parthia, and the Jews had no further trouble from Syria. ✻

JOHN SUCCEEDS SIMON

Now Ptolemaeus son of Abubus had been appointed 11 commander for the plain of Jericho. He had great wealth, for he was the high priest's son-in-law. But he became 12,13 over-ambitious; he proposed to make himself master of the country and plotted to put Simon and his sons out of the way. In the course of a tour to inspect the towns in 14 that region and to attend to their needs, Simon came to Jericho with his sons Mattathias and Judas in the year 177,[a] in the eleventh month, the month of Shebat. The son of 15 Abubus, with treachery in his heart, received them at the small fort called Dok which he had built, and entertained them lavishly. But he had men in concealment there, and 16 when Simon and his sons had drunk freely, Ptolemaeus and his accomplices jumped up, seized their weapons, and rushed in to the banquet. They attacked Simon and killed him, along with his two sons and some of his servants. It 17 was an act of base treachery in which evil was returned for good.

Ptolemaeus sent news of this in a dispatch to the king, 18 asking him to send troops to his assistance and to give him authority over the country and its towns. He sent some 19

[a] *That is* 134 B.C.

of his men to Gazara to kill John, and wrote to the army
officers urging them to join him, and offering them silver
20 and gold and presents. Other troops he sent to take Jeru-
21 salem and the temple hill. But someone ran ahead and
reported to John at Gazara that his father and brothers
had been murdered, and that Ptolemaeus had sent men
22 to kill him as well. When John heard this he was beside
himself; he arrested the men who came to kill him, and
put them to death, because he had discovered their plot
against his life.

23 The rest of the story of John, his wars and the deeds of
valour he performed, the walls he built, and his exploits,
24 are written in the annals of his high-priesthood from the
time when he succeeded his father.

* Simon is killed by his son-in-law, ambitious for power, but
Simon's son John succeeds in gaining control, and 1 Maccabees ends with a brief reference to his high-priesthood.

11. *Ptolemaeus:* the name suggests an Egyptian Jew, or
perhaps the grandchild of a man born during the Egyptian
rule of Judaea (it was quite common to give a child his grandfather's name). *Abubus* is a hellenized form of a semitic name
meaning 'beloved'. The *plain of Jericho*, with its alluvial soil,
tropical heat and humidity, and irrigation schemes, is even now
rich and fertile, besides being of great strategic importance, and
it is not surprising to find a *commander* – he had the same rank
as John at Gazara (13: 53) – in charge.

12. *great wealth:* the author takes it for granted that the high
priest (and his family) would enjoy wealth. The Hasmonaeans
behaved like other hellenistic kings, with their drinking parties,
mistresses, and tendency to eliminate rivals.

14. The *year 177* began in spring 135 B.C., and *Shebat* (see
p. 7) would be January–February 134 B.C.

15. *small fort called Dok:* on the top of what is now called the Mount of Temptation, overlooking Jericho.

16. Josephus says that the sons were kept as hostages, along with Simon's wife (*Antiquities* XIII. 7. 4). The author of I Maccabees, who does not intend to narrate the events of John's high-priesthood, foreshortens the story without intending to deceive.

18. *sent... to the king:* Ptolemaeus knew that he would not command personal *authority over the country and its towns*, which supported Simon and the Maccabees, and he hoped to establish himself as Syria's official ruler. He was perhaps relying on the fact that Antiochus would seize such an opportunity to *send troops* into Judaea.

19. The *coup d'état* takes its usual course; Ptolemaeus attempts to remove loyal *army officers* and win over the rest.

20. Control of the capital, with its fortified temple hill (13 : 52), was similarly vital to Ptolemaeus' success.

21. Ptolemaeus failed because someone at Dok disliked him sufficiently to get prompt news to John. The distance from Jericho to Gazara as the crow flies is about 55 km (30 miles), and John apparently managed to reach Jerusalem from Gazara (32 km, 20 miles) before Ptolemaeus had reached it from Jericho (a similar distance). John was accepted by the people 'because of his father's good deeds and the masses' hatred of Ptolemaeus' (Josephus, *Antiquities* XIII. 7. 4). Ptolemaeus retreated to Dok, where John besieged him, and from there he escaped to Ammon.

23–4. Simon has lost his life, but the Maccabaean succession has been preserved, and here the author of I Maccabees ends his story. Its climax is Simon's rule and the acceptance of Simon's family as the new high-priestly family. Having vindicated the Maccabaean family by portraying their devotion and success in a righteous cause, and by showing that military and priestly functions could be combined successfully in one man (a point which was not easily accepted in the reign of Alexander Jannaeus, 103–76 B.C.), the author writes his final sentence in the style of the historian of 1 and 2 Kings (cp., e.g., 2 Kings 14: 28–9). The author could apparently refer to *annals* much as the historian of 1 and 2 Kings could, but any such records were probably destroyed when the Romans took Jerusalem in A.D. 70. These last two verses suggest (though they do not state) that when they were written John's reign was past; if so, the final touches were added to the book after 104 B.C. Most scholars believe that the work was originally written in John's reign (134–104 B.C.), and this gives further reason for the book's close with the death of the author's hero. ✳

THE SECOND BOOK OF THE

MACCABEES

✳   ✳   ✳   ✳   ✳   ✳   ✳   ✳   ✳   ✳   ✳   ✳   ✳

THE ORIGINAL TEXT AND ITS DATE

2 Maccabees was originally written in Greek. Our oldest
manuscript is the fifth-century A.D. Codex Alexandrinus. (The
book does not occur in the Codex Sinaiticus.) There are also
'Old Latin' and Syriac versions.

2 Maccabees is prefaced by some letters which bear dates.
The latest date given is 124 B.C., and if these letters were
bound up with the book from a very early stage of its life,
we would have some indication of the period in which the
book was written. The author himself claims that his book is
a 'summary' of the five-volume work of a certain Jason of
Cyrene (2: 19–32, probably the original opening of the book).
If Jason's work ended with the reign of Eupator (161 B.C.;
cp. 2: 20–1), as indeed 2 Maccabees does, then we know the
earliest possible date for Jason's work, and thus for 2 Maccabees.
But the earliest possible date is not necessarily the right one.
Some scholars claim that the author of 2 Maccabees knew
1 Maccabees and wrote to convey a different interpretation.
It is also suggested that the Pharisaic ideas prominent in the
book – the emphasis on keeping the sabbath (5: 25; 8: 26;
12: 38; 15: 1), the idea of retribution and discipline (cp. 6:
12–17), the prominence of martyrdom and the doctrine of
resurrection (6: 18 – 7: 42) – all reflect the first century B.C.
rather than the second. But none of these points can be used
with certainty, and the book may belong almost anywhere in
the last 150 years B.C. It is more generally agreed that the
book's home may have been the Jewish community at Alexandria.

THE AUTHOR'S APPROACH TO THE WORK

The author himself describes this in his preface (2: 19–32) and
in his tail-piece (15: 38–9) and the reader should see the commentary on these passages. But the author has not told us
everything.

In some ways his approach is very Greek. He is writing the
sort of history known to scholars as 'pathetic historiography';
that is, he is attempting to arouse the reader's sympathy or
dislike for the persons and the causes he describes. Thus Jason,
Menelaus, Antiochus, Alcimus and Nicanor are seen by the
reader as villains of the blackest dye, while Onias, Judas,
Eleazar and Razis are heroes who suffer most unjustly for their
people. The enemy's cruelties are vividly described (6: 18 – 7:
42), as are also God's dramatic interventions on behalf of the
Jews (cp. 3: 23–40). The deaths of Eleazar, the seven brothers
and their mother, Menelaus and Razis are described with every
rhetorical art; the death of Antiochus is a minor Greek tragedy
of its own (see the commentary on 9: 1–10).

In other ways, however, the author's approach is very
Jewish. In contrast to 1 Maccabees, 2 Maccabees sees the
religious aspect of the struggle as much more important than
the political one. There is more prayer before battle, the
sabbath is more strictly observed, the idea of martyrdom for
the cause is given great prominence, together with the belief
in the resurrection of the faithful for reward and of the wicked
for punishment. Again in some contrast to 1 Maccabees,
2 Maccabees contains much comment from the author by way
of theological explanation of what is happening (cp. 5: 17–20;
6: 12–17). But most noticeable of all is the way the author
focuses his whole history on the temple. The first half of
Judas' work is the recapture of the temple, its purification and
the institution of the feast of rededication (cp. 10: 1–8), and
the second ends with the death of the blasphemer Nicanor
who had threatened to destroy the temple, and the institution
of the feast of Nicanor's Day (15: 28–37). The letters added

at the beginning of the work are also concerned with the celebration of the purification of the temple.

THE HISTORICAL VALUE OF 2 MACCABEES

This subject has been much debated. The more obvious liking of the author of 2 Maccabees, compared with the author of 1 Maccabees, for legendary material and theological explanation has tended to make many modern scholars value 1 Maccabees more highly as a historical source. But it has become clear that 2 Maccabees does contain much genuine and valuable historical material, particularly in his account of the early stages of the hellenizing process in Jerusalem. 2 Maccabees sometimes places events in a different order from that given by 1 Maccabees; thus in 2 Maccabees Antiochus robs the temple after his second Egyptian campaign, while in 1 Maccabees this happens after the first Egyptian campaign. In 2 Maccabees Antiochus' death comes before the rededication of the temple, in 1 Maccabees after it. In fact, 2 Maccabees may actually be right here, but the re-arrangement has had the effect of throwing other events out of place. (Further details are discussed in the commentary at the appropriate point; cp. p. 286.) Again, one is not always sure whether similar stories in the two books describe the same event or two different ones. Thus producing a clear sequence of events from the material in 1 and 2 Maccabees is far from easy; some think it virtually impossible. However, the datings given and the general political and military trends of events make the establishment of a reasonable sequence much more possible than it is in the case of the gospels, and this commentary makes some attempt at the task.

As in the case of 1 Maccabees, the documents quoted are particularly interesting and important in an assessment of 2 Maccabees' historical value. The documents are as follows:

(1)	1: 1 – 2: 18	Two, or three, letters
(2)	9: 18–27	Antiochus' letter recommending his son to his citizens
(3)	11: 16–21	Letter of Lysias to the Jews
(4)	11: 22–26	Letter of Antiochus V to Lysias
(5)	11: 27–33	Letter of Antiochus IV to the Jews
(6)	11: 34–38	Letter of the Romans to the Jews

For these documents in detail, see the commentary. No. 2 in its present form and context causes several difficulties. No. 4 is clearly out of place in its present context, and its setting here in the context of events of 164 B.C. has probably led to 2 Maccabees' early placing of the death of Antiochus. But all the letters may contain genuine elements; the problem is to get them into the right context and interpret them accurately. This is always a difficulty when only one side of a correspondence is available.

THE AUTHOR

As in the case of 1 Maccabees, we do not know his name. But there is much about his work that suggests he was a Jew of the Dispersion, perhaps living in Alexandria. He is apparently familiar with the imperial administration, which the Syrian kings had taken over largely from their Egyptian predecessors. He knows the work of Jason of Cyrene, a North African Jew whose work might well become popular in Alexandrian Jewry. He does not show the nationalism of the author of 1 Maccabees, but rather emphasizes the distinctive features of Judaism, so important to a Jew living abroad; indeed, he speaks in terms of 'Judaism' and 'Hellenism'. He is greatly interested in the institution of feasts, as are also two other books much concerned with foreign Jews, Esther (in the Old Testament) and 3 Maccabees (see p. 13). He writes in Greek, apparently his native language, and approaches history in a particularly Greek way, as his preface shows. The preface also shows that he has not the discernment or judgement of the author of 1 Maccabees. But we remain grateful to him for his 'toil and late nights' (2: 27) for much that would otherwise have been lost.

*   *   *   *   *   *   *   *   *   *   *   *   *

Foreword:
letters to the Jews in Egypt

The author's preface to 2 Maccabees does not appear until 2: 19, which refers to 'the history of Judas Maccabaeus and his brothers, the purification of the great temple, and the dedication of the altar'. The book ends with the account of the establishment of a feast on the day Nicanor fell (15: 36), and, as it stands, begins with two, or possibly three, letters about the observance of the feast of 'the purification of the temple' (2: 16). These letters, probably translated from an original Aramaic form by the author, are festal letters, to be compared with those sent 'to all the Jews... binding them to keep the fourteenth and fifteenth days of the month Adar' (Esther 9: 20-2, 29-32). Possibly such letters were sent annually; the letters here come from different years.

The division and dating of the letters is not as easy as it seems at first sight. The following suggestions have been made:

(a) verses 1–10a (to 'the year 188') in ch. 1 are a letter written in 124 B.C., referring to, and quoting, or summarizing, an earlier letter of 143 B.C. A second letter, beginning with 'From the people...' in verse 10, is undated. This is the interpretation followed by the N.E.B.;

(b) verses 1–9 are a letter written in 143 B.C.; verse 10 begins a second letter which it thus dates to 124 B.C.;

(c) 'in the year 169' (verse 7) ends the first letter, and 'in the year 188' (verse 10) ends the second. A third letter follows. In cases (*b*) and (*c*) 'wrote' is translated 'write' and a full stop inserted after 'to you', in verse 7. 'During the persecution... shed innocent blood' then become subordinate clauses describing the circumstances in which 'we prayed to the Lord'.

A LETTER TO THE JEWS IN EGYPT

1 TO THEIR JEWISH KINSMEN in Egypt, the Jews who are in Jerusalem and those in the country of Judaea send brotherly greeting.

2 May God give you peace and prosperity and remember his covenant with Abraham, Isaac, and Jacob, his faithful
3 servants. May he give to you all a will to worship him, to
4 fulfil his purposes eagerly with heart and soul. May he give you a mind open to his law and precepts. May he
5 make peace and answer your prayers, and be reconciled
6 to you and not forsake you in an evil hour. Here and now we are praying for you.

7 In the reign of Demetrius, in the year 169,*a* we the Jews wrote to you during the persecution and the crisis that came upon us in those years since the time when Jason and his partisans revolted from the holy land and the
8 kingdom. They set the porch of the temple on fire and shed innocent blood. Then we prayed to the Lord and were answered. We offered a sacrifice and fine flour, we
9 lit the lamps, and set out the Bread of the Presence. And now, you are to observe the celebration of a Feast of Tabernacles in the month Kislev.

10 Written in the year 188.*b*

[*a*] *That is* 143 B.C.   [*b*] *That is* 124 B.C.

✻ The Jews of Jerusalem and Judaea, probably in a time of peace under John Hyrcanus (see the suggested dating under (*a*) above), write to encourage Jews of Egypt 'in an evil hour' (verse 5) and to tell them to observe a feast commemorating the Maccabaean rededication of the temple.

1. *kinsmen in Egypt.* Jews went to Egypt after the fall of Jerusalem in 586 B.C. (see Jer. 43: 1–7). We know of a Jewish military colony at Elephantine near Aswan in the fifth century B.C. (see *Old Testament Illustrations* in this series, pp. 99–101). In 312 B.C. Ptolemy I deported some Jews to Alexandria; the community flourished and according to Josephus (*Jewish War* II. 18. 8) in A.D. 66 some 50,000 Jews were killed there. About 160 B.C. Onias IV founded a small Jewish military colony and temple at Leontopolis (see the note on 1 Macc. 10: 55). *Jerusalem* and *the country of Judaea* were always mentioned separately; they had made an uneasy partnership in Jewish history.

2. The greeting is followed, as in Paul's letters, by a prayer. *peace and prosperity* perhaps implies that the Egyptian Jews at the time had neither (cp. verses 5–6).

3–4. *will, heart,* and *mind* all translate the original 'heart'. The prayer may imply a certain criticism of the Egyptian Jews' worship and observance of the law.

5. *evil hour:* perhaps persecution by Ptolemy VIII (145–116 B.C.) is in mind.

6. *and now* in the original might have been the phrase common in letters introducing the main point after the preamble. If so, this would be an argument in favour of suggestion (*c*) above about the dating and division of the letters.

7. *Demetrius* II (145–138 B.C.) is meant; *the year 169* began spring 143 B.C. On the dating and division of the letters, see above. The roots of the *persecution* and *crisis* are, interestingly, traced back, not to an act of Antiochus IV, but to the revolt of *Jason and his partisans . . . from the holy land and the kingdom.* If his political revolt is meant, see 5: 5–10 and the commentary on 1 Macc. 1: 29–40; if Jason's hellenizing is meant, see 4: 7–17; 1 Macc. 1: 11–15.

8. *set the porch of the temple on fire:* cp. 8: 33; 1 Macc. 4: 38. *innocent blood:* see 5: 6. *we prayed... and were answered* covers events up to the regaining of the temple (10: 1–8; 1 Macc. 4: 36–59). *flour* refers to the grain-offering described in Lev. 2, offered with an animal *sacrifice* (cp. Isa. 19: 21). For the *lamps* and *Bread of the Presence* see the notes on 1 Macc. 4: 51, 59.

9. *and now:* see the note on verse 6. The original feast of rededication had been 'like the Feast of Tabernacles' (10: 6); see the commentary on 1 Macc. 4: 36–59. Feasts were often named after their character and their month, as here. The feast was held on the twenty-fifth day of Kislev (1 Macc. 4: 52, 59), in mid-December.

10. *the year 188:* beginning spring 124 B.C. *

A LETTER TO ARISTOBULUS AND THE JEWS
IN EGYPT

* This letter, like the previous one, urges the celebration of the festival of 'the purification of the temple' (2: 16). Quoting scripture and legend, the author tries to show the similarity of this temple rededication with the dedications by Nehemiah and Solomon, at which the sacrifices were consumed by heavenly fire. The author of the letter perhaps saw this as the background to the lighting of the lamps (1 Macc. 4: 50) which gave this feast its name of 'Lights' (cp. 1: 8; 10: 3).

For the purpose of comment, this letter is divided into convenient sections. *

From the people of Jerusalem and Judaea, from the Senate, and from Judas, to Aristobulus, the teacher of King Ptolemy and a member of the high-priestly family, and to the Jews in Egypt, greeting and good health.

11   We have been saved by God from great dangers, and give him all thanks, as men standing ready to resist the

king. It was God who drove out the enemy force in the 12
holy city.

For when the king went into Persia with an army that 13
seemed invincible, they were cut to pieces in the temple
of Nanaea through a stratagem employed by Nanaea's
priests. Antiochus, along with his Companions, arrived at 14
the temple to marry the goddess, in order to secure the
considerable treasure by way of dowry. After this had 15
been laid out by the priests, he went into the temple
precinct with a small retinue. When Antiochus entered,
the priests shut the sanctuary, opened a secret door in the 16
panelling, and hurled stones at them. The king fell, as if
struck by a thunderbolt. They hacked off limbs and heads
and threw them to those outside. Blessed in all things be 17
our God, who handed over the evil-doers to death!

* 10 *b*. A standard formula of greeting is used. *from the Senate,
and from Judas* (or perhaps this should be 'from the Senate of
the Jews') is added to *From the people of Jerusalem and Judaea*,
for whom see the note on verse 1. *Aristobulus* was probably the
Jewish apologist of that name at the court of Ptolemy VI
(180–145 B.C.); if so, it is difficult to accept the suggestion
which dates this letter to 124 B.C. (see above, p. 219). If *Judas*
(cp. 2: 14) is the right, and the original, reading here, then
this letter might be dated between December 164 B.C. (Antiochus' death, cp. verses 13–17) and May 160 B.C. (Judas'
death).

11–12. The letter would be easier to date if we could deter-
mine the historical reference of these verses. If verse 12 refers
to the expulsion of the citadel garrison (142 B.C.) we must
explain the mention of Judas and Aristobulus in verse 10.
Possibly the defeat of Lysias (1 Macc. 4: 28–35) is meant. Some
refer the verse to the withdrawal of Antiochus VII after his
siege of Jerusalem in 134 B.C.

13. See the commentary on 1 Macc. 6: 1–17. *the king* here is clearly meant to be Antiochus IV, though it was Antiochus III who died temple-raiding. *Nanaea* was originally a Sumerian goddess of love and fertility, 'Lady of Heaven'.

14. *to marry the goddess:* the ceremonial marriage of the king with the goddess of fertility in the ancient world was intended to secure fertility for the land in the coming year. Here the king is credited with other motives.

15. *secret door:* see Daniel, Bel, and the Snake, verse 21.

17. Here is the moral: God punishes sacrilegious enemies like Antiochus. ✳

LETTER (CONTINUED): FIRE CONSUMES NEHEMIAH'S SACRIFICE

18 We are about to celebrate the purification of the temple on the twenty-fifth of Kislev, and think it right to inform you, so that you also for your part may celebrate a Feast of Tabernacles, in honour of the fire which appeared when Nehemiah offered sacrifices, after he had built the 19 temple and the altar. When our fathers were carried off to Persia, the pious priests of those days secretly took fire from the altar and concealed it in a dry well. It proved a 20 safe hiding-place and remained undiscovered. After many years had passed, in God's good time, Nehemiah was sent back by the king of Persia. He then dispatched the descendants of the priests who had hidden it to get the fire, and they informed our people that they found, not 21 fire, but a thick liquid. Nehemiah ordered them to draw some out and bring it to him. When the materials of the sacrifice had been presented, he ordered the priests to sprinkle this liquid over the wood and the things laid 22 upon it, and this was done. Some time passed; then the

sun, which earlier had been hidden by clouds, shone out and the altar burst into a great blaze, so that everyone marvelled. As the sacrifice was burning, the priests offered 23 prayer, they and all those present: Jonathan began and the rest responded, led by Nehemiah.

The prayer was in this style: 'O Lord God, creator of all 24 things, thou the terrible, the mighty, the just, and the merciful, the only King, the only gracious one, the only 25 giver, the only just, omnipotent, and everlasting one, who dost deliver Israel from every evil, who didst choose the patriarchs and set them apart: accept this sacrifice 26 on behalf of thy whole people Israel; they are thy own, watch over them and sanctify them. Gather the dispersed, 27 free those who are in slavery among the heathen, look favourably on the despised and detested; let the heathen know that thou art our God. Punish our oppressors for 28 their insolent brutality and make them suffer torment; but plant thy people in thy holy place, as Moses said.'   29

Then the priests chanted the hymns. After the materials 30, 31 of the sacrifice had been consumed, Nehemiah further ordered what remained of the liquid to be poured over some great stones.[a] At this a flame shot up, but burnt itself 32 out as soon as the fire on the altar outshone it.[b]

These events became widely known. The king of Persia 33 was told that, in the place where the priests who were departed had hidden the fire, a liquid had appeared, and that Nehemiah and his companions had used it to burn up the materials of the sacrifice. When he had verified 34

[a] what remained... stones: *so some witnesses; others read* that great stones should enclose what remained of the liquid.   [b] *Or* but hardly had the light been reflected from the altar, when it burnt itself out.

the fact, the king enclosed the site and made it sacred.
35 The custodians he appointed received a share of the very
36 substantial revenue that the king derived from it. Nehemiah and his companions called the liquid 'nephthar',
which means 'purification'; but most people call it
'naphtha'.

* The author recounts a legend about the fire which burnt
the sacrifices on the pre-exilic temple altar of burnt-offering,
and connects it with the new feast of the purification of the
temple by means of an etymology (verse 36).

18. *about to celebrate:* some have thought that this refers to
the very first celebration in 164 B.C.; but if so, the verses
describing Antiochus' death (verses 13–17) cannot be part of
the original letter, for his death would not be known by the
date the letter would have been written. *twenty-fifth of Kislev:*
cp. 1 Macc. 4: 52, 59. *a Feast of Tabernacles:* cp. 1 Macc. 4:
52–9. *fire which appeared:* for heavenly fire consuming sacrifices (a sign that the sacrifices were accepted), cp. Judg. 6: 21,
1 Kings 18: 33–8.

The historical references in this passage are curious. It was
not *Nehemiah* who *built the temple and the altar* (cp. Ezra 3: 1 ff.;
5: 1 ff.). They were built about seventy years and ninety years
respectively before Nehemiah arrived.

19. *to Persia:* the exiles were taken to Babylon, which later
became part of the Persian empire. *a safe hiding-place:* apparently somewhere in the place of exile (cp. verses 33–4).

20. Nehemiah was sent to Jerusalem in 444 B.C.

23. Jonathan appears to be high priest: but Eliashib was
high priest in Nehemiah's time (Neh. 3: 1; 13: 4).

24–5. *The prayer,* like other Hebrew prayers (cp., e.g., Neh.
9: 5–37, or the Prayer of Manasseh), contains reference to God
as creator, saviour, chooser of the patriarchs, but is notable
for its long series of epithets and emphasis on the uniqueness
of God.

26–8. The requests are appropriate for the Maccabaean situation (e.g. *in slavery among the heathen:* cp. 1 Macc. 5), but not for Nehemiah's; the Persians were not *oppressors* of *insolent brutality*.

29. *as Moses said:* cp. Exod. 15: 17.

31. The point seems to be, whichever translation is adopted, that the liquid was divinely appointed for use on the altar and nowhere else.

33–5. The basis of fact behind the legend is perhaps momentarily revealed by the note that the Persian king established a state monopoly in this commodity. The Greek geographer Strabo (first century A.D.) speaks of naphtha in Assyria and Babylon, and recounts that Alexander the Great nearly killed a boy by dousing him in it and bringing a lamp near him.

36. '*nephthar*' may have meant something like 'oil of fire', fire ('*atar*') being for the Persians a purifying agent. The meaning '*purification*' provides for the author the link between the legendary fire and the new feast of rededication, whose purificatory aspect he emphasizes more than 1 Maccabees (cp. 2:18; 10: 3; 14: 36).

LETTER (CONTINUED): FIRE CONSUMES SOLOMON'S SACRIFICE

The records show that it was the prophet Jeremiah who **2** ordered the exiles to hide the fire, as has been mentioned; also that, having given them the law, he charged them 2 not to neglect the ordinances of the Lord, or be led astray by the sight of images of gold and silver with all their finery. In similar words he appealed to them not to aban- 3 don the law.

Further, this document records that, prompted by a 4 divine message, the prophet gave orders that the Tent of Meeting and the ark should go with him. Then he went

away to the mountain from the top of which Moses saw
5 God's promised land. When he reached the mountain,
Jeremiah found a cave-dwelling; he carried the tent, the
ark, and the incense-altar into it, then blocked up the
6 entrance. Some of his companions came to make out the
7 way, but were unable to find it. When Jeremiah learnt of
this he reprimanded them. 'The place shall remain unknown', he said, 'until God finally gathers his people
8 together and shows mercy to them. Then the Lord will
bring these things to light again, and the glory of the Lord
will appear with the cloud, as it was seen both in the time
of Moses and when Solomon prayed that the shrine
might be worthily consecrated.'

9   It was also related that Solomon, having the gift of
wisdom, offered the dedication sacrifice at the completion
10 of the temple; and that, just as Moses prayed to the Lord
and fire came down from heaven and burnt up the
sacrificial offerings, so Solomon prayed and the fire came
11 down and consumed the whole-offerings. (Moses said:
'The sin-offering was burnt up in the same way because
12 it was not eaten.') Solomon celebrated the feast for eight
days.

＊ The author traces the history of the altar-fire back through
legends about Jeremiah to the sacrifices of Solomon and Moses,
consumed by fire from heaven. The author sees the new feast
of rededication or purification as belonging to a famous series
of dedicatory sacrifices, marked by the descent of heavenly fire.

    1. *The records:* cp. verse 4. Jeremiah's letter to the exiles
(Jer. 29) says nothing about hiding the fire; possibly the lost
Apocryphon of Jeremiah contains the legends recounted in
verses 1, 4 ff. The Jewish historian Eupolemus, of Macca-

baean times (see the note on 1 Macc. 8: 17), mentioned Jeremiah's removal of the ark in 586 B.C.

2. *images:* the exiles are warned against idolatry by the Letter of Jeremiah (not genuine) in the Apocrypha.

4–5. The construction of the *Tent of Meeting, the ark,* and *the incense-altar* are described in Exod. 25–7; 30: 1–10, and the introduction of the tent and the ark to Solomon's temple in 2 Chron. 5: 5–10. *the mountain* was Mount Nebo (Deut. 34: 1); the idea seems to be that Israel's sacred cult-objects were appropriately concealed with Moses, whose grave was also 'unknown' (verse 7, cp. Deut. 34: 6).

6–7. This story is hardly consistent with the real expectation of the historical Jeremiah, who prophesied (Jer. 3: 16) that 'In those days...says the LORD, men shall speak no more of the Ark of the Covenant of the LORD; they shall not think of it nor remember it nor resort to it; it will be needed no more.'

8. *the glory of the Lord will appear with the cloud:* such an appearance meant the presence of God's majesty, and was the mark of great moments in the life of Israel, e.g., Sinai (Exod. 24: 16 ff.) or the dedication of Solomon's temple (1 Kings 8: 10–11, 2 Chron. 5: 14).

9–10. When Solomon dedicated the first temple, 'fire came down from heaven and consumed the whole-offering and the sacrifices, while the glory of the LORD filled the house' (2 Chron. 7: 1), and after the hallowing and installation of the priests, 'Moses and Aaron entered the Tent of the Presence, and when they came out, they blessed the people, and the glory of the LORD appeared to all the people. Fire came out from before the LORD and consumed the whole-offering' (Lev. 9: 23–4).

11. The point for the present argument, of this detail taken from an intricate legal question in Lev. 10: 16 ff., is obscure.

12. *eight days:* the period of Solomon's dedication and the Maccabees' rededication of the temple (2 Chron. 7: 9, 1 Macc. 4: 56). ✳

THE LETTER'S CONCLUSION

13 These same facts are set out in the official records and in
the memoirs of Nehemiah. Just as Nehemiah collected
the chronicles of the kings, the writings of prophets, the
works of David, and royal letters about sacred offerings,
14 to found his library, so Judas also has collected all the
books that had been scattered as a result of our recent
15 conflict. These are in our possession, and if you need any
of them, send messengers for them.

16 As, then, we are about to celebrate the purification of
the temple, we are writing to impress upon you the duty
17 of celebrating this festival. God has saved his whole people
and granted to all of us the holy land, the kingship, the
18 priesthood, and the consecration, as he promised by the
law; and in him we have confidence that he will soon
be merciful to us and gather us from every part of the
world to the holy temple. For he has delivered us from
great evils and purified the temple.

* The writer names his authorities, states his purpose in
writing, and ends with a statement of the people's faith in God.
   13. *official records:* preserved in the temple. *the memoirs of
Nehemiah:* Neh. 1: 1 – 7: 72; 11: 1–2; 12: 27–43; 13: 4–31.
The author does not seem to have used much of this material,
however. *Nehemiah collected. . . to found his library:* it is possible
that Nehemiah, when he rebuilt Jerusalem, made such a collection to preserve the writings, but Nehemiah does not tell us
so. It is also possible that this is part of the later enhancement
of Nehemiah's reputation, as also witnessed by the legendary
material in 2 Macc. 1: 18–36. *the chronicles of the kings:* perhaps
the books of Samuel and Kings. *the works of David:* the psalms.
royal letters about sacred offerings: probably the Persian docu-

ments of Ezra 6: 3–12; 7: 12–26. Nehemiah is not credited with collecting any books of the law with which Ezra was connected.

14. Which books Judas managed to collect we cannot tell; copies of the law had been burnt by order of Antiochus IV. Possibly verse 13 is more informative about Judas' collection than Nehemiah's, and indicates what was available to the author of the letter. The passage is interesting for our knowledge of the growth of the Hebrew canon: see *The Making of the Old Testament* in this series, pp. 105–32.

16. See 1: 18, 36 and the notes on these verses.

17. *promised by the law:* perhaps Exod. 19: 5–6 is in mind, 'you shall become my special possession... my kingdom of priests, my holy nation'.

18. *gather us:* for the promise that God will gather Israel see Deut. 30: 1–5. The idea of the centrality of the *temple* at the final ingathering is an old one; see Isa. 2: 2–3. The author stresses that this is a purified temple. *

Preface to this abridgement

* The author's personal preface is rare in biblical literature, belonging to the hellenistic rather than to the Jewish tradition. We may compare the prologue to those of Ecclesiasticus, Luke's gospel and the Acts of the Apostles. *

IN FIVE BOOKS Jason of Cyrene has set out the history 19 of Judas Maccabaeus and his brothers, the purification of the great temple, and the dedication of the altar. He has 20 described the battles with Antiochus Epiphanes and with his son Eupator, and the apparitions from heaven which 21 appeared to those who vied with one another in fighting

manfully for Judaism. Few though they were, they ravaged
22 the whole country and routed the foreign hordes; they
restored the world-renowned temple, freed the city of
Jerusalem, and reaffirmed the laws which were in danger
of being abolished. All this they achieved because the
Lord was merciful and gracious to them.

23 These five books of Jason I shall try to summarize in a
24 single work; for I was struck by the mass of statistics and
the difficulty which the bulk of the material causes to
25 those wishing to grasp the narratives of this history. I have
tried to provide for the entertainment of those who read
for pleasure, the convenience of students who must com-
mit the facts to memory, and the profit of even the casual
26 reader. The task which I have taken upon myself in making
this summary is no easy one. It means toil and late nights,
27 just as it is no light task for the man who plans a dinner-
party and aims to satisfy his guests. Nevertheless, I will
gladly undergo this hard labour for the benefit of[a] readers
28 in general. I shall leave to the original author the minute
discussion of every detail, and concentrate on the main
29 points of my outline. As the architect of a new house must
concern himself with the whole of the structure, while the
man who paints in encaustic on the walls needs to discover
only what is necessary for the ornamentation, so, I judge,
30 it is with me also. It is the province of the original author
of a history to take possession of the field, to spread himself in discussion, and to inquire closely into particular
31 questions. The man who makes a paraphrase must be
allowed to aim at conciseness of expression and to omit
a full treatment of the subject-matter.

[a] for...of: *so some witnesses; others read* to win the gratitude of...

232

Here, then, without adding anything further, I begin 32
my narrative. It would be absurd to make a lengthy introduction to the history and cut short the history itself.

* The author of 2 Maccabees describes Jason's work and his
own approach to summarizing it.

19. The *five books* have not survived. *Jason* (cp. the high
priest Jason) was a Greek name used as an equivalent of the
Hebrew Joshua. *Cyrene*, about 500 miles west of Alexandria,
was a hellenistic city with a large Jewish population (see 1
Macc. 15: 23, and cp. Simon of Cyrene, Mark 15: 21). *the
history...purification...dedication:* the themes here listed are
those that the author of 2 Maccabees himself emphasizes; the
purification and dedication have already been brought to our
notice by the two letters prefixed to the work.

20. The *battles* in 2 Maccabees are not limited to those of
the two reigns mentioned; the events of 3: 1 – 4: 6 belong to
the reign of Seleucus IV and those of 14: 1 ff. to the reign of
Demetrius I.

21. *apparitions:* 2 Maccabees makes a regular feature of
these (cp. 3: 23–40; 5: 1–4; 10: 29; 11: 8). 2 Maccabees also
conveys that Judas' partisans were *Few* and very destructive
(cp. 8: 5–7), and that they were fighting against *foreign hordes*
for *Judaism* (cp. 8: 1; 14: 38, and Gal. 1: 13). The word is a
new one, typically Greek in its formation, summarizing a way
of life and belief for which Jews would fight *manfully* (the
phrase expresses a very Greek virtue).

23. *summarize:* Greek *epitemnein*; the author is often called
'the Epitomist', i.e. the summarizer.

27. *toil and late nights:* the translator of Ecclesiasticus (see his
prologue) commented that he had spent 'some energy and
labour', working 'night and day' to complete his translation.

28. *main points:* Syrian oppression of the Jews; Judas' revolt;
the final defeat of Nicanor. We must be prepared to find that
2 Maccabees is selective and gets the course of events out of
perspective.

29. The author means that he, like the decorator, is concerned with high-lighting the important things, rather than with the basic planning.

32. This is a remark perhaps made at the expense of other more pompous historians. *

Syrian oppression of the Jews

* This section, chs. 3–7, describes the breakdown of good relations between Jerusalem and Antioch and its results for the Jewish population. There is much material here which is not found in 1 Maccabees, including some detail of great value to the historian. *

JEWISH RIVALRIES AND THE TEMPLE TREASURY

3 DURING THE RULE of the high priest Onias, the holy city enjoyed complete peace and prosperity, and the laws were still observed most scrupulously, because he was 2 a pious man and hated wickedness. The kings themselves held the sanctuary in honour and used to embellish the 3 temple with the most splendid gifts; even Seleucus, king of Asia, bore all the expenses of the sacrificial worship from his own revenues.

4 But a certain Simon, of the clan Bilgah,*a* who had been appointed administrator of the temple, quarrelled with the 5 high priest about the regulation of the city market. Unable to get the better of Onias, he went to Apollonius son of Thrasaeus, then governor of Coele-syria and Phoenicia, 6 and alleged that the treasury at Jerusalem was full of

[a] *So some witnesses (compare Nehemiah 12. 5, 18); others read* Benjamin.

untold riches—indeed the total of the accumulated balances was incalculable and did not correspond with the account for the sacrifices; he suggested that these balances might be brought under the control of the king. When Apollo- 7 nius met the king, he reported what he had been told about the riches. The king selected Heliodorus, his chief minister, and sent him with orders to remove these treasures.

Heliodorus set off at once, ostensibly to make a tour of 8 inspection of the cities of Coele-syria and Phoenicia, but in fact to carry out the purpose of the king. When he 9 arrived at Jerusalem and had been courteously received by the high priest and the citizens, he explained why he had come: he told them about the allegations and asked if they were in fact true. The high priest intimated that 10 the deposits were held in trust for widows and orphans, apart from what belonged to Hyrcanus son of Tobias, a 11 man of very high standing; the matter was being misrepresented by the impious Simon. In all there were four hundred talents of silver and two hundred of gold. It was 12 unthinkable, he said, that wrong should be done to those who had relied on the sanctity of the place, on the dignity and inviolability of the world-famous temple. But Helio- 13 dorus, in virtue of the king's orders, replied that these deposits must without question be handed over to the royal treasury.

* 1 Maccabees begins with a description of the growing hellenization of Judaea, 2 Maccabees with an internal dispute in the Jerusalem priesthood.

1. Under Onias III (removed from office 175 B.C., cp. 4: 7) Jerusalem is peaceful, prosperous, and law-abiding. Onias is praised for his good Jewish qualities; but elsewhere the author

praises his Greek qualities (cp. 15: 12, 'that great gentleman of modest bearing and mild disposition, apt speaker, and exponent from childhood of the good life').

2–3. *The kings themselves:* Antiochus III and *even Seleucus* supported the temple (see note on 1 Macc. 10: 44–5). The Greeks are not seen as such an evil influence as they are in 1 Maccabees.

4. *Simon:* brother of the later Syrian-appointed high priest Menelaus (4: 23) and of Lysimachus (4: 29, 39 ff.). *the clan Bilgah:* see the footnote. A man from such a priestly family would be more likely than a Benjamite to become *administrator of the temple. quarrelled:* that two such important men, probably with overlapping spheres of authority, should quarrel, is not unlikely. Quarrels were even more likely if Simon favoured Syria and Onias Egypt. *about the regulation of the city market:* whether Simon coveted this job, or, having it, disputed with Onias some detail of its management, is not clear. Perhaps Simon was a hellenizer, prepared to sacrifice principles of Mosaic law in the execution of his office. As administrator of a temple whose treasury was as much concerned with secular as with religious financial affairs, Simon was probably largely responsible for the complete finances of Judaea under Syria.

5. *son of Thrasaeus:* if, by a slight change, we translate this as 'of Tarsus', a contradiction with 4: 4, 21, which mention Apollonius son of Menestheus, is eased. For Syrian officials, see pp. 8–10.

6. Simon points out that the temple treasury acted as a civic as well as a religious treasury and that the funds not needed for the temple might with profit be controlled by the king. *untold riches:* certainly a very large amount, cp. verse 11.

7. The king needed money to pay the Roman fine levied on Antiochus III by the treaty of Apamea (188 B.C.). *Heliodorus* is known to us from an inscription erected in his honour on the island of Delos (cp. 1 Macc. 15: 23) 'for his friendly disposition and love to the king'.

9. *courteously received:* the Jews had so far found the Seleucids friendly enough, and the visit would be something of a great event.

10. *for widows and orphans:* caring for these was a basic Jewish religious duty; cp. Deut. 26: 12–13.

11. *Hyrcanus son of Tobias* was the son of Joseph of the Tobiad family from Transjordan (cp. p. 4). He was related to, and perhaps friendly with, Onias; their Egyptian sympathies were probably exploited on this occasion and afterwards (cp. 4: 1 ff.) by Simon.

12. *sanctity ... dignity ... inviolability:* unlikely to impress a king whose father, Antiochus III, died robbing a temple to gain funds. ✻

ATTEMPT TO ROB THE TREASURY

He fixed a day and went into the temple to make an 14
inventory. At this there was great distress throughout the
whole city. The priests, prostrating themselves in their 15
vestments before the altar, prayed to Heaven, to the Law-
giver who had made deposits sacred, to keep them intact
for their rightful owners. The high priest's looks pierced 16
every beholder to the heart, for his face and its changing
colour betrayed the anguish of his soul. Alarm and shud- 17
dering gripped him, and the pain he felt was clearly
apparent to the onlookers. The people rushed pell-mell 18
from their houses to join together in supplication because
of the dishonour which threatened the holy place. Women 19
in sackcloth, their breasts bare, filled the streets; un-
married girls who were kept in seclusion ran to the gates
or walls of their houses, while others leaned out from the
windows; all with outstretched hands made solemn 20
entreaty to Heaven. It was pitiful to see the crowd all 21

lying prostrate in utter confusion, and the high priest in an agony of apprehension.

22 While the people were calling upon the Lord Almighty to keep the deposits intact and safe for those who had 23 deposited them, Heliodorus proceeded to carry out his 24 decision. But at the very moment when he arrived with his bodyguard at the treasury, the Ruler of spirits and of all powers produced a mighty apparition, so that all who had the audacity to accompany Heliodorus were faint with 25 terror, stricken with panic at the power of God. They saw a horse, splendidly caparisoned, with a rider of terrible aspect; it rushed fiercely at Heliodorus and, rearing up, attacked him with its hooves. The rider was wearing 26 golden armour. There also appeared to Heliodorus two young men of surpassing strength and glorious beauty, splendidly dressed. They stood on either side of him and 27 scourged him, raining ceaseless blows upon him. He fell suddenly to the ground, overwhelmed by a great darkness, and his men snatched him up and put him on a litter. 28 This man, who so recently had entered the treasury with a great throng and his whole bodyguard, was now borne off by them quite helpless, publicly compelled to acknowledge the sovereignty of God.[a]

29 While he lay speechless, deprived by this divine act of 30 all hope of recovery, the Jews were praising the Lord for the miracle he had performed in his own house. The temple, which a short time before was full of alarm and confusion, now overflowed with joy and festivity, because the Lord Almighty had appeared.

[a] was now... of God: *so some witnesses; others read* they, recognizing the sovereignty of God, now bore off quite helpless.

✳ 2 Maccabees gives a highly dramatic picture of Heliodorus' attempt to rob the treasury, the Jewish reaction, and the divine intervention.

14. *into the temple:* a Gentile might go only into the outer court of the Gentiles, as even Antiochus III had decreed (Josephus, *Antiquities* XII. 3. 4). To reach the treasury Heliodorus had to enter the inner court, and this would add to the general dismay.

15. *deposits* were *sacred*, and under the care, therefore, of *Heaven*. (This is an example of the avoidance of using the name of God.) There was perhaps also a general fear that Heliodorus might wish to remove the temple vessels, as Antiochus IV later did (1 Macc. 1: 21–4). The priests therefore appeared *in their vestments*, as they had done when Alexander arrived before Jerusalem (Josephus, *Antiquities* XI. 8. 5).

16. The high priest was above all responsible for the preservation of the temple's holiness.

19. *in sackcloth* (cp. Esther 4: 1), *their breasts bare* (for beating: cp. Luke 23: 48): the marks of mourning.

23 ff. 2 Maccabees is fond of the 'apparition' of a horseman with 'golden armour' (verse 26; cp. 5: 2), bridles (10: 29) or weapons (11: 8). For the vision of a horseman, symbolizing the victory of heaven over opposing powers, compare Zech. 1: 8 ff., Rev. 6: 2.

26. *two young men:* compare, e.g., Luke 24: 4; in Ezek. 9: 2 six men come to smite those who do not oppose the abominations committed in Jerusalem.

28. As the footnote shows, the Greek textual tradition is divided as to whether Heliodorus or his bearers acknowledged the *sovereignty of God*.

30. *because the Lord Almighty had appeared:* in Old Testament style, the distinction between the Lord and his messengers is not sharply drawn. Cp. Gen. 18: 1, 'The LORD appeared to Abraham... he looked up and saw three men standing in front of him.' ✳

HELIODORUS' RECOVERY AND WITHDRAWAL

31 Some of Heliodorus's companions hastily begged Onias
to pray to the Most High, and so to spare the life of their
32 master now lying at his very last gasp. The high priest,
fearing that the king might suspect that Heliodorus had
met with foul play at the hands of the Jews, brought a
33 sacrifice for the man's recovery. As the high priest was
making the expiation, the same young men, dressed as
before, again appeared to Heliodorus. They stood over
him and said: 'Be very grateful to Onias the high priest;
34 for his sake the Lord has spared your life. You have been
scourged by God; now tell all men of his mighty power.'
When they had said this, they vanished.

35 Heliodorus offered a sacrifice and made lavish vows to
the Lord who had spared his life; then, after taking friendly
36 leave of Onias, he led his troops back to the king. He bore
witness to everyone of the miracles of the supreme God
which he had seen with his own eyes.

37 When the king asked him what sort of man would be
suitable to send to Jerusalem another time, Heliodorus
38 replied: 'If you have an enemy or someone plotting
against your government, that is the place to send him;
you will receive him back soundly flogged, if he survives
at all, for beyond doubt there is a divine power surround-
39 ing the temple. He whose habitation is in heaven watches
over it himself and gives it his aid; those who approach
the place with evil intent he strikes and destroys.'

40 So runs the story of Heliodorus and the preservation of
the treasury.

✶ Heliodorus is saved by the intercession of the virtuous Onias, and returns to Seleucus.

31. Onias is asked to intercede for Heliodorus, just as Moses had been asked to intercede for Pharaoh (Exod. 8: 28-9) and Job for his friends (Job 42: 7-10).

32. *foul play:* as indeed Simon alleged (4: 1). Heliodorus' setback created an embarrassment for Onias' relations with Syria, which Simon exploits.

33. The high priest could make *expiation* 'for himself and for the people' (Lev. 16: 24) annually on the day of atonement, and a priest could make expiation by means of a sin-offering for 'a man of standing' or for a commoner for 'doing inadvertently what is forbidden in any commandment of the LORD' (Lev. 4: 22-35). But here it seems that the personal worth of Onias is thought of as a factor in the successful expiation (though his motives were hardly selfless, verse 32). The intercessor's quality could make a difference; Moses and Samuel were famous intercessors, though on one occasion 'Even if Moses and Samuel stood before me, I would not be moved to pity this people' (Jer. 15: 1).

35. Foreigners could pray to God in the Jerusalem temple (cp. 1 Kings 8: 41-3). *offered a sacrifice:* this seems unlikely, in view of the Jewish prohibition of Gentiles from the inner court, though Josephus (*Antiquities* XI. 8. 5) says that Alexander the Great sacrificed under the high priest's guidance, and 2 Macc. 13: 23 says that Antiochus V offered sacrifice.

36. *bore witness... supreme God:* a Gentile could worship the supreme, most high god, without becoming a Jew, as an inscription from Syria mentioning 'Zeus Supreme, Most High' shows. 'Most High' (Greek *hupsistos*, cp. verse 31) translated a title used from of old by Israel (cp. Gen. 14: 18, Ps. 9: 2).

37. Seleucus perhaps blamed the failure of the mission on the character of Heliodorus: he was not *suitable* for the task.

38. Heliodorus' answer may be intended as ironic, for it was Heliodorus who conspired against Seleucus and brought about his death. Heliodorus' remarks about the divine

protection of the temple certainly express the viewpoint of
the author of 2 Maccabees, and the theme reappears later
(9: 11–17; 14: 31–6; 15: 34). *

SIMON ACCUSES ONIAS

4 But the Simon mentioned earlier, the man who had made
allegations against his country about the money, slandered
Onias, alleging that he had attacked Heliodorus and had
2 been the author of these troubles. He had the effrontery
to accuse him of conspiracy against the government – this
benefactor of the holy city, this protector of his fellow-
3 Jews, this zealot for the laws. The enmity grew so great
that one of Simon's trusted followers even resorted to
4 murder. Onias, realizing that Simon's rivalry was dangerous and that Apollonius son of Menestheus, governor
of Coele-syria and Phoenicia, was encouraging his evil
5 ways, paid a visit to the king. He did not appear as an
accuser of his fellow-citizens, but as concerned for the
interests of all the Jews, both as a nation and as individuals.
6 For he saw that unless the king intervened there could not
possibly be peace in public affairs, nor could Simon be
stopped in his mad course.

* The scene of the political struggle between Simon and
Onias moves to Syria as each opponent seeks Syrian support.
Simon and his party have gained the advantage, and Onias is
on the defensive.

1. *mentioned earlier:* 3: 4–7. *alleging:* see 3: 32. Onias himself had thought it worthwhile to allay any Syrian suspicions
of foul play. Possibly behind the dramatic picture of three
angelic young men attacking Heliodorus there lies a violent

assault by ardent pre-Maccabaean defenders of the faith which Onias may have connived at or tacitly supported.

2. *conspiracy against the government:* probably Onias' alleged part in the Heliodorus episode, supported by Onias' known pro-Egyptian sympathies. Jason of Cyrene and his epitomist saw Onias in a different light: *benefactor* was normally used in Greek cities of citizens who made some notable contribution to the city's life or wealth. *protector:* perhaps in his defence of the temple. *zealot for the laws* may be meant to imply that Onias respected the Syrian government as well as the Jewish law.

3. Who was murdered and why we do not know, but clearly there was considerable political pressure against Onias in Jerusalem.

4. *Apollonius:* see the note on 3: 5. His support of Simon was a serious matter for Onias.

5. *paid a visit to the king:* probably a strategic error. It put him in a defensive position, left Jerusalem open to his rivals, and created a dangerous precedent. *did not appear as an accuser:* 2 Maccabees defends Onias against someone's criticism that he was accusing *his fellow-citizens* (he very likely was) by pointing to Onias' concern for the nation as a whole. *

JASON'S REFORMS

But when Seleucus was dead and had been succeeded 7 by Antiochus, known as Epiphanes, Jason, Onias's brother, obtained the high-priesthood by corrupt means. He 8 petitioned the king and promised him three hundred and sixty talents in silver coin immediately, and eighty talents from future revenue. In addition he undertook to pay 9 another hundred and fifty talents for the authority to institute a sports-stadium, to arrange for the education of young men there, and to enrol in Jerusalem a group to be

10 known as the 'Antiochenes'.[a] The king agreed, and, as soon as he had seized the high-priesthood, Jason made the Jews conform to the Greek way of life.

11 He set aside the royal privileges established for the Jews through the agency of John, the father of that Eupolemus who negotiated a treaty of friendship and alliance with the Romans. He abolished the lawful way of life and
12 introduced practices which were against the law. He lost no time in establishing a sports-stadium at the foot of the citadel itself, and he made the most outstanding of the
13 young men assume the Greek athlete's hat. So Hellenism reached a high point with the introduction of foreign customs through the boundless wickedness of the impious
14 Jason, no true high priest. As a result, the priests no longer had any enthusiasm for their duties at the altar, but despised the temple and neglected the sacrifices; and in defiance of the law they eagerly contributed to the expenses of the wrestling-school whenever the opening
15 gong called them. They placed no value on their hereditary dignities, but cared above everything for Hellenic
16 honours. Because of this, grievous misfortunes beset them, and the very men whose way of life they strove after, and tried so hard to imitate, turned out to be their vindictive
17 enemies. To act profanely against God's laws is no light matter, as will become clear in due time.

✶ Onias is replaced by Jason, a new constitution for Jerusalem is negotiated, and a new way of life introduced to Jerusalem. Compare 1 Macc. 1: 10–15.

7. Antiochus IV Epiphanes succeeded in 175 B.C. 'by dissimulation and intrigue in time of peace' (Dan. 11: 21).

[a] *Or* enrol the inhabitants of Jerusalem as citizens of Antioch.

Heliodorus had killed Seleucus, perhaps proclaiming the
infant son of Seleucus king. The real heir was the elder son
Demetrius, a hostage in Rome. Antiochus was Seleucus'
brother, and he seized the throne with the help of Eumenes of
Pergamum. Insecure, Antiochus had to get rid of Heliodorus,
his minister Andronicus (cp. 4: 38), and his nephew, the real
heir. The pro-Egyptian Hyrcanus committed suicide, and the
pro-Egyptian Onias was exchanged for Jason, presumably a
pro-Syrian hellenizer.

8. Antiochus would not see Jason's offer of increased tribute
(from 300 to 360 silver talents annually, with further payment
promised) as 'corrupt means' (verse 7); indeed, he may well
have demanded increased tribute. But the important new
feature here is that in these events the high priest has become
dependent for his security and office on the Syrian king, and
with the replacement of Jason by Menelaus soon after (4:
23–5) even heredity ceases to be a necessary qualification for
office. Before the exile the high priest had been the officer of
the Davidic king; now, after a period of increased status
within Judaism, the high priest was the officer of a foreign
king.

9. *sports-stadium:* see note on 1 Macc. 1: 14. *to enrol in
Jerusalem...the 'Antiochenes':* the precise translation of this
phrase is debated. It seems to mean either to draw up a list
of hellenizers and so form a group or corporation of 'Antiochenes' with certain privileges in Jerusalem, or (as in the N.E.B.
footnote) to recognize the people of Jerusalem as Antiochenes,
i.e. as citizens of the new Greek city 'Antioch-at-Jerusalem'.
Both N.E.B. translations perhaps contain part of the truth;
only some of the people of Jerusalem became citizens of the
new Greek city (on the basis of 4: 40 some have argued for a
citizen list of something over 3,000 men – women would not
be citizens), but on the other hand the old Jerusalem as a
whole became the new city of 'Antioch-at-Jerusalem' (though
some have argued that this new city was restricted to the
citadel and its Syrian garrison and Jewish supporters). For this

new status of Jerusalem, and for the stadium which educated the citizens, Jason paid a large sum, because this change was expected to bring financial rewards to the city.

11. This placing of Jerusalem on a par with other Greek cities in the Syrian empire automatically *set aside the royal privileges* granted by Antiochus III, by which the Jews 'could have a form of government in accordance with the laws of their country' (Josephus, *Antiquities* XII. 3. 3). *Eupolemus:* see the notes on 1 Macc. 8: 17 and 2 Macc. 2: 1. *abolished:* in the sense that the Mosaic law was no longer the law of the nation. But no Jew, as yet, was punished for observing Jewish practices; even Jewish envoys to a state occasion at Tyre were able to put money sent for pagan sacrifices to other purposes (4: 18–20). Rather, Greek practices were allowed where they had not been before, and presumably the law code in operation, like the constitution, became hellenistic in form.

12. The *citadel* (Greek *acropolis*) was probably the fort on the north-west corner of the temple area, the later Roman Antonia to which Paul was taken (Acts 22). The stadium just below it was thus most convenient for the priests (verse 14). *assume the Greek athlete's hat:* a phrase perhaps meaning simply 'to enter upon the training of the sports-stadium'. If it is to be taken literally, the Jewish youths had to wear a brimmed hat (the *petasos*) associated with the Greek god Hermes; traditional Jewish head-dress was either something like the Arab's *keffiyeh* (a cotton square folded and wound round the head) or like a turban or stocking cap. But such training would be expensive and restricted to the wealthier classes, as would also be the citizenship.

13. *Hellenism:* a way of life contrasted by 2 Maccabees with *Judaism* (2: 21). The word was a new one, perhaps invented by Jason or his epitomist, meaning 'imitation of the Greeks' (whose common name was 'Hellenes'). *wickedness of the impious Jason:* contrasted with Onias, who 'was a pious man and hated wickedness' (3: 1). *no true high priest:* because he was a usurper and a hellenizer.

14–15. Hellenism corrupted even the priests and under-mined the traditional importance of its *hereditary* nature. Menelaus, Jason's successor in office, was not of the high-priestly family. This hellenizing of the priesthood and temple may be one reason for the rise of the Qumran community and its sharp separation from Jerusalem (see p. 12).

16. Compare the idea that 'the instruments of a man's sin are the instruments of his punishment' (Wisd. of Sol. 11: 16). *the very men*: perhaps Jason and Menelaus (cp. 4: 26; 5: 6–10; 13: 3–8), Callisthenes (8: 33) and Nicanor (15: 32) are in mind, or perhaps the reference is a general one to the hellenistic world. Such comments on the meaning of events are a feature of 2 Maccabees: cp. 5: 17–20; 6: 12–17. ✳

THE NEW JERUSALEM IN THE SYRIAN EMPIRE

When the quinquennial games were being held at Tyre 18 in the presence of the king, the blackguard Jason sent, as 19 envoys to represent Jerusalem, Antiochenes carrying three hundred drachmas in cash for the sacrifice to Hercules. Even the bearers thought it improper that this money should be used for a sacrifice, and considered that it should be spent otherwise. So, thanks to the bearers, the money 20 designed by the sender for the sacrifice to Hercules went to fit out the triremes.

When Apollonius son of Menestheus was sent to Egypt 21 for the enthronement of King Philometor, Antiochus learnt that Philometor was now hostile to his state, and became anxious for his own security. So he went to Joppa, and then on to Jerusalem, where he was lavishly 22 welcomed by Jason and the city and received with torch-light and ovations. After this, he quartered his army in Phoenicia.

✻ Two events are now recounted which illustrate Jerusalem's new status in Antiochus' empire.

18–19. The *quinquennial games*, held each fifth year, were an important occasion, gathering athletes and *envoys* from a wide area, like the Olympic games themselves on which these were modelled. At Tyre, they were held in honour of the city's god, Melkart, whose Greek equivalent was taken to be *Hercules*. On the opening day the competitors would offer *sacrifice* to him. The new city of Antioch-at-Jerusalem would send its *envoys* with some pride; their presence would be a sign of Jerusalem's acceptance within the community of important cities of the empire.

Even the hellenizing Jews who represented Jerusalem were uneasy at sacrificing to Hercules. Political reform at Jerusalem, it seems, did not compel any Jew to abandon his traditional scruples.

20. If the *triremes* were part of Antiochus' fleet, Antiochus would hardly object to the arrangement.

21. *Apollonius:* cp. verse 4, and 3: 5. *the enthronement of King Philometor*, aged fourteen, took place in 172 B.C. His ministers were planning to recover Palestine for Egypt (see I Macc. I: 16–19).

22. Antiochus, 'anxious for his own security' (verse 21), visited the sea-port of Joppa and the new city of Jerusalem, both front-line defences against Egypt, to assure himself of their loyalty and preparedness. With Onias in exile, and Hyrcanus dead, the pro-Egyptian party was leaderless, and Jerusalem gave Antiochus an official welcome which, though not necessarily representative of popular feeling, may have reassured him. He brought his army to the coast of *Phoenicia* in preparation for action. (For the campaign see I Macc. I: 16–19.) ✻

MENELAUS SUPPLANTS JASON

Three years later, Jason sent Menelaus, brother of the 23
Simon mentioned above, to convey money to the king
and to carry out his directions about urgent business. But 24
Menelaus established his position with the king by acting
as if he were a person of great authority, outbid Jason by
three hundred talents in silver, and so diverted the high-
priesthood to himself. He arrived back with the royal 25
mandate, but with nothing else to make him worthy of
the high-priesthood; he still had the temper of a cruel
tyrant and the fury of a savage beast. Jason, who had 26
supplanted his own brother, was now supplanted in his
turn and forced to flee to Ammonite territory. As for 27
Menelaus, he continued to hold the high-priesthood but
without ever paying any of the money he had promised
the king, although it was demanded by Sostratus, the
commander of the citadel, who was responsible for collect- 28
ing the revenues. In consequence they were both summoned by the king. As their deputies, Menelaus left his 29
brother Lysimachus, and Sostratus left Crates, the commander of the Cypriots.

* As Simon had caused Onias' downfall, so now Simon's
brother caused that of Onias' brother. Jason had perhaps been
a moderate politician, the tool of the hellenizing party, and
was now to be replaced by a man with fewer scruples and no
hereditary right to the office. Menelaus, however, had difficulty
in keeping his promises to the king.

23. *Three years later* probably reckons from the beginning
of the reign of Antiochus or Jason's high-priesthood. The date
is thus the end of 172 or the beginning of 171 B.C.

24. Menelaus succeeded by his pose of *authority* and over-ambitious promise of nearly double tribute (see verse 8).

25. In Jewish eyes, not even *the royal mandate* could make a man with Menelaus' moral and hereditary failings *worthy of the high-priesthood*. The Greek Jew who wrote 2 Maccabees describes Menelaus with the harshest epithets a Greek could use – *tyrant* and *savage beast*. The Greeks hated tyranny and barbarism, and prized freedom and civilized culture.

26. *to Ammonite territory:* perhaps to the region of Hyrcanus' estates, or to the Nabataeans (see 5: 7–8) to await an opportunity to return. He was, according to Josephus (*Antiquities* XII. 5. 1), more popular than Menelaus.

28. *citadel:* cp. verse 12.

29. *Lysimachus:* see verses 39–42 below. *commander of the Cypriots* (i.e. mercenary troops): cp. Nicanor, 'chief of the Cypriot mercenaries' (12: 2) and Apollonius, 'general of the Mysian mercenaries' (5: 24). *

THE MURDER OF ONIAS

30 It was at this point that the inhabitants of Tarsus and Mallus revolted, because their cities had been handed over
31 as a gift to the king's concubine, Antiochis. The king hastened off to restore order, leaving as regent Androni-
32 cus, one of his ministers. Menelaus, thinking he had obtained a favourable opportunity, made a present to Andronicus of some of the gold plate belonging to the temple which he had appropriated. He had already sold
33 some of it to Tyre and to the neighbouring cities. When Onias heard this on good authority, he withdrew to sanctuary at Daphne near Antioch and denounced him.
34 As a result, Menelaus approached Andronicus privately and urged him to kill Onias. The regent went to Onias bent on treachery; he greeted him, gave him assurances

on oath, and persuaded him, though still suspicious, to leave the sanctuary. Then at once, with no respect for justice, he made away with him.

His murder filled not only Jews, but many from other 35 nations as well, with alarm and anger. So when the king 36 returned from Cilicia, the Jews of Antioch sent him a petition about the senseless killing of Onias, the Gentiles sharing in their detestation of the crime. Antiochus was 37 deeply grieved, and was moved to pity and tears as he thought of the prudence and disciplined habits of the dead man. In a burning fury, he immediately stripped Andro- 38 nicus of the purple, tore off his clothes, led him round the whole city to that very place where he had committed sacrilege against Onias, and there disposed of the mur- derer. Thus the Lord repaid him with the retribution he deserved.

* Onias' denunciation of the selling of the temple plate by Menelaus leads to his assassination by the king's regent, who supported Menelaus. This removes the legitimate high-priest; Jason is in exile, and Menelaus is in disfavour. Meanwhile, a temporary deputy officiates in Jerusalem.

30. *Tarsus* (Paul's city) and *Mallus* were in Cilicia, across Syria's border to the north-west. Cities did not always enjoy being *handed over as a gift* to another master or mistress; later Alexander Balas gave Jonathan Accaron (1 Macc. 10: 89), and Mark Antony gave Cleopatra Jericho. The Syrian kings were sensitive to the loyalty of Cilicia, which was often ready to support a rival to the Syrian throne (cp. 1 Macc. 11: 14, and the note on 1 Macc. 10: 67).

31. *as regent:* similarly, Antiochus IV, away on campaign, left Lysias in charge (1 Macc. 3: 32). Andronicus had been the murderer (on behalf of Antiochus) of the young son of Seleucus IV in 175 B.C.

32. Menelaus seeks the support of Andronicus by bribery, at the same time implicating him in his own acts of sacrilegious embezzlement.

33. *sanctuary at Daphne near Antioch:* Daphne had a famous shrine of Apollo, but there is some evidence that a Jewish synagogue might have existed there (for Jews at Antioch, see verse 36), which would be a more likely place for the high priest to seek sanctuary. *denounced him:* Onias was doubtless shocked by the sacrilege, but used the story to discredit both Andronicus and Menelaus in the king's eyes in the hope of winning his own return to Jerusalem.

36. *Jews at Antioch:* the Jewish colony there seems to have grown steadily from the early days of the Seleucid monarchy. Those who settled there for economic reasons were added to by Jewish captives settled there. The strong early Christian community at Antioch was probably founded on the Jewish community.

37. *deeply grieved:* the king's regret may have owed something to the thought that Onias was a useful card to hold in reserve against a too independent Menelaus. *prudence and disciplined habits:* virtues especially to the Greek mind.

38. Antiochus took the opportunity of removing an unscrupulous man who was a potential threat to his own security. Andronicus is dismissed with the sentiment that his punishment fitted his crime (see verse 16 and the note there). *purple:* worn by the King's Friends (cp. 1 Macc. 10: 20). *

UNPOPULARITY OF LYSIMACHUS AND MENELAUS

39 Lysimachus committed many acts of sacrilegious plunder in Jerusalem with the connivance of Menelaus. When the news of them became public and the people heard that much of the gold plate had been disposed of, they

40 banded together against Lysimachus. Since the crowds were seething with rage and getting out of hand, Lysima-

chus armed three thousand men and began to launch a
vicious attack, led by a certain Auranus, a man advanced
in years and no less in folly. Realizing that the attack came 41
from Lysimachus, some of the crowd seized stones and
others blocks of wood, while others again took handfuls
of the ashes that were lying round, and there was complete confusion as they all hurled them at Lysimachus and
his men. As a result, they wounded many, killed some, 42
and routed them all; the sacrilegious man himself they
dispatched near the treasury.

An action was brought against Menelaus in connection 43
with this incident. When the king came to Tyre, the 44
three men sent by the Jewish senate pleaded the case
before him. Menelaus's cause was as good as lost; but he 45
promised a large sum of money to Ptolemaeus son of
Dorymenes to win over the king. So Ptolemaeus led the 46
king aside into a colonnade, as if to take the air, and persuaded him to change his mind. The king acquitted Mene- 47
laus, the cause of all the mischief, dismissed the charges
brought against him, and condemned his unfortunate
accusers to death, men who would have been discharged
as entirely innocent had they appeared even before Scythians. Without more ado those who had pleaded for 48
their city, their people, and their sacred vessels, suffered
the unjust penalty. At this, even some of the Tyrians 49
showed their detestation of the crime by providing a
splendid funeral for the victims. Menelaus, thanks to the 50
greed of those in power, remained in office. He went from
bad to worse, this arch-plotter against his own fellow-
citizens.

✳ Lysimachus continued Menelaus' policy of plundering the temple plate (cp. verse 32), presumably to pay the promised tribute to Antiochus. The real culprits were Menelaus (cp. verses 39, 43) and Antiochus himself (cp. 5: 15-21, 1 Macc. 1: 21-4). Such disposal of the national treasures enraged the Jews and led to a public riot and an official protest to Antioch.

39. *connivance*: Lysimachus acts for the absent Menelaus, who probably made the arrangements for the secret disposal of the plate.

40. *some three thousand men*: they were *armed* for the occasion, and were perhaps drawn from the young men trained in the sports-stadium. The number may give some indication of the size of the citizen body. The mass of the people would see the plunder of the plate as the action of the king, the high priest and the small but privileged citizen body. *Auranus* is unknown; the name is possibly a hellenized form of the Hebrew name Avaran (cp. 1 Macc. 2: 5).

41. *ashes*: from the sacrificial fires in the priests' court of the temple. Lysimachus' men were trapped in a relatively small space and had to cut their way out.

42. The *treasury* was in the women's court, part of the central complex to which a Gentile was not admitted.

43. Such an *incident* could hardly pass without complaint.

44. *senate*: see the note on 1 Macc. 12: 6. Though the senate probably favoured a hellenizing policy, it was prepared to sacrifice the unpopular Menelaus for the sake of the city's peace and prosperity. Their plea (verse 48) was for 'their city, their people, and their sacred vessels'; they probably accused Menelaus of embezzlement, sacrilege, and otherwise acting beyond his legal powers. They hoped that the king would take the opportunity of letting Menelaus suffer as a scapegoat for his own mistaken policy.

45-6. *Ptolemaeus* (cp. 8: 8; 1 Macc. 3: 38), successor to Apollonius as governor of Coele-syria and Phoenicia, perhaps persuaded Antiochus by pointing out that any alternative to Menelaus might be pro-Egyptian, by suggesting that the attack on Menelaus was really an attack on the king's policy, and by pointing to the king's need for money (cp. 'the greed of those in power', verse 50).

47. The senate's deputies were executed, presumably on the technical grounds of having brought false accusations. Menelaus and Ptolemaeus probably urged that a dissident Jerusalem senate was a security risk to the king. The *Scythians* were notorious barbarians (cp. Col. 3: 11).

49. The *Tyrians* had some independence as a city in the Syrian empire. 2 Maccabees contrasts the behaviour of barbarian and Greek alike with that of Antiochus and Menelaus. *

JASON TRIES TO REGAIN CONTROL

About this time Antiochus undertook his second in- 5 vasion of Egypt. Apparitions were seen in the sky all over 2 Jerusalem for nearly forty days: galloping horsemen in golden armour, companies of spearmen standing to arms, swords unsheathed, cavalry divisions in battle order. 3 Charges and countercharges were made on each side, shields were shaken, spears massed and javelins hurled; breast-plates and golden ornaments of every kind shone brightly. All men prayed that this apparition might portend good. 4

Upon a false report of Antiochus's death, Jason collected 5 no less than a thousand men and made a surprise attack on Jerusalem. The defenders on the wall were driven back and the city was finally taken; Menelaus took refuge in the citadel, and Jason continued to massacre his fellow- 6 citizens without pity. He little knew that success against one's own kindred is the greatest of failures, and he imagined that the trophies he raised marked the defeat of enemies, not of fellow-countrymen. He did not, however, 7 gain control of the government; he gained only dishonour

as the result of his plot, and returned again as a fugitive to
8 Ammonite territory. His career came to a miserable end;
for, after being imprisoned by Aretas the ruler of the
Arabs, he fled from city to city, hunted by all, hated as a
rebel against the laws, and detested as the executioner of
his country and his fellow-citizens, and finally was driven
9 to take refuge in Egypt. In the end the man who had
banished so many from their native land himself died in
exile after setting sail for Sparta, where he had hoped to
obtain shelter because of the Spartans' kinship with the
10 Jews. He who had cast out many to lie unburied was himself unmourned; he had no funeral of any kind, no resting-
place in the grave of his ancestors.

11   When news of this reached the king, it became clear to
him that Judaea was in a state of rebellion. So he set out
from Egypt in savage mood, took Jerusalem by storm,
12 and ordered his troops to cut down without mercy everyone they met and to slaughter those who took refuge in
13 the houses. Young and old were murdered, women and
14 children massacred, girls and infants butchered. At the
end of three days their losses had amounted to eighty
thousand: forty thousand killed in action, and as many
sold into slavery.

* With Menelaus unpopular in Jerusalem, and Antiochus
involved in Egypt, Jason, perhaps with some help from
Ammonite or Nabataean territory, made an attempt to regain
control in Jerusalem. His failure seems to have been due to his
treatment of the civilian population. 1 Maccabees does not
mention the episode.

    1. *About this time...second invasion of Egypt:* Dan. 11: 25–30
describes two Egyptian campaigns. The first, omitted by

2 Maccabees but described in 1 Macc. 1: 16–19, took place in 169 B.C., the second in 168 B.C.

2. *apparitions*: see the note on 3: 23 ff. The period of *nearly forty days* heightens the expectancy that something tremendous is afoot by reminding the reader of the Old Testament divine appearances on Sinai and Horeb (Exod. 24: 18; 1 Kings 19: 8–18). The reader would also be reminded of the great battle expected at the end between God and the forces of evil (see Ezek. 38–9).

4. The meaning of this apparition was uncertain, apparently, but the author of 2 Maccabees is certainly indicating that this moment marked the arrival of crisis for Jerusalem.

5. *city...taken*: according to 1: 8, Jason's men 'set the porch of the temple on fire and shed innocent blood'.

6. *citadel*: see the note on 4: 12. Notice the author's typical moralizing comment on Jason's failure.

7. This verse may suggest that Jason was driven out of Jerusalem before Antiochus took reprisals on the city and reinstated Menelaus. Some scholars think that for a time the people gained control, rejecting both Jason and Menelaus; hence the king rightly accused them of 'rebellion' (verse 11).

8. *Aretas*: Harith I, king of the Nabataeans. See the note on 1 Macc. 5: 25. *imprisoned*: the leader of a failed *coup d'état* is an embarrassment to a neighbouring power: before failure he can be something of an asset. *refuge in Egypt*: like others before him; cp. 1 Kings 11: 14–25.

9. *Sparta* had long connections with Egypt, but her *kinship with the Jews* was a diplomatic fiction (see the commentary on 1 Macc. 12: 1–23).

10. This is another example of the author's liking for appropriate punishments (cp. 4: 16, 38).

11. The removal of Menelaus by Jason, or the removal of both by the people, meant *rebellion* to Antiochus. Ejected from Egypt by Rome (cp. Dan. 11: 30), he had no wish to lose Judaea.

12–14. The picture is exaggerated; such a devastation would hardly leave much work for Apollonius (verses 24–6). The author is portraying the extreme villainy of Antiochus and the extreme loyalty of the Jews. ✻

FURTHER PUNITIVE MEASURES OF ANTIOCHUS

15 Not satisfied with this, the king had the audacity to enter the holiest temple on earth, guided by Menelaus, who had turned traitor both to his religion and his 16 country. He laid impious hands on the sacred vessels; his desecrating hands swept together the votive offerings which other kings had set up to enhance the splendour and fame of the shrine.

17 The pride of Antiochus passed all bounds. He did not understand that the sins of the people of Jerusalem had angered the Lord for a short time, and that this was why 18 he left the temple to its fate. If they had not already been guilty of many sinful acts, Antiochus would have fared like Heliodorus who was sent by King Seleucus to inspect the treasury; like him he would have been scourged and his 19 insolent plan foiled at once. But the Lord did not choose the nation for the sake of the sanctuary; he chose the 20 sanctuary for the sake of the nation. Therefore even the sanctuary itself first had its part in the misfortunes that overtook the nation, and afterwards shared its good fortune. It was abandoned when the Lord Almighty was angry, but restored again in all its spendour when he became reconciled.

21 Antiochus, then, carried off eighteen hundred talents from the temple and hastened back to Antioch. In his arrogance he was rash enough to think that he could make

ships sail on dry land and men walk over the sea. He left 22
commissioners behind to oppress the Hebrews: in Jerusalem Philip, by race a Phrygian, by disposition more barbarous than his master, and in Mount Gerizim, Androni- 23
cus, to say nothing of Menelaus, who was more brutally
overbearing to the citizens than the others. Such was the
king's hostility towards the Jews that he sent Apollonius, 24
the general of the Mysian mercenaries, with an army of
twenty-two thousand men, and ordered him to kill all
the adult males and to sell the women and boys into
slavery. When Apollonius arrived at Jerusalem, he posed 25
as a man of peace; he waited until the holy sabbath day
and, finding the Jews abstaining from work, he ordered a
review of his troops. All who came out to see the parade 26
he put to the sword; then, charging into the city with his
soldiers, he killed a great number of people.

* 2 Maccabees recounts the king's pillage of the temple,
passing his own comment on the meaning of this act, and then
Antiochus' imposition of direct rule by his own commissioners
and army on Jerusalem.

15–16. Verses 15, 16, and 21 pose a problem of dating, for
1 Macc. 1: 20–4 put the king's entry into the temple in 169
B.C. after the first Egyptian campaign. Dan. 11: 28 is not speci-
fic about what happened in 169 B.C. but the desecration of the
sanctuary in Dan. 11: 31 which followed the second Egyptian
campaign might be the event of 1 Macc. 1: 54 (cp. 2 Macc.
6: 1 ff.) rather than that of 2 Macc. 5: 15. It is likely that the
temple robbery of verses 15, 16, 21 really belongs, as 1 Maccabees says, to the end of the first Egyptian campaign in 169
B.C., which is not described in 2 Maccabees. If so, and if the
action brought against Menelaus (4: 43–50) belongs between
the two Egyptian campaigns (cp. 'about this time', verse 1),

the king's acquittal of Menelaus and execution of the accusers
has all the more point.

audacity (cp. 1 Macc. 1: 21, 'arrogance'): Antiochus, however, would probably claim the right to enter the temples
of cities in his empire. From a Jewish viewpoint his action is
impious and *desecrating*. *votive offerings:* cp. 3: 2.

17. The author embarks on an extended explanation of this
apparent failure of God to protect his temple and people.
Antiochus was proud; but the blame lay not with him but
with *the sins of the people of Jerusalem*, i.e. the adoption of
Hellenism. Jerusalem needed punishing.

19–20. God could use *the sanctuary* as a means of disciplining
the nation, and the fate of *the sanctuary* was a guide to the
pleasure or displeasure of God. Compare 6: 12: 'such penalties were inflicted for the discipline of our race and not for its
destruction.'

21. This verse probably belongs with 15–16. Antiochus'
pride (cp. verse 17) is described with much hyperbole. Dan.
11: 36 says of him that 'The king will do what he chooses;
he will exalt and magnify himself above every god.' Coins of
Antiochus from some mints did bear the inscription 'God
manifest' (Greek *theou epiphanous*), but the coins do not, as
was once thought, portray Antiochus impersonating Zeus,
and that Antiochus thought of himself as a living god is now
considered unlikely.

22. *commissioners:* these were the king's personal representatives, also found elsewhere in the empire, connecting the
independent cities with the central government. At Jerusalem,
Philip replaced, in effect, Menelaus, though as high priest
Menelaus still had much power. *a Phrygian:* the Phrygians
lived in west central Asia Minor, and Antiochus III (according
to a letter of his recorded by Josephus, *Antiquities* XII. 3. 4)
had settled Jews in Phrygia, which was in a state of revolt,
to act as 'loyal guardians of our interests'. The situation is now
reversed. *more barbarous than his master:* as a cultured hellenist,
Antiochus would not have liked this comment.

23. *Mount Gerizim:* the Samaritan religious centre near Shechem (cp. 6: 2, John 4: 20).

24. The barbarous and overbearing behaviour of Philip and Menelaus may have led to some further violent reaction or threat of violence; otherwise the king would have had no cause to send Apollonius on a punitive expedition (though he might have sent him as support for Philip). For this expedition see 1 Macc. 1: 29–32 and the commentary there.

25. *waited until the holy sabbath day:* Apollonius appears to take the opportunity of an easy massacre, and is painted even blacker than in 1 Maccabees. This event was followed by the turning of the city of David into a Syrian garrison (see 1 Macc. 1: 33–6). *

THE SUPPRESSION OF JUDAISM

But Judas, also called Maccabaeus, with about nine others, 27 escaped into the desert, where he and his companions lived in the mountains, fending for themselves like the wild animals. They remained there living on what vegetation they found, so as to have no share in the pollution.

Shortly afterwards King Antiochus sent an elderly 6 Athenian to force the Jews to abandon their ancestral customs and no longer regulate their lives according to the laws of God. He was also commissioned to pollute 2 the temple at Jerusalem and dedicate it to Olympian Zeus, and to dedicate the sanctuary on Mount Gerizim to Zeus God of Hospitality, following the practice of the local inhabitants.

This evil hit them hard and was a severe trial. The 3, 4 Gentiles filled the temple with licentious revelry: they took their pleasure with prostitutes and had intercourse with women in the sacred precincts. They also brought forbidden things inside, and heaped the altar with impure 5

6 offerings prohibited by the law. It was forbidden either
to observe the sabbath or to keep the traditional festivals,
7 or to admit to being a Jew at all. On the monthly celebration of the king's birthday, the Jews were driven by brute
force to eat the entrails of the sacrificial victims; and on
the feast of Dionysus they were forced to wear ivy-
8 wreaths and join the procession in his honour. At the
instigation of the inhabitants of Ptolemais*a* an order was
published in the neighbouring Greek cities to the effect
that they should adopt the same policy of compelling
9 the Jews to eat the entrails and should kill those who
refused to change over to Greek ways.

10   Their miserable fate was there for all to see. For instance,
two women were brought to trial for having had their
children circumcised. They were paraded through the
city, with their babies hanging at their breasts, and then
11 flung down from the fortifications. Other Jews had
assembled in caves near Jerusalem to keep the sabbath in
secret; they were denounced to Philip and were burnt
alive, since they scrupled to defend themselves out of
regard for the holiness of the day.

* N.E.B. begins this section with the flight of Judas to the
desert; then comes the climax of the policy of hellenization –
the rededication of the temple to Olympian Zeus and the
proscription of traditional Jewish behaviour. The reader should
compare this passage carefully with 1 Macc. 1: 41–64.

27. Compare 1 Macc. 2; 2 Maccabees sets the flight of Judas
(nothing is said of his father or of the incident at Modin)
before, not after, the 'decree' of Antiochus. The date is probably early in 167 B.C. The *desert* was a place of *wild animals* –

[a] *Some witnesses read* At the instigation of Ptolemaeus...

only recently a large panther was shot on the west shore of the Dead Sea – but most of them were by Jewish law regarded as unclean (cp. Lev. 11). So the refugees lived on *vegetation*, refusing to *share* the hellenizers' *pollution* by 'eating any unclean food' (1 Macc. 1: 62).

6: 1. *Shortly afterwards:* autumn 167 B.C. *elderly Athenian:* 'Geron the Athenian', 'an elder of Athens', 'Athenaios the elder' have all been suggested as alternative translations. The man is perhaps one of the 'superintendents' sent to enforce the decree (1 Macc. 1: 51). *to force the Jews:* as punishment for the 'rebellion' (5: 11) the king is withdrawing the privilege granted to the Jews by Antiochus III of being allowed to *regulate their lives according to the laws of God* (see Josephus, *Antiquities* XII. 3. 3). From now on the authorized form of religion was the hellenized Judaism; from now on a Jew could be punished for obeying his traditional scruples (see the note on 4: 11).

2. See the note on 1 Macc. 1: 54. *Olympian Zeus* was the head of the Greek pantheon; he dwelt on Mount Olympus in north Greece, whose summit was believed to reach into heaven. *God of Hospitality* was one of many ancient attributes of Zeus. *following the practice:* possibly, by a slight change in the Greek, 'following the request'. Josephus (*Antiquities* XII. 5. 5) says that the Samaritans, seeing the Jews' misfortunes, asked Antiochus for permission to give the name of *Zeus Hellenios* to their temple. But both 2 Maccabees and Josephus may reflect Jewish bias against the Samaritans at this point.

3–4. The introduction of typically Syrian (verses 3 f.) or Greek (verses 7 f.) religious behaviour was one thing; their compelled adoption, and the persecution of traditionally Jewish religious practice another (verse 6). Temple prostitution had featured in Israelite religion before, incurring the anger of the prophets (e.g. Hos. 4: 14); by it the worshippers actively participated in the sacred marriage of the god and his bride, thus helping to ensure the year's fertility.

5. *forbidden things...impure offerings:* there was a general

failure to observe the ceremonial laws of wholeness and clean-ness in objects brought into the temple, whether for sacrifice or not. Surprisingly, 2 Maccabees does not mention 'the abomi-nation of desolation' (1 Macc. 1: 54).

6. *sabbath . . . traditional festivals:* see 1 Macc. 1: 45.

7. Jewish sufferings on *the monthly celebration of the king's birthday* (for which compare the monthly inquisition of 1 Macc. 1: 58) are apparently illustrated by 2 Macc. 7, which calls itself the 'account of the eating of the entrails and the monstrous outrages that accompanied it' (7: 42). *the entrails* would by Jewish law be burnt, either on the altar (Lev. 1: 9) or at some other place (Lev. 4: 11–12); the fat around them belonged to God and could not be eaten (Lev. 3: 3–4, 8–10). *Dionysus* (cp. 14: 33) was the Greek god of the vine, perhaps originally of all vegetation; his worshippers went in procession carrying wands (*thursoi*) and *ivy-wreaths* (*kissoi*). 2 Macc. 10: 7 says that at the new feast of the purification of the sanctuary the Jews 'carried garlanded wands' (*thursoi*) 'and branches' in a feast like that of Tabernacles, and the similarities and connections between these feasts have been much discussed.

8. The city of *Ptolemais* (particularly hostile to the Jews, cp. 1 Macc. 5: 15), or, if we follow the reading given by the N.E.B. footnote, Ptolemaeus, governor of Coele-syria and Phoenicia (cp. 4: 45; 1 Macc. 3: 38), ensured that Jews living in Greek cities also had to celebrate the king's birthday or face the consequences.

10. Compare 1 Macc. 1: 60–1.

11. Compare 1 Macc. 2: 31–8; 2 Maccabees' story seems to tell of Jerusalem Jews under the jurisdiction of Philip (cp. 5: 22) hiding locally to keep the sabbath; 1 Maccabees' story tells of rebels in the desert, complete with families and cattle, attacked on the sabbath, perhaps for tactical advantage. Per-haps Heb. 11: 38, in its list of men of faith, has these passages in mind: 'They were refugees in deserts and on the hills, hiding in caves and holes in the ground.' *

A THEOLOGICAL DIGRESSION

Now I beg my readers not to be disheartened by these 12
calamities, but to reflect that such penalties were inflicted
for the discipline of our race and not for its destruction.
It is a sign of great kindness that acts of impiety should not 13
be let alone for long but meet their due recompense at
once. The Lord did not see fit to deal with us as he does 14
with the other nations: with them he patiently holds his
hand until they have reached the full extent of their sins,
but upon us he inflicted retribution before our sins 15
reached their height. So he never withdraws his mercy 16
from us; though he disciplines his people by calamity, he
never deserts them. Let it be enough for me to have 17
recalled this truth; after this short digression, I must continue with my story.

---

* In 5: 17–20 the author demonstrated the Lord's anger with
the sins of the people, as shown by the fate of the temple. Now,
the author points to the purpose of the Lord's anger – 'discipline', not 'destruction' (verse 12).

14–15. Other nations are, so to speak, given enough rope
to hang themselves; Israel is punished *before our sins reached
their height* and incur the death-penalty. We are reminded of
Prov. 3: 12,

> for those whom he loves the LORD reproves,
> and he punishes a favourite son.

16. *disciplines his people:* 2 Maccabees sees the people or
nation (5: 20) as a whole as guilty, while 1 Maccabees emphasizes the role of the 'renegades'. 2 Maccabees blames the
Gentiles and even Antiochus in person as the instruments of
Jewish suffering (together with the traitor Menelaus, cp. 5: 15,
23) to a greater extent than 1 Maccabees. *

THE EXAMPLE OF ELEAZAR

18 There was Eleazar, one of the leading teachers of the law, a man of great age and distinguished bearing. He
19 was being forced to open his mouth and eat pork, but preferring an honourable death to an unclean life, he spat
20 it out and voluntarily submitted to the flogging, as indeed men should act who have the courage to refuse to eat
21 forbidden food even for love of life. For old acquaintance' sake, the officials in charge of this sacrilegious feast had a word with Eleazar in private; they urged him to bring meat which he was permitted to eat and had himself prepared, and only pretend to be eating the sacrificial
22 meat as the king had ordered. In that way he would escape death and take advantage of the clemency which
23 their long-standing friendship merited. But Eleazar made an honourable decision, one worthy of his years and the authority of old age, worthy of the grey hairs he had attained to and wore with such distinction, worthy of his perfect conduct from childhood up, but above all, worthy of the holy and God-given law. So he answered at once:
24 'Send me quickly to my grave. If I went through with this pretence at my time of life, many of the young might believe that at the age of ninety Eleazar had turned apos-
25 tate. If I practised deceit for the sake of a brief moment of life, I should lead them astray and bring stain and pollu-
26 tion on my old age. I might for the present avoid man's punishment, but, alive or dead, I shall never escape from
27 the hand of the Almighty. So if I now die bravely, I shall
28 show that I have deserved my long life and leave the young a fine example, to teach them how to die a

good death, gladly and nobly, for our revered and holy laws.'

When he had finished speaking, he was immediately dragged away to be flogged. Those who a little while be- 29 fore had shown him friendship now became his enemies because, in their view, what he had said was madness. When he was almost dead from the blows, Eleazar sighed 30 deeply and said: 'To the Lord belongs all holy knowledge. He knows what terrible agony I endure in my body from this flogging, though I could have escaped death; yet he knows also that in my soul I suffer gladly, because I stand in awe of him.'

So he died; and by his death he left a heroic example 31 and a glorious memory, not only for the young but also for the great body of the nation.

✱ 2 Maccabees now tells the story of the martyrdom of Eleazar, emphasizing his devotion to the law and refusal to turn apostate. The story was perhaps told originally to encourage Jews suffering persecution, as were also the rather more legendary stories of Shadrach, Meshach and Abed-nego (Dan. 3) and of Daniel in the lions' pit (Dan. 6).

18. *Eleazar* is otherwise unknown; cp. Eleazar Avaran, son of Mattathias (1 Macc. 2: 5; 6: 43). Another form of the name, which means 'God has helped', is Lazarus. *leading teachers of the law*: perhaps the Hasidaeans (see the note on 1 Macc. 2: 42). *pork*: the pig was regarded as unclean (Lev. 11: 7). Just after the exile 'eating swine's flesh' was condemned along with such irregular practices as 'offering sacrifice in gardens, burning incense on brick altars, crouching among graves, keeping vigil all night long' (Isa. 65: 3–4).

19. *flogging*: an uncertain translation. The verb from the noun here used (Greek *tumpanon*) is translated by the N.E.B. at Heb. 11: 35 (which may reflect this passage) 'tortured to death'.

21. The Greek behind *sacrilegious feast* refers to eating the entrails (cp. verse 7), and the occasion therefore may be 'the monthly celebration of the king's birthday' (cp. also 7: 42).

22. *clemency:* the Greek word is *philanthropia*. The Syrian king (whatever the Jews thought) seems to have prided himself on this virtue. The word, in different forms, lies behind 'the royal privileges established for the Jews' (4: 11), Antiochus' claim to 'benevolence' (9: 27), and his successor's paying 'honour to the sanctuary' (13: 23).

24. Eleazar's clear-sighted reply can only be admired. It reminds us of the famous reply (which it perhaps influenced) of another elderly martyr, Polycarp, 'Eighty and six years have I served him, and he has done me no wrong; how then can I blaspheme my king who saved me?'

26. Eleazar reckons with the possibility of punishment or judgement in the next life, if not in this, if he practises deceit. The Maccabaean martyrdoms seem to have stimulated men's thought about divine rewards and punishments, as we can see from Dan. 12: 1–3:

> But at that moment your people will be delivered,
>> every one who is written in the book:
> many of those who sleep in the dust of the earth will wake,
>> some to everlasting life
> and some to the reproach of eternal abhorrence.
> The wise leaders shall shine like the bright vault of heaven,
>> and those who have guided the people in the true path
>> shall be like the stars for ever and ever.

The idea that the martyrs will have their reward and the persecutors their punishment is particularly emphasized in the story of 2 Macc. 7.

28. Eleazar, like others in 2 Maccabees (cp. 8: 21; 13: 14), is prepared to die for the *revered and holy laws*, leaving *the young a fine example*. 2 Maccabees goes on to describe vividly how some young men followed it in ch. 7.

29. *madness:* cp. Wisd. of Sol. 3: 1: 'But the souls of the just are in God's hand, and torment shall not touch them. In the eyes of foolish men they seemed to be dead; their departure was reckoned as defeat, and their going from us as disaster. But they are at peace, for though in the sight of men they may be punished, they have a sure hope of immortality; and after a little chastisement they will receive great blessings, because God has tested them and found them worthy to be his.' *

THE SEVEN BROTHERS AND THEIR MOTHER

* The story of the seven brothers and their mother dying in hope of a resurrection has some points in common with the story told by the Sadducees ridiculing the idea of a resurrection (Luke 20: 27–38). The story reappears in 4 Maccabees (for which see p. 13), where the sufferings of the seven brothers and their mother are described in great detail. What particular martyrdom, if any, lay behind this story we do not know – no names are given. But the motif of the seven brothers, the presence of the king, the theological progression of the brothers' dying words with their climax in the speech of the youngest all indicate the art of the story-teller. The theme of exemplary loyalty to the law in the face of persecution has appeared in the story of Eleazar, and frequently throughout 1 and 2 Maccabees; cp. the speech of Mattathias (1 Macc. 2: 49–64). But 2 Maccabees, in describing the example of these young men, also expresses the theology which has appeared in 5: 17–20; 6: 12–17, carrying it a stage further by indicating that with the death of the martyrs the Lord's 'anger' against Israel might 'be ended' (verse 38).

For the purpose of comment, this long story is divided into two sections. *

Again, seven brothers with their mother had been **7** arrested, and were being tortured by the king with whips

269

2 and thongs to force them to eat pork, when one of them, speaking for all, said: 'What do you expect to learn by interrogating us? We are ready to die rather than break
3 the laws of our fathers.' The king was enraged and
4 ordered great pans and cauldrons to be heated up, and this was done at once. Then he gave orders that the spokesman's tongue should be cut out and that he should be scalped and mutilated before the eyes of his mother and
5 his six brothers. This wreck of a man the king ordered to be taken, still breathing, to the fire and roasted in one of the pans. As the smoke from it streamed out far and wide, the mother and her sons encouraged each other to die
6 nobly. 'The Lord God is watching', they said, 'and without doubt has compassion on us. Did not Moses tell Israel to their faces in the song denouncing apostasy: "He will have compassion on his servants"?'

7 After the first brother had died in this way, the second was subjected to the same brutality. The skin and hair of his head were torn off, and he was asked: 'Will you eat,
8 before we tear you limb from limb?' He replied in his native language, 'Never!', and so he in turn underwent
9 the torture. With his last breath, he said: 'Fiend though you are, you are setting us free from this present life, and, since we die for his laws, the King of the universe will raise us up to a life everlastingly made new.'

10 After him the third was tortured. When the question was put to him, he at once showed his tongue, boldly
11 held out his hands, and said courageously: 'The God of heaven gave me these. His laws mean far more to me than they do, and it is from him that I trust to receive them
12 back.' When they heard this, the king and his followers

were amazed at the young man's spirit and his utter disregard for suffering.

When he too was dead, they tortured the fourth in the 13
same cruel way. At the point of death, he said to the king: 14
'Better to be killed by men and cherish God's promise to
raise us again. There will be no resurrection to life for
you!'

Then the fifth was dragged forward for torture. Look- 15,16
ing at the king, he said: 'You have authority over men,
mortal as you are, and can do as you please. But do not
imagine that God has abandoned our race. Wait and see 17
how his great power will torment you and your descendants.'

Next the sixth was brought and said with his dying 18
breath: 'Do not delude yourself. It is our own fault that
we suffer these things; we have sinned against our God
and brought these appalling disasters upon ourselves. But 19
do not suppose you will escape the consequences of
trying to fight against God.'

* 2. *pork:* see the note on 6: 18.

4. *scalped:* the Greek word is *periskuthizo*, 'to scalp in
Scythian fashion'. For Scythians, cp. 4: 47. The young men's
punishment seems to have been scalping, cutting off the
tongue and hands (cp. verses 10–11) as the offending members,
and then roasting alive. Compare the punishment of Zedekiah
and Ahab, Jer. 29: 22.

6. The first comment, a quotation from Deut. 32: 36 *in
the song denouncing* Israel's *apostasy*, is that God *will have compassion on his servants*, with whom the martyrs identify themselves. This just hints at their future vindication.

8. *native language:* cp. verses 21, 27, and 12: 37 where it is
used in a battle-cry. Its use expresses national and religious

pride. The language was probably Hebrew in contrast to the
generally spoken Aramaic (cp. 15: 29, 36).

9. The second brother explains the 'compassion' (verse 6)
in terms of freedom from the present life and resurrection *to a
life everlastingly made new*. Apart from Dan. 12: 1–3 (quoted
above, p. 268) there is very little in the Old Testament which
suggests any general belief in resurrection. Israelites expected
to join their fathers in the shadowy existence of Sheol. Belief
about the after-life, however, was increasingly affected by
discussion of the problem of how God rewarded the just and
punished the wicked. Man could not escape God even in Sheol
(Ps. 139: 8). An unknown, somewhat nationalistic post-exilic
prophet, distinguishing between Israel and her enemies, could
say that 'The dead will not live again...But thy dead live,
their bodies will rise again' (Isa. 26: 14, 19). Dan. 12: 1–3
portrays those who have died on each side in the Maccabaean
struggle rising to receive their appropriate reward in the
imminent kingdom. That is the view expressed in this chapter.
Wisdom of Solomon, perhaps a century later, discusses the
fate after death of the just and the wicked, but without the
urgency and immediate application to present circumstances
so vividly present in Daniel and 2 Maccabees.

11. The third brother appears to suggest that the resurrection will be a bodily resurrection; he expects to have hands
and tongue restored.

14. The fourth brother's words remind us of Matt. 10: 28,
'Do not fear those who kill the body, but cannot kill the
soul.' He takes the theme of resurrection a stage further by
denying *resurrection to life* to the king and his servants.

15–17. The fifth brother emphasizes the limited authority
of the king, and hints at his pride (see the note on 5: 21). *do not
imagine:* compare the author's comment in 6: 16. The fourth
brother's negative threat (verse 14) becomes a positive one:
God's power *will torment* Antiochus and his descendants. Antiochus himself, according to 9: 28, died in torment. His son
was murdered by Demetrius' supporters (14: 2; 1 Macc. 7: 4).

His alleged son Alexander Balas was beheaded (1 Macc. 11: 17). Alexander's son was killed by Trypho (1 Macc. 11: 39–40; 13: 31).

18–19. The sixth brother makes the author's point (cp. 5: 17; 6: 15) that the Jews have brought suffering upon themselves, but that the Syrians, even though they are acting as God's instrument in punishing the Jews, will be punished for *trying to fight against God*. Jewish writers from times of persecution naturally found it hard to see the Gentiles as having any share in God's final rule. The place of the Gentiles in God's dispensation has always been a major Jewish theological problem, and it is not often that the heights reached by Second Isaiah ('Look to me and be saved, you peoples from all corners of the earth', Isa. 45: 22) are found elsewhere. See the note on verse 37 below. ✳

The mother was the most remarkable of all, and 20 deserves to be remembered with special honour. She watched her seven sons all die in the space of a single day, yet she bore it bravely because she put her trust in the Lord. She encouraged each in turn in her native language. 21 Filled with noble resolution, her woman's thoughts fired by a manly spirit, she said to them: 'You appeared in my 22 womb, I know not how; it was not I who gave you life and breath and set in order your bodily frames. It is the 23 Creator of the universe who moulds man at his birth and plans the origin of all things. Therefore he, in his mercy, will give you back life and breath again, since now you put his laws above all thought of self.'

Antiochus felt that he was being treated with contempt 24 and suspected an insult in her words. The youngest brother was still left, and the king, not content with appealing to him, even assured him on oath that the moment

he abandoned his ancestral customs he would make him
rich and prosperous, by enrolling him as a King's Friend
25 and entrusting him with high office. Since the young man
paid no attention to him, the king summoned the mother
26 and urged her to advise the lad to save his life. After much
urging from the king, she agreed to persuade her son.
27 She leaned towards him, and flouting the cruel tyrant, she
said in their native language: 'My son, take pity on me.
I carried you nine months in the womb, suckled you three
years, reared you and brought you up to your present
28 age. I beg you, child, look at the sky and the earth; see
all that is in them and realize that God made them out
of nothing, and that man comes into being in the same
29 way. Do not be afraid of this butcher; accept death
and prove yourself worthy of your brothers, so that by
God's mercy I may receive you back again along with
them.'

30   She had barely finished when the young man spoke out:
'What are you all waiting for? I will not submit to the
king's command; I obey the command of the law given
31 by Moses to our ancestors. And you, King Antiochus,
who have devised all kinds of harm for the Hebrews,
32 you will not escape God's hand. We are suffering for our
33 own sins, and though to correct and discipline us our
living Lord is angry for a short time, yet he will again be
34 reconciled to his servants. But you, impious man, foulest
of the human race, do not indulge vain hopes or be carried
away by delusions of greatness, you who lay hands on
35 God's servants. You are not yet safe from the judgement
36 of the almighty, all-seeing God. My brothers have now
fallen in loyalty to God's covenant, after brief pain leading

to eternal life;[a] but you will pay the just penalty of your
insolence by the verdict of God. I, like my brothers, sur- 37
render my body and my life for the laws of our fathers.
I appeal to God to show mercy speedily to his people and
by whips and scourges to bring you to admit that he alone
is God. With me and my brothers may the Almighty's 38
anger, which has justly fallen on all our race, be ended!'

The king, exasperated by these scornful words, was 39
beside himself with rage. So he treated him worse than
the others, and the young man died, putting his whole 40
trust in the Lord, without having incurred defilement.
Then finally, after her sons, the mother died. 41

This, then, must conclude our account of the eating of 42
the entrails and the monstrous outrages that accompanied
it.

* 22–3. The mother returns to the theme of the third brother
(verse 11). God gave life and will give back life to those who
put his laws above all thought of self. The mother's words are
reminiscent of Ps. 139: 13–14:

> Thou it was who didst fashion my inward parts;
> thou didst knit me together in my mother's womb,

or Job 10: 10–12:

> Didst thou not...clothe me with skin and flesh
> and knit me together with bones and sinews?
> Thou hast given me life and continuing favour,
> and thy providence has watched over my spirit.

24–6. The king tries to bribe the youngest brother to
apostatize (compare the officers' approach to Mattathias, 1
Macc. 2: 18, where the offer of the title of *King's Friend* is also

[a] in loyalty...life: *or* after a brief time of pain, in loyalty to God's
covenant of everlasting life.

made), and finally urges the mother to persuade her son. All this is part of the story-teller's craft, heightening the drama.

27-9. The mother reverts to the theme of creation and re-creation; if God can make the universe, and man in particular, *out of nothing*, then mother and child may be sure that she may *receive* the brothers *back again*. This last point makes a further contribution to the picture of resurrection.

31-5: these verses repeat thoughts already expressed: God is disciplining the Jews for their sins, but will soon be reconciled (cp. 6: 12-17, and 7: 6, 18), and Antiochus will be punished (7: 14-19).

36. *eternal life:* these words in the Greek are not easy to fit into the grammar of the sentence, and both translations offered by the N.E.B. are a little forced. Possibly we should translate (by a slight change of the Greek): 'My brothers have now drunk of eternal life, after enduring brief pain in loyalty to God's covenant.' For *eternal life* cp. 'life everlastingly made new' (verse 9).

37-8. A new thought is introduced. The brothers' deaths are to be *for* (in the cause of) *the laws*, and instrumental in ending the discipline that the people are now undergoing. They will effect this (perhaps) by completing the total of suffering to be undergone. Similarly Paul writes to the Colossians that 'It is now my happiness to suffer for you. This is my way of helping to complete, in my poor human flesh, the full tale of Christ's afflictions still to be endured, for the sake of his body which is the church' (Col. 1: 24). The author saw the martyrs' suffering as more than just an example to their compatriots; it made a difference to the progress of events. It did not lessen God's anger with his people; but by the brothers' acceptance of the discipline God's *mercy* could come *speedily* and his *anger* could *be ended*. There is a hint, too, that in the future the Gentiles might be brought *to admit* (even if *by whips and scourges*) *that he alone is God*. Neither Jewish nor gentile suffering, the author sees, is pointless.

42. *eating of the entrails:* see the notes on 6: 7, 21. *

The revolt of Judas Maccabaeus

✻ The author of 2 Maccabees has taken nearly half his book to describe the background to his account of the campaigns of Judas Maccabaeus, which now follows. This next major section in the N.E.B. tells of military action to the death of Antiochus, and of the purification of the temple. ✻

JUDAS' REVOLT AND SYRIAN REACTION

MEANWHILE JUDAS, also called Maccabaeus, and his **8** companions were making their way into the villages unobserved. They summoned their kinsmen and enlisted others who had remained faithful to Judaism, until they had collected about six thousand men. They invoked the 2 Lord to look down and help his people, whom all were trampling under foot, to take pity on the temple profaned by impious men, and to have mercy on Jerusalem, which 3 was being destroyed and would soon be levelled to the ground. They prayed him also to give ear to the blood that cried to him for vengeance, to remember the in- 4 famous massacre of innocent children and the deeds of blasphemy against his name, and to show his hatred of wickedness.

Once his band of partisans was organized, Maccabaeus 5 proved invincible to the Gentiles, for the Lord's anger had changed to mercy. He came on towns and villages 6 without warning and burnt them; he occupied the key positions, and inflicted many severe reverses on the enemy, choosing the night-time as being especially favourable 7

for these attacks. His heroism[a] was talked about every-
8 where. When Philip realized that the small gains made by
Judas were occurring with growing frequency, he wrote
to Ptolemaeus, the governor of Coele-syria and Phoenicia,
9 asking for his help in protecting the royal interests. Ptolemaeus immediately selected Nicanor, son of Patroclus, a
member of the highest order of King's Friends, and sent
him at the head of at least twenty thousand troops of
various nationalities to exterminate the entire Jewish race.
With him Ptolemaeus associated Gorgias, a general of
10 wide experience. Nicanor determined to pay off the two
thousand talents due from the king as tribute to the
Romans, by the sale of the Jews he would take prisoner;
11 and he at once made an offer of Jewish slaves to the coastal
towns, undertaking to deliver them at the price of ninety
to the talent. But he did not expect the vengeance of the
Almighty, which was soon to be at his heels.

* 2 Maccabees omits most of the material in 1 Macc. 2: 1 – 3:
24, describes briefly the gathering and early activities of the
partisans, and the first serious Syrian attempt to meet the
problem.

1. *Meanwhile:* during the persecution described in chs. 6
and 7. The author first mentioned Judas in 5: 27. *six thousand:*
an approximate figure; cp. 1 Macc. 3: 16, 'a handful', and
4: 6, 29 which mention first 3,000 and then 10,000 men.
Numbers in fact fluctuated according to success or failure.

2. *temple profaned:* see 6: 2–5, and 5: 15–16.

3. *Jerusalem...destroyed and...levelled:* see 1 Macc. 1: 29–32.

4. *massacre of innocent children:* cp. 5: 13; 6: 10. *deeds of
blasphemy against his name:* probably the dedication of the

[a] *Or* His numerous force.

temple ('this place of which thou didst say, "My Name shall be there"', 1 Kings 8: 29) to Olympian Zeus (6: 2).

5. *the Lord's anger had changed to mercy:* see 7: 38. From now on 2 Maccabees portrays the progressive victory of Judas.

6. *towns and villages:* see 1 Macc. 2: 45–8. *the key-positions* will include Beth-horon, and the *severe reverses* Judas' victories over Apollonius and Seron (see 1 Macc. 3: 10–24).

7. *talked about everywhere:* it is at this point that 1 Maccabees also notes Judas' growing fame (1 Macc. 3: 25–6). The date is probably 165 B.C.

8. For verses 8–11, see the commentary on 1 Macc. 3: 38–41. *Philip* (commissioner in Jerusalem, 5: 22) is ignored by 1 Maccabees. *Ptolemaeus:* the son of Dorymenes (4: 45).

9. *Nicanor* is for 2 Maccabees the 'double-dyed villain' (8: 34; 15: 3) and the major foe of Judas. 2 Maccabees portrays Judas' revolt beginning with Nicanor's defeat and ending with his defeat and death (15: 1 ff.). *Gorgias* is here merely *associated* with Nicanor; his attacks on Israel are briefly mentioned in another context in 10: 14. (In 1 Maccabees' version of this campaign, Gorgias leads a small Syrian detachment from the main army, whose commander could have been Nicanor, though this is not said.)

The objects of this campaign – *to exterminate the entire Jewish race* and 'to pay off' the 'tribute' owed to Rome (verse 10) – are also given by 1 Macc. 3: 41–2. Complete suppression rather than extermination was probably in mind, and slavery was a means to that end.

10–11. Enslaving 180,000 people (or even half that figure, if the correct text, as some think, reads 'one' *thousand talents*) was perhaps an over-ambitious project. The *price of ninety* (slaves) *to the talent* was low; fifteen to the talent would be more normal. *tribute* of 12,000 talents, payable in annual instalments of 1,000 talents, had been demanded by Rome in the Treaty of Apamea, 188 B.C.; in 173 B.C. Syria apologized for getting behindhand. This seems to have been an attempt to complete the payment. ✱

PREPARATION FOR BATTLE

12 Word of Nicanor's advance reached Judas, and he in-
13 formed his men that the enemy was at hand. The cowards
who doubted God's justice took themselves off and fled.
14 But the rest disposed of their remaining possessions, and
they prayed together to the Lord to save them from the
impious Nicanor, who had sold them even before they
15 met in battle; and if they could not ask this for their own
merits, they did so on the ground of the covenants God
had made with their ancestors, and of his holy and majes-
16 tic Name which they bore. Maccabaeus assembled his
followers, six thousand in number, and appealed to them
not to flee in panic before the enemy nor to be afraid of
the great host which was attacking them without just
17 cause. Rather they should fight nobly, having before their
eyes the wicked crimes of the Gentiles against the temple,
their callous outrage upon Jerusalem, and, further, their
18 suppression of the traditional Jewish way of life. 'They
rely on their weapons and their audacity,' he said, 'but
we rely on God Almighty, who is able to overthrow
with a nod our present assailants and, if need be, the
19 whole world.' He went on to recount to them the
occasions when God had helped their ancestors: how,
in Sennacherib's time, one hundred and eighty-five
20 thousand of the enemy had perished, and also how, on
the occasion of the battle against the Galatians in Babylonia, all the Jews engaged in the combat had numbered
no more than eight thousand, with four thousand Macedonians, yet, when the Macedonians were hard pressed,
the eight thousand through heaven's aid had destroyed

one hundred and twenty thousand and taken much
booty.

* The Jews prepare themselves for battle by drawing up a
picked force of men, offering prayer, and hearing Judas'
exhortation. Compare 1 Macc. 3: 42–60; 4: 8–11.

13. *cowards:* compare 1 Macc. 3: 56.

14. *disposed of...possessions:* this showed their determination, made them more mobile, and less vulnerable to reprisals.

15. *on the ground of the covenants...with their ancestors:* i.e.
Abraham, Isaac and Jacob. God had promised that 'As an everlasting possession I will give you and your descendants after
you the land in which you are now aliens' (Gen. 17: 8). *his...
Name which they bore:* Jeremiah had also appealed to this
(14: 9):

> Thou art in our midst, O LORD,
> and thou hast named us thine; do not forsake us.

16–18. The first part of Judas' speech makes much the same
points as the equivalent speech in 1 Macc. 3: 58–60.

19–20. Compare Judas' speech in 1 Macc. 4: 8–11. The
major difference is that in 2 Maccabees Judas gives as examples
of God's help not the defeat of Pharaoh but the failure of
Sennacherib's attack on Jerusalem in 701 B.C. (cp. 2 Kings 19:
35–6) and an otherwise unknown victory of the Jewish forces
in Babylonia. Judas quoted the failure of Sennacherib, according to 1 Macc. 7: 41 and 2 Macc. 15: 22, in his prayer before
his final battle with Nicanor, from which 2 Maccabees may
have introduced it here. The *Galatians* were Gauls from
western Europe who arrived in Asia Minor in 278 B.C., and
the Jewish forces may have assisted Antiochus I (281–261 B.C.)
against their invasions or Antiochus III against Galatian mercenaries helping the rebellious satrap of Media (221 B.C.).
Macedonians here probably means Antiochus and his subjects,
seen as part of the empire founded by Alexander of Macedon. *

DEFEAT OF NICANOR

21 His words put them in good heart and made them ready to die for their laws and for their country. He then 22 divided the army into four and gave each of his brothers, Simon, Josephus, and Jonathan, command of a division 23 of fifteen hundred men. Besides this, he appointed Eleazar to read the holy book aloud,*a* and giving the signal for battle with the cry 'God is our help', and taking command of the leading division in person, he engaged 24 Nicanor. The Almighty fought on their side, and they slaughtered over nine thousand of the enemy, wounded and disabled the greater part of Nicanor's forces, and 25 routed them completely. They seized the money of those who had come to buy them as slaves. After chasing the enemy a considerable distance, they were forced to break 26 off because it was late, for it was the day before the sab- 27 bath, and for that reason they called off the pursuit. When they had collected the enemy's weapons and stripped the dead, they turned to keep the sabbath. They offered thanks and praises loud and long to the Lord who had kept the first drops of his mercy to shed on them that day.*b* 28 After the sabbath was over, they distributed some of the spoils among the victims of persecution and the widows and orphans; the remainder they divided among them- 29 selves. This done, all together made supplication to the merciful Lord, praying him to be fully reconciled with his servants.

[a] Besides...aloud: *probable reading; Gk. obscure.*
[b] kept...day: *so some witnesses; others read* brought them safely to that day and had appointed it as the beginning of mercy for them.

* Final preparations, the battle, and consequent Jewish activity are described, with considerable emphasis on the reading of the law, the aid of the 'Almighty', the keeping of the 'sabbath', and the needs of 'victims of persecution and the widows and orphans'.

22–3. *Josephus* is not named in 1 Macc. 2: 1–5 as one of Judas' brothers, and some scholars suggest reading 'John'. Eleazar would be the other remaining brother (1 Macc. 2: 5). But for Eleazar the Latin manuscript tradition reads 'Esdras', possibly the 'Esdrias' of 12: 36 (= Azarias of 1 Macc. 5: 56, who is associated with a Josephus). Perhaps here, then, we have mentioned the three main Maccabees, Judas, Simon and Jonathan, with the pair Josephus and Azarias who were later left in charge of Jerusalem. This would give four division commanders and a reader; though there is some textual evidence for making Judas himself the reader, in which case Eleazar/Azarias would be a divisional commander. But we would then have five commanders for four divisions (for Judas himself led the first division). As the N.E.B. footnote says, the passage is 'obscure'. Whether *Eleazar* or Azarias is correct here, the battle-cry '*God is our help*' is a play on his name (see the note on 6: 18). The reading of the *holy book* may be parallel to the reference of 1 Macc. 3: 48 to seeking guidance before battle by unrolling the law scroll.

24. The battle and its aftermath are barely described; contrast 1 Macc. 4: 13–25. *nine thousand:* 1 Macc. 4: 15 says 'about three thousand'.

26. *for that reason:* 1 Macc. 4: 16–17 gives a different reason. 2 Maccabees is emphasizing the Jewish obedience to the law.

27. On either reading of the text (see the footnote) 2 Maccabees regards this battle as the beginning of the Lord's mercy on the Jews (see 7: 28 and 8: 5). Thus prayer is made (verse 29) for God 'to be *fully* reconciled with his servants'.

28. *distributed some of the spoils:* according to 1 Sam. 30: 24 ff. David established the principle that spoils were to be shared

among non-combatant as well as combatant participants in a
campaign. Here those who have suffered from the Syrian
king's policy are given some relief. This would help establish
their allegiance to the cause. But 2 Maccabees is making a
point of the Maccabees' devotion to the demands of the
Jewish law and tradition (for *widows and orphans* see the note
on 3: 10). ✷

THE DEFEAT OF TIMOTHEUS AND ESCAPE OF NICANOR

30 The Jews now engaged the forces of Timotheus and
Bacchides and killed over twenty thousand of them. They
gained complete control of some high strongholds, and
divided the immense booty, giving shares equal to their
own to the victims of persecution, to the widows and
31 orphans, and to the old men as well. They carefully collected all the enemy's weapons and stored them at strategic
points; the remainder of the spoils they brought into
32 Jerusalem. They killed the officer commanding the forces
of Timotheus, an utterly godless man who had caused the
33 Jews great suffering. During the victory celebrations in
their capital, they burnt alive the men who had set fire
to the sacred gates, including Callisthenes, who had taken
refuge in a small house; he thus received the due reward
of his impiety.

34,35   Thus, by the Lord's help, Nicanor, that double-dyed
villain who had brought the thousand merchants to buy
the Jewish captives, was humiliated by the very people
whom he despised above all others. He threw off his
magnificent uniform, and all alone like a runaway slave
made his escape through the interior, and was, indeed,
very lucky to reach Antioch after losing his whole army.

So the man who had undertaken to secure tribute for the 36
Romans by taking prisoner the inhabitants of Jerusalem
showed the world that the Jews had a champion and were
therefore invulnerable, because they kept the laws he had
given them.

* Verses 30–3 are clearly out of place here and belong to the
context of the Ammonite campaign of Judas mentioned in
1 Macc. 5: 6, 24–54. The authors of 1 and 2 Maccabees do not
seem entirely clear about the placing of the campaigns involving Timotheus; see the note below on 10: 24–31. This paragraph perhaps falls here because of its reference to sharing the
spoil with the 'victims of persecution' and 'widows and
orphans' (verse 30, cp. verse 28 above). The author of 2 Maccabees is less concerned with the chronology than with the
theological picture he is drawing of the Maccabaean struggle.

30. *Timotheus:* see 1 Macc. 5: 6–7, and the note on 10:
24–38. This reference apart, *Bacchides* first appears in 161 B.C.
(1 Macc. 7: 8).

31. *the spoils they brought into Jerusalem:* but hardly before
the recapture of the temple at the end of 164 B.C.

32. *the officer commanding:* perhaps an Arab (cp. 1 Macc. 5:
39). *suffering:* perhaps that described in the letter of 1 Macc.
5: 11–13.

33. *victory celebrations:* after the campaign of Gilead, Pentecost 163 B.C. (1 Macc. 5: 54; 2 Macc. 12: 31–2). *Callisthenes:*
the name stands awkwardly in the Greek text, which has no
word for the English *including*, and possibly its intrusion
influenced the textual tradition of the number of the relative
who and the verbs *had taken...received;* both singular and plural
versions are found. The event referred to may be that of 1: 8,
from 168 B.C. *due reward of his impiety:* cp. 4: 16, 38.

34–6. The narrative returns to Nicanor who similarly is
shown as receiving his due reward; he who tried to enslave
the Jews (verse 10) escaped *like a runaway slave. the thousand*

merchants is doubtless a piece of story-telling embellishment and the careful contrasts drawn in the paragraph show that this is a deliberate piece of 'ornamentation' (cp. 2: 29). ✻

A NOTE ON THE CHRONOLOGY OF 9: 1-12: 2

✻ The order of events in 9: 1 – 12: 2 differs from that given in 1 Maccabees. The major difference is that the death of Antiochus is described (ch. 9) before the Maccabaean recovery of the temple (10: 1-8); contrast 1 Macc. 4: 36-61; 6: 1-16. In fact the two events were almost contemporary, at the end of 164 B.C. (see the note on 1 Macc. 6: 1-16). However, the author of 2 Maccabees may have been led to give this order by the wrong insertion of the letter of Antiochus V mentioning his father's death (11: 22-6) into a collection of letters otherwise dated early 164 B.C. These letters in ch. 11 (apart from the letter of Antiochus V, and perhaps the Roman letter, verses 34-8) and the campaign and peace negotiations which precede them (11: 1-15; cp. 1 Macc. 4: 28-35) belong to the period before the death of Antiochus and the Maccabaean recovery of the temple, and should be read at this point, between chs. 8 and 9. ✻

THE LAST CAMPAIGN OF ANTIOCHUS

9 It so happened that, about this time, Antiochus had
2 returned in disorder from Persia. He had entered the city of Persepolis and attempted to plunder its temples and assume control. But the populace rose and rushed to arms in their defence, with the result that Antiochus was routed by civilians and forced to beat a humiliating re-
3 treat. When he was near Ecbatana, news reached him of what had happened to Nicanor and the forces of Timo-
4 theus. Transported with fury, he conceived the idea of making the Jews pay for the injury inflicted by those who

had put him to flight, and so he ordered his charioteer
to drive without stopping until the journey was finished.

But riding with him was the divine judgement! For in
his arrogance he said: 'When I reach Jerusalem, I will
make it a common graveyard for the Jews.' But the all- 5
seeing Lord, the God of Israel, struck him a fatal and
invisible blow. As soon as he had said the words, he was
seized with incurable pain in his bowels and with sharp
internal torments – a punishment entirely fitting for one 6
who had inflicted many unheard-of torments on the
bowels of others. Still he did not in the least abate his 7
insolence; more arrogant than ever, he breathed fiery
threats against the Jews. After he had given orders to
speed up the journey, it happened that he fell out of his
chariot as it hurtled along, and so violent was his fall that
every joint in his body was dislocated. He, who in his 8
pretension to be more than man had just been thinking
that he could command the waves of the sea and weigh
high mountains on the scales, was brought to the ground
and had to be carried in a litter, thus making God's power[a]
manifest to all. Worms swarmed even from the eyes of 9
this godless man and, while he was still alive and in agony,
his flesh rotted off, and the whole army was disgusted by
the stench of his decay. It was so unbearably offensive 10
that nobody could escort the man who only a short time
before had seemed to touch the stars in the sky.

✳ See 1 Macc. 3: 31–7; 6: 1–4. Antiochus left for the east in
spring 165 B.C., and campaigned in Armenia and the Persian
Gulf regions. 2 Maccabees emphasizes the painful nature of
his death, and sees it as divine punishment fitting his crimes.

[a] *Some witnesses read* litter. God made his power...

2. *Persepolis:* see the note on 1 Macc. 6: 3.

3. *Ecbatana:* the capital of Media (see Ezra 6: 2). 1 Macc. 6: 5–6 says that the *news* which reached Antiochus was of the defeat of Lysias (1 Macc. 4: 28–35), which 2 Maccabees puts later (11: 1–15). For *what had happened to Nicanor and... Timotheus,* see ch. 8. Timotheus' defeat is wrongly placed, and news of it could not have reached Antiochus.

6. *a punishment entirely fitting:* this continues a theme already illustrated in the cases of Andronicus (4: 38), Callisthenes (8: 33), and Nicanor (8: 34–5). For Antiochus' *torments,* cp. 7: 17.

8. *command the waves... and weigh high mountains:* the Hebrew wisdom tradition similarly contrasts man's feebleness with God's power in creation; cp. Isa. 40: 12,

> Who has gauged the waters in the palm of his hand,
> or with its span set limits to the heavens?
> Who has held all the soil of earth in a bushel,
> or weighed the mountains on a balance
>   and the hills on a pair of scales?

9. *Worms:* Herod Agrippa I suffered a similar fate after his persecution of the church 'because he had usurped the honour due to God' (Acts 12: 23).

10. *touch the stars:* cp. the song of derision over the king of Babylon (Isa. 14: 13–15):

> 'You thought in your own mind...
> I will set my throne high above the stars of God...
> Yet you shall be brought down to Sheol.'

This story also illustrates the Greek idea of *hubris* (violence to others based on pride) which meets its *nemesis* (divine vengeance). There is a dreadful inevitability about the sequence of events. Antiochus tries to plunder temples, is humiliated, needs to restore his self-esteem by 'making the Jews pay', urges on his charioteer, utters a threat which brings on 'internal torments', gives orders 'to speed up the journey', and, falling out of his chariot, has to be carried in a litter, in an advanced state of decay. He who wanted 'to be more than man' ended as rotting flesh as a result of his own 'insolence' (verse 7), 'pretension' (verse 8) and 'arrogance' (verse 11, cp. 7). The passage is a Greek tragedy in miniature. *

PENITENCE AND PROMISES

In this broken state, Antiochus began to abate his great 11 arrogance. Under God's lash, and racked with continual pain, he began to see things in their true light. He could 12 not endure his own stench and said, 'It is right to submit oneself to God and, being mortal, not to think oneself equal to him.' Then the villain made a solemn promise to 13 the Lord, who had no intention of sparing him any longer, and it was to this effect: Jerusalem the holy city, which he 14 had been hurrying to level to the ground and to transform into a graveyard, he would now declare a free city; to all the Jews, whom he had not considered worthy of 15 burial but only fit to be thrown out with their children as prey for birds and beasts, he would give privileges equal to those enjoyed by the citizens of Athens. The holy 16 temple which he had earlier plundered he would adorn with the most splendid gifts; he would replace all the sacred utensils on a much more lavish scale; he would meet the cost of the sacrifices from his own revenues. In 17 addition to all this, he would even turn Jew and visit every inhabited place to proclaim God's might.

* The tragedy ends with Antiochus' remorse and attempts at restitution, but (as our author sees it) in true tragic style Antiochus has by his own arrogance brought upon himself a fate which even submission to God cannot alter. This under-

lying Greek understanding of Antiochus' fate is given Jewish clothing by the author, who speaks of God's control over the king's fate and of God's 'just judgement' (verse 18). The author is largely governed by his thesis that Antiochus must suffer 'as he had made others suffer' (verse 28).

11. *abate his great arrogance:* cp. verse 7.

12. *being mortal:* see the note on 5: 21. Compare Dan. 4, where Nebuchadnezzar is made to eat grass to learn the lesson that 'the Most High is sovereign over the kingdom of men' (4: 32). Compare, too, Herod Agrippa I (see the note on verse 9).

14. *Jerusalem...a free city:* the precise nature of this freedom is not clear. Later Demetrius I promised that Jerusalem should be 'sacred and tax-free', perhaps implying that it should have certain privileges as a holy city (cp. 1 Macc. 10: 31), and this may be the case here. To *transform* the city *into a graveyard* (cp. verse 3) would make it the opposite of holy in Jewish eyes.

15. *privileges equal to those...of Athens:* presumably the author means that the Jews were to enjoy the democracy – or the freedom: Athens was not in the Syrian empire – traditionally *enjoyed by Athens.* Yet the new Greek constitution, supervised by an Athenian (cp. 6: 1) and originally introduced by Jason, had caused all the trouble. Coming from Antiochus this offer, if genuine, is hardly tactful.

16–17. Such *gifts* and provisions for the temple are consistent with previous Seleucid policy (cp. 3: 2–3). But the king's promise to *turn Jew* and *proclaim God's might* is most unlikely; stories of the acknowledgement of God's power by heathen kings and rulers appear frequently in ancient Jewish literature; compare the story of Israel in Egypt, which ends with Pharaoh saying 'go; and ask God's blessing on me also' (Exod. 12: 31–2), and the story in Dan. 4, which ends with Nebuchadnezzar's words, 'Now I, Nebuchadnezzar, praise and exalt and glorify the King of heaven; for all his acts are right and his ways are just and those whose conduct is arrogant he can bring low.' *

ANTIOCHUS' LETTER AND DEATH

When his pains in no way abated, because the just 18
judgement of God had fallen on him, he was in despair
and, as a kind of olive branch, wrote to the Jews the letter
here copied:

To my worthy citizens, the Jews, warm greetings 19
and good wishes for their health and prosperity from
Antiochus, King and Chief Magistrate.

May you and your children flourish and your affairs 20
go as you wish. Having my hope in heaven, I keep an 21
affectionate remembrance of your regards and goodwill.

As I was returning from Persia, I suffered a tiresome
illness, and so I have judged it necessary to provide for
the general safety of you all. Not that I despair of my 22
condition – on the contrary I have good hopes of
recovery – but I observed that my father, whenever he 23
made an expedition east of the Euphrates, appointed a
successor, so that, if anything unexpected should hap- 24
pen or if some tiresome report should spread, his subjects would not be disturbed, since they would know
to whom the empire had been left. Further, I know well 25
that the neighbouring princes on the frontiers of my
kingdom are watching for an opportunity and waiting
on events. So I have designated as king my son Antiochus, whom I frequently entrusted and recommended
to most of you during my regular visits to the satrapies
beyond the Euphrates. I have written to him what is
here copied. Wherefore I pray and entreat each one 26

of you to maintain your existing goodwill towards myself and my son, remembering the services I have rendered to you both as a community and as indivi-
27 duals. For I am sure my son will follow my own policy of moderation and benevolence and will accommodate himself to your wishes.

28 Thus this murderer and blasphemer, suffering the worst of agonies, such as he had made others suffer, met a pitiable
29 end in the mountains of a foreign land. His body was brought back by Philip, his intimate friend; but he was afraid of Antiochus's son and went over to Ptolemy Philometor in Egypt.

* This letter, which seems designed to introduce Antiochus V to loyal and friendly subjects as the successor to Antiochus IV, seems inappropriate to the situation in Judaea in 164 B.C. If it does derive ultimately from Antiochus, it may have been written for the people of Antioch, of which city Antiochus was 'King and Chief Magistrate' (verse 19).

18. *just judgement:* see the note on verse 6. The letter does not read like one written *in despair* and *as a kind of olive branch. copied:* from where, we do not know.

19. *the Jews:* perhaps an addition by the author of 2 Maccabees or his source. For the style and contents of the opening of the letter, compare, e.g., Paul's letter to the Philippians.

21. *from Persia:* see the notes on 1 Macc. 6: 1–4. *tiresome illness:* compare the lurid picture which the author draws in verses 5–12.

23. *my father . . . appointed a successor:* Antiochus III took this precaution in 210 B.C. before marching to Media, Parthia, Bactria and the Kabul valley.

25. *neighbouring princes:* Ptolemy VI of Egypt and Arsakes of Parthia, in particular. *designated as king my son Antiochus:*

Philip, appointed regent 'to educate his son Antiochus for the kingship' (1 Macc. 6: 15, 55), is not mentioned. If Antiochus made *regular visits* to eastern *satrapies* (for these see p. 8) we know nothing of them; he does not seem to have visited the east before this campaign.

26–7. These words would hardly be agreeable to the king's Jewish opponents, though many Greek cities – Athens, Delos, Olympia and others – could attest the *services* Antiochus had *rendered* in the form of handsome gifts, and many eastern cities would approve of the advantages derived from their new status in his empire. *moderation and benevolence* were Greek virtues: see the note on 6: 22.

28. For the idea of *agonies* suffered appropriate to agonies inflicted, see the note on verse 6. For the place of Antiochus' death, see the note on 1 Macc. 6: 3.

29. *intimate friend:* a title, given to Seleucus' minister Heliodorus (cp. 3: 7) by an inscription at Delos, and to Manaen at the court of Herod Antipas (Acts 13: 1, though the N.E.B. paraphrases and obscures the title). *Philip* tried 'to take over the government' (1 Macc. 6: 56), took possession of Antioch (1 Macc. 6: 63, cp. 2 Macc. 13: 23), and it was presumably after his defeat by Lysias, probably autumn 163 B.C. (1 Macc. 6: 63), that he went over to Egypt. Josephus, however (*Antiquities* XII. 9. 7), says that he was killed by Antiochus V. *

THE PURIFICATION OF THE SANCTUARY

Maccabaeus with his men, led by the Lord, recovered **10** the temple and city of Jerusalem. He demolished the 2 altars erected by the heathen in the public square, and their sacred precincts as well. When they had purified the 3 sanctuary, they constructed another altar; then, striking fire from flints, they offered a sacrifice for the first time for two whole years, and restored the incense, the lights, and the Bread of the Presence. This done, they prostrated 4

themselves and prayed the Lord not to let them fall any
more into such disasters, but, should they ever happen to
sin, to discipline them himself with clemency and not
hand them over to blasphemous and barbarous Gentiles.
5 The sanctuary was purified on the twenty-fifth of Kislev,
the same day of the same month as that on which
6 foreigners had profaned it. The joyful celebration lasted
for eight days; it was like the Feast of Tabernacles, for
they recalled how, only a short time before, they had
kept that feast while they were living like wild animals in
7 the mountains and caves; and so they carried garlanded
wands and branches with their fruits, as well as palm-
fronds, and they chanted hymns to the One who had so
triumphantly achieved the purification of his own temple.
8 A measure was passed by the public assembly to the effect
that the entire Jewish race should keep these days every
year.

✻ See 1 Macc. 4: 36–59 and the commentary there. The date
is December 164 B.C. This event is particularly important to
the author of 2 Maccabees as the basis for the celebration of a
feast (cp. 1: 9, 18). We may compare his treatment of the
victory over Nicanor (15: 36).

1–2. *temple and city:* 1 Maccabees does not mention the
recovery of the city, which was under the control of the
Syrian garrison (1 Macc. 6: 18), but only of the temple area,
which Judas then fortified. Thus 1 Maccabees does not record
the destruction of *altars...in the public square*, though it mentions their erection, with idols and sacred precincts (1 Macc.
1: 47, 54–5).

3. *purified:* for the author's emphasis in this theme, see the
note on 2: 19. *another altar:* see 1 Macc. 4: 44–7. The importance of heavenly *fire* at the dedicatory sacrifices for a new

altar is stressed by the letter of 1: 10 – 2: 18; the use of *flints* guaranteed fire which owed nothing to any previous man-made fire. *two whole years* is a year short (cp. 1 Macc. 1: 54; 4: 52), perhaps because 2 Maccabees has brought forward the date of Antiochus' death.

4. *to discipline them:* the idea has already appeared in 6: 12–17.

6–7. The author tries to explain the ceremonial of the new feast by reference to a celebration of Tabernacles by the Maccabees in their desert period (5: 27). *branches*, *fruits* and *palm-fronds* are connected with the feast by the law of Lev. 23: 40, but *garlanded wands* (Greek *thursoi*) belonged to the ceremonies of the worship of Dionysus (see the note on 6: 7), and it is surprising to find them adopted by the strictly orthodox Maccabees. Possibly the author is using the Maccabaean tabernacles to explain and justify practices of his own time.

8. *the entire Jewish race:* the author is concerned with foreign as well as Palestinian Jews. *

The campaign against Eupator

* The N.E.B. prints the text from this point to the end of ch. 13 as a separate section, covering events during the reign of Antiochus V (December 164 B.C. to spring 161 B.C.). Much of the material here is paralleled by material in 1 Maccabees, but comparison of the two books suggests that 2 Maccabees has not put all the events in the right sequence. See the chrono-logical note on p. 286. *

EUPATOR'S ACCESSION

WE HAVE ALREADY recounted the end of Antiochus 9 called Epiphanes. Now we will describe what hap- 10 pened under that godless man's son, Antiochus Eupator,

in a brief summary of the principal evils brought about
11 by his wars. At his accession, Eupator appointed as vicegerent a man called Lysias who had succeeded Ptolemaeus Macron as governor-general of Coele-syria and
12 Phoenicia. For Ptolemaeus had taken the lead in reversing
the former unjust treatment of the Jews and had attempted
13 to maintain peaceful relations with them, and as a result
he was denounced by the King's Friends to Eupator. On
every side he was called traitor, because he had already
abandoned Cyprus, entrusted to him by Philometor, and
had gone over to Antiochus Epiphanes. He still enjoyed
power, but no longer respect, and in despair he ended his
life by poison.

* The changes at Antioch consequent upon the death of
Antiochus IV are briefly described.

9. The author is clearly aware that he is re-arranging his
material.

10. *Eupator:* cp. 1 Macc. 6: 17. *his wars* appear to include
campaigns of Gorgias, Timotheus, and Lysias against Judas,
but the first campaign of Lysias and the subsequent negotiations probably belong to the previous reign (11: 1-21, 27 - 12:
2; cp. 1 Macc. 4: 26-35).

11. *Eupator appointed...Lysias:* 1 Macc. 3: 33; 6: 17 more
realistically say that Lysias put Eupator on the throne. By his
re-arrangement of material 2 Maccabees puts all Lysias'activity
into Eupator's reign. *who had succeeded Ptolemaeus Macron as:*
these words are not in the original Greek of this verse, though
verses 12-13 may imply this succession. 1 Macc. 3: 32 says
that Lysias was 'viceroy of the territories between the Euphrates and the Egyptian frontier', which might be the same
as *governor-general of Coele-syria and Phoenicia*, apparently a
higher dignitary than the 'governor' of that area, who was
Ptolemaeus (8: 8).

12–13. *Ptolemaeus* Macron ('long-head'), himself the son of a Ptolemaeus, was probably the successor of Ptolemaeus son of Dorymenes (1 Macc. 3: 38; 2 Macc. 4: 45; 8: 8). Previously Egyptian governor of *Cyprus*, Macron had *gone over to Antiochus* when Antiochus invaded Cyprus in 168 B.C. He had perhaps influenced the peace proposals of 164 B.C. described in 11: 13–21, 27–38, and was thus vulnerable to attack from political rivals. The change of reign brought about his downfall. The power in Syria was now held by Lysias. ✻

CAMPAIGNS IN IDUMAEA

When Gorgias became governor, he engaged mercen- 14 aries and took every opportunity of attacking the Jews. At the same time the Idumaeans, who were in control of 15 strategic fortresses, were also harassing them; they harboured the fugitives from Jerusalem and tried to carry on the war. Maccabaeus and his men made public suppli- 16 cation and prayed God to fight on their side. They made an assault on the Idumaean fortresses, pressed the attack 17 vigorously, and captured them; they drove off all who were manning the walls, and killed all they met, to the number of at least twenty thousand.

Nine thousand or more of the enemy took refuge in 18 two towers, very strongly fortified and fully equipped against a siege. Maccabaeus himself set out for the places 19 which were being hard pressed, but left Simon and Josephus behind, with Zacchaeus and his men, enough to prosecute the siege. But Simon's men were too fond of 20 money, and when they were bribed with seventy thousand drachmas by some of those in the towers, they let them slip through their lines. When Maccabaeus was 21 informed of this, he assembled the leaders of the army

and denounced these men for having sold their brothers
22 for money by letting their enemies escape. Then he
executed the men who had turned traitor, and imme-
23 diately the two towers fell to him. His military operations
were completely successful; in the two fortresses he destroyed over twenty thousand of the enemy.

* Compare 1 Macc. 5: 3–5, 65. 2 Maccabees gives a confused
account; the numbers of verses 17, 18 and 23 are improbable
and no places are named. The author seems concerned mainly
to distinguish between those who are faithful, and so successful,
and those who are not.

14. *Gorgias* was *governor* (or 'general', 12: 32; the same
Greek word is used) of Idumaea, stationed at Jamnia (1 Macc.
5: 58–9). His *mercenaries* perhaps came from the hellenistic
cities of the coast and coastal plain such as Joppa or Marisa.

15. *strategic fortresses:* in particular Hebron (1 Macc. 5: 65)
over against Bethsura, held by the Jews (1 Macc. 4: 61).

16. For prayer before battle, cp. verse 26 below; see the
note on 1 Macc. 3: 44.

18. *two towers:* perhaps compare the Baeanite forts, 1 Macc.
5: 5.

19. *left Simon and Josephus behind, with Zacchaeus:* compare
in some respects 1 Macc. 5: 18–20, 55–62. In 1 Maccabees
Josephus is 'son of Zacharias' and his fellow officer is one
Azarias: Simon is in Galilee. *places...hard pressed:* probably in
Gilead (1 Macc. 5: 9 ff.).

20. *drachmas:* Greek silver coins weighing about 4.4 gram-
mes each (see Luke 15: 8).

23. 9,000 men in two besieged towers is improbable
enough (verse 18); 20,000 (plus those who escaped, verse 20)
impossible. A total of 40,000 (verses 17, 23) killed by a Jewish
army of perhaps 11,000 (1 Macc. 5: 20) is most unlikely. *

CAMPAIGN AGAINST TIMOTHEUS

After his previous defeat by the Jews, Timotheus col- 24
lected a huge force of mercenaries and Asian cavalry, and
advanced to take Judaea by storm. As he approached, 25
Maccabaeus and his men made their prayer to God. They
sprinkled dust on their heads and put sackcloth round
their waists; they prostrated themselves on the altar-step 26
and begged God to favour them, 'to be an enemy of
their enemies and an opponent of their opponents', as
the law clearly states.

When they had finished their prayer, they took up their 27
weapons, advanced a good distance from Jerusalem, and
halted near the enemy. At first light the two armies joined 28
battle. For the Jews, success and victory were guaranteed
not only because of their bravery but even more because
the Lord was their refuge, whereas the Gentiles had only
their own fury to lead them into battle. As the fighting 29
grew hot, the enemy saw in the sky five magnificent
figures riding horses with golden bridles, who placed
themselves at the head of the Jews, formed a circle round 30
Maccabaeus, and kept him invulnerable under the protection of their armour. They launched arrows and thunder-
bolts at the enemy, who, confused and blinded, broke up
in complete disorder. Twenty thousand five hundred 31
of the infantry, as well as six hundred cavalry, were
slaughtered.

Timotheus himself fled to a fortress called Gazara, com- 32
manded by Chaereas and strongly garrisoned. Maccabaeus 33
and his men welcomed this, and for four days they laid
siege to the place. The garrison, confident in the strength 34

of their position, hurled horrible and impious blasphemies
35 at them, until, at dawn on the fifth day, twenty young
men from the force of Maccabaeus, burning with rage at
the blasphemy, courageously stormed the wall and in
36 savage anger cut down all they met. Under cover of this
distraction others got up the same way, attacked the
defenders, set light to the towers, and started fires on
which they burnt the blasphemers alive. Others broke
down the gates and let in the rest of the army, and thus
37 the city was occupied. Timotheus had hidden himself in
a cistern, but he was killed along with his brother
38 Chaereas and Apollophanes. To celebrate their achievement, the Jews praised with hymns and thanksgivings the
Lord who showers blessings on Israel and gives them the
victory.

✱ 1 and 2 Maccabees between them present us with a very
confused picture of the campaigns against Timotheus (for
whom see the note on 1 Macc. 5: 6). 1 Maccabees describes
two campaigns: (a) in Ammon, ending with the capture of
Jazer (5: 6–8); (b) in Gilead, where Timotheus is twice defeated (5: 9–44). 2 Maccabees describes (1) a campaign against
Timotheus and Bacchides (8: 30–3), perhaps part of 1 Maccabees' campaign in Ammon; (2) an attack by Timotheus, a
battle 'a good distance from Jerusalem', and Timotheus'
death at Gazara (= Jazer of 1 Macc. 5: 8?); (3) a campaign
against Timotheus in Gilead (12: 10–25) which ends in Timotheus' capture and release, and clearly parallels 1 Maccabees'
campaign in Gilead.

This suggests two main campaigns. If the campaign in
Gilead came first, and the campaign in Ammon (involving
Bacchides and ending with Timotheus' death at Gazara/Jazer)
second, then the course of events becomes intelligible. The
passage 1 Macc. 5: 3–8 is probably a summary originally

independent of the rest of 1 Macc. 5, and we need not necessarily assume from it that the campaign in Ammon preceded
the campaign in Gilead. The order of 2 Maccabees is clearly
wrong, as Timotheus' death in 10: 37 followed by his capture
and release in 12: 24 shows.

24. *previous defeat:* the author refers to 8: 30–3. The *mercenaries* were from the Arab tribes (cp. 12: 10; 1 Macc. 5: 39),
and the *Asian cavalry* perhaps from Iran; the Parthians of this
area were later famous for their cavalry. An advance on Judaea
is not in fact unlikely, if Timotheus was the Syrian general or
governor (cp. 12: 2) in Transjordan; the attack would comple-
ment the work of Gorgias and the Idumaeans.

26. *as the law clearly states*: see Exod. 23: 22.

27. Where the battle took place is unknown, but it was
possibly in Ammon, east of the Jordan, if Gazara (verse 32) is
a mistake for the Jazer of 1 Macc. 5: 8.

28. *the Lord was their refuge:* compare verse 16 above.

29. For similar visions, see 3: 25–6; 5: 2–3.

32. *Gazara*, between Joppa and Jerusalem, was first taken
for the Jews by Simon in 142 B.C. (1 Macc. 13: 43). There is
no other evidence that Judas took it or that Timotheus campaigned west of the Jordan, and so Gazara here has often been
thought a mistake for Jazer. If the author did write Gazara
here, he was perhaps crediting his hero Judas with an exploit
that really belonged to Simon.

36. *burnt...alive:* cp. the fate of Callisthenes, 8: 33.

37. A dry *cistern* – a hole hollowed out of the rock and
plastered – made a useful hiding place. *Chaereas* and *Apollophanes* are Greek names, as also is Timotheus; they are probably soldiers of the Syrian army. ✳

LYSIAS BESIEGES BETHSURA

Very shortly afterwards, Lysias the vicegerent, the **11**
king's guardian and relative, angered by these events,
collected about eighty thousand troops, in addition to his 2

entire cavalry, and advanced on the Jews. He reckoned
3 on making Jerusalem a settlement for Gentiles, subjecting
the temple to taxation like all gentile shrines, and putting
4 up the high-priesthood for sale annually. He reckoned
not at all with the might of God, but was elated with his
myriads of infantry, his thousands of cavalry, his eighty
5 elephants. Penetrating into Judaea, he approached Bethsura, a fortified place about twenty miles from Jerusalem,
and closely invested it.

6   When Maccabaeus and his men learnt that Lysias was
besieging their fortresses, they and all the people, wailing
and weeping, prayed the Lord to send a good angel to
7 deliver Israel. Maccabaeus was the first to arm himself,
and he urged the rest to share his danger and come to the
help of their brothers. One and all, they set out eagerly.
8 They were still in the neighbourhood of Jerusalem when
there appeared at their head a horseman arrayed in white,
9 brandishing his golden weapons. Then with one voice
they praised their merciful God and felt so strong in spirit
that they could have attacked not only men but also the
10 most savage animals, and even walls of iron. They came
on fully armed, with their heavenly ally, under the mercy
11 of the Lord. They hurled themselves like lions against the
enemy, cut down eleven thousand of them, as well as
sixteen hundred cavalry, and put all the rest to flight.
12 Most of those who escaped lost their weapons and were
wounded, and Lysias saved his life only by running away.

* Lysias besieges Bethsura and is beaten off. The dating given
to the following negotiations (see verses 16–21 below) and the
parallel account of this campaign in 1 Macc. 4: 28–35 both
suggest that these events belong to the late autumn or winter

of 165-164 B.C., and so to the period of the absence of Antiochus IV in the east, when Lysias was vicegerent. However,
some think that this campaign is a fictional duplication of
Lysias' later campaign against Bethsura (13: 19). See the
comment on 1 Macc. 4: 28-35.

1. *vicegerent:* see the note on 10: 11. *guardian:* see 1 Macc.
3: 33. *relative:* the Greek word is elsewhere translated 'kinsman' by the N.E.B. (cp. 1 Macc. 11: 31-2; 10: 89) and is a
title of honour.

2. Compare the numbers given by 1 Macc. 4: 28.

3. Compare 1 Macc. 3: 36; the intention is the forcible
hellenization of Jerusalem. But apart from the already-estab-
lished citadel garrison, Jerusalem did not become *a settlement
for Gentiles.* The temple probably was taxed; Demetrius I
offered to repeal the taxation in 152 B.C. (cp. 1 Macc. 10: 31).
The high-priesthood for the time depended on Syrian support,
but was not *for sale annually.*

4. *elephants:* cp. 1 Macc. 3: 34; 6: 34 ff.

6. *prayed:* cp. 1 Macc. 4: 30-3. *to send a good angel:* cp. 15: 23.

8. *a horseman:* see the note on 3: 23 ff.

11-12. 2 Maccabees gives higher casualty figures than 1
Maccabees, and pictures Lysias, like Nicanor (8: 34-5), *running
away.* ✱

NEGOTIATIONS

✱ 11: 13 – 12: 2 contains an account of various negotiations
and their result, together with four letters. These are not all
concerned with the same situation, and will be considered
separately. ✱

Lysias was no fool, and as he took stock of the defeat 13
he had suffered he realized that the Hebrews were invincible, because the mighty God fought on their side. So he
proposed a settlement on terms entirely acceptable, pro- 14
mising also to win the king over by putting pressure on

15 him to show friendship to the Jews. Maccabaeus agreed
to all the proposals of Lysias out of regard for the general
welfare, for the king had accepted all the proposals from
the Jewish side which Maccabaeus had forwarded to
Lysias in writing.

16   The letter of Lysias to the Jews ran as follows:

Lysias to the Jewish community, greeting.

17   Your representatives John and Absalom have handed
to me the document here copied and have asked me

18   to ratify what is contained in it. Whatever needed to
be brought to the king's knowledge, I have communicated to him, and what was within my own competence,

19   I have granted. If, therefore, you maintain your goodwill towards the empire, I for my part will endeavour

20   to promote your welfare for the future. I have ordered
your representatives and mine to confer with you about

21   the details. Farewell.

The twenty-fourth of Dioscorus in the year 148.[a]

＊ If the date in verse 21 is trustworthy some negotiations took
place late in 165 B.C. or early in 164 B.C., though 1 Maccabees
does not mention them. See the note on 1 Macc. 4: 35. The
negotiations brought no lasting peace, for the Maccabaean
seizure of the temple at the end of 164 B.C. and the campaigns
in Gilead and Galilee re-opened hostilities.

13. *Hebrews:* cp. 7: 31; 15: 37. The term has a religious
rather than a political content; 2 Maccabees is emphasizing the
divine support for the Jewish people, and perhaps gently
reminding his Jewish readers of their history as God's people.

16. *to the Jewish community:* this may be primarily the
hellenizing government party and the Jewish majority, ready
to 'maintain...goodwill towards the empire' (verse 19).

[a] *That is* 164 B.C.

17. What *the document here copied* was, or what its contents were, we do not know. It was probably from the hellenizing party; Lysias seems to accept its proposals easily enough. If, however, it was from the Maccabaeans, *John* might be the Maccabaean brother of 1 Macc. 2: 2 and *Absalom* the Maccabaean supporter of 1 Macc. 11: 70; 13: 11.

18. *I have communicated to him:* probably to the absent Antiochus IV.

19. These words are unlikely from Lysias to the Maccabees. Either they were originally addressed to the hellenizing party, or this letter has been composed to show Lysias' readiness to recognize that 'the Hebrews were invincible, because...God fought on their side' (verse 13).

21. *Dioscorus:* a Cretan name for the third month, or perhaps the name of an intercalary month. But the name is uncertain here, being conjectured from a difficult Greek text. Other suggestions are that either the Macedonian Dios (October) or Dystros (February) is meant. The date may be October 165 B.C. or February 164 B.C. ✶

The king's letter ran as follows: 22

King Antiochus to his brother Lysias, greeting.

Now that our royal father has gone to join the gods, 23 we desire that our subjects be undisturbed in the conduct of their own affairs. We have learnt that the Jews 24 do not consent to adopt Greek ways, as our father wished, but prefer their own mode of life and request that they be allowed to observe their own laws. We 25 choose, therefore, that this nation like the rest should be left undisturbed, and decree that their temple be restored to them and that they shall regulate their lives in accordance with their ancestral customs. Have the 26 goodness, therefore, to inform them of this and ratify it, so that, knowing what our intentions are, they may settle down confidently and quietly to manage their own affairs.

* This letter, as verse 23 shows, is from Antiochus V to Lysias, and does not belong with the letters that accompany it, but rather to the situation described in 13: 23 and I Macc. 6: 55–63, and dates therefore from early in 162 B.C. See the chronological note on p. 286.

22. *brother:* the title implied honour but not necessarily kinship.

23. *gone to join the gods:* i.e. died. The expression is appropriate for the officially deified rulers of Syria and Egypt.

24. The king refers to the choice between a hellenistic city's constitution, adopted under Jason, and the Jews' previous constitution.

25. Cp. I Macc. 6: 59, 'Let us guarantee their right to follow their laws and customs as they used to do.' Lysias has realized that Antiochus IV's decree suppressing the law was a major mistake which infuriated an already disturbed country people. He now hopes that the decree's repeal will bring peace. He will therefore leave the nation *undisturbed, have their temple* (already captured by the Maccabees) *restored*, probably cancelling the Syrian garrison's right to worship there (see the note on I Macc. I: 33–4), and allow the Jews to live by their *ancestral customs*. In short, he was restoring the privileges which the Jews enjoyed under Antiochus IV's predecessors. The Jews, of course, were still politically part of the Syrian empire and militarily under the eye of the Syrian garrisons in Jerusalem and Bethsura, and financially bound to pay taxes to Syria. Naturally, this Syrian decision would be bitterly resented by the hellenizing party, but the arrival of Demetrius I (14: 1 ff.) soon gave them a new opportunity. *

To the people the king's letter ran thus: 27

    King Antiochus to the Jewish Senate and people, greeting.

    We hope that you prosper. We too are in good health. 28
Menelaus has informed us of your desire to return to 29
your own homes. Therefore we declare an amnesty 30
for all who return before the thirtieth of Xanthicus.
The Jews may follow their own food-laws as heretofore, 31
and none of them shall be charged with any previous
infringement. I am sending Menelaus to reassure you. 32
Farewell.   33

    The fifteenth of Xanthicus in the year 148.[a]

* This letter, dated 12 March 164 B.C., was written by Antiochus IV (though 2 Maccabees, by putting it here, ascribes it to Antiochus V) and was perhaps the result of the conference at Antioch to which the following letter refers (verse 36).

27. The address is to the government (the hellenizing Senate) and people of the Jews, not to the Maccabees.

28. *in good health:* Antiochus writes before his illness (9: 4–10).

29. *Menelaus* was the high priest, the hellenizers' champion, later discarded by Lysias (13: 3–8) as 'responsible for all Antiochus' troubles'.

30–1. The policy of the king and the hellenizers was to weaken Judas' position by encouraging his supporters to return home with the promise of an amnesty and the repeal of the prohibition on Jewish food-laws. In fact it probably worked for a time; the country farmers did want to return home to repair the damage caused by the Syrian campaigns. But in the autumn, after the harvest, Judas and his supporters gathered to regain the temple; the king's offer did not go far enough (contrast the later letter of Antiochus V, verses 22–6).

[a] *That is* 164 B.C.

33. *Xanthicus:* the Macedonian name for the Babylonian
and Jewish month Adar. The *fifteenth* and *thirtieth* days would
be 12 and 27 March 164 B.C. Jews taking advantage of the
amnesty could thus celebrate passover (Nisan 14) peacefully.
But the dates contain the difficulty that they allow only fifteen
days between the writing of the letter somewhere in the east
where Antiochus is campaigning and the final date for the
amnesty. The author of 2 Maccabees probably thought Antiochus was at Antioch, and perhaps provided (on the basis
of verse 30) an erroneous date.

34 The Romans also sent the Jews the following letter:

> Quintus Memmius and Titus Manius, Roman legates,
> to the Jewish people, greeting.

35 We give our assent to all that Lysias, the king's rela-
36 tive, has granted you. But examine carefully the questions which he reserved for reference to the king; then
send someone immediately, so that we may make suitable proposals, for we are proceeding to Antioch.
37 Send messengers therefore without delay, so that we
38 also may know what your opinion is. Farewell.

> The fifteenth of Xanthicus in the year 148.[a]

12 When these agreements had been concluded, Lysias
went off to the king, and the Jews returned to their farm-
2 ing. But some of the governors in the region, Timotheus
and Apollonius son of Genaeus and also Hieronymus and
Demophon, and in addition Nicanor, chief of the Cypriot
mercenaries, would not allow them to enjoy security and
live in quiet.

[a] *That is* 164 B.C.

✻ The letter in verses 34–8 is the first evidence of direct Roman contact with the Jews, though Rome had been concerned with Syria since the days of Antiochus III. Whichever party had asked Rome to exert pressure on their behalf at Antioch, Rome was probably well enough pleased to have an excuse for intervention. But even so, Rome cannot do much more than 'assent' to what Lysias grants, and ask for further briefing on the matters reserved for the king's attention. But some confusion in the Roman names (verse 34), the letter's knowledge of the contents of Lysias' letter (verse 36, cp. verse 18), and the use of a Seleucid dating (verse 38) have made some scholars doubt the letter's genuineness.

34. We know of a Titus Manlius Torquatus as consul in 165 B.C. and in Egypt in 164 B.C., and of an envoy to Antiochus IV called Manius Sergius in 164 B.C., between whom there may be some confusion here (*Titus Manius*). But *Quintus Memmius* remains otherwise unknown.

35. *king's relative:* cp. 11: 2.

36. *questions which he reserved:* cp. verse 18. *we are proceeding to Antioch:* from where, we can only guess – possibly Egypt.

38. If genuine, this letter might be dated shortly after Lysias' letter (verses 16–21) and a little before Antiochus IV's letter (verses 27–33), which perhaps reflects the deliberations to which the Roman legates were going. The Seleucid dating here given might have been derived from verse 33.

12: 1. *to the king:* if this verse refers to events early in 164 B.C., Antiochus IV is meant. But he was in the east. Lysias would have returned to Antioch. *to their farming:* farming would occupy the summer of 164 B.C.; see the note on verses 30–1.

2. *Timotheus:* see above on 10: 24–38. The others are unknown to us, unless Nicanor is to be identified with the general of 1 Macc. 3: 38 etc. For *Cypriot mercenaries* cp. 4: 29. This verse suggests that renewed fighting was provoked by the Syrian governors, but the following story shows (cp. 12: 10 ff.; 1 Macc. 5) that the Jews were not popular in the surrounding areas. ✻

AN ATROCITY AT JOPPA

3 I must now describe an atrocity committed by the inhabitants of Joppa. They invited the Jews living in the town to embark with their wives and children in boats which they provided, with no indication of any ill will towards 4 them. As it was a public decision by the whole town, and because they wished to live in peace and suspected nothing, they accepted; but when they were out at sea, the people of Joppa sank the boats, drowning no fewer than two 5 hundred of them. When Judas learnt of this brutal treatment of his fellow-countrymen, he alerted his troops, 6 invoked God, the just judge, and fell upon their murderers. He set the harbour of Joppa on fire by night, burnt the shipping, and put to the sword those who had taken 7 refuge there. But finding the town gates closed, he withdrew, meaning however to return and root out the entire 8 community. When he learnt that the people of Jamnia intended to do the same to the Jews who lived among 9 them, he attacked Jamnia by night and set fire to its harbour and fleet; the light of the flames was visible in Jerusalem thirty miles away.

* The hostility of Joppa to the Jews is perhaps part of the general hostility recorded in 1 Macc. 5 (see especially 1 Macc. 5: 15, which mentions the coastal towns). 1 Macc. 5: 55–62, 68 tells of an attack on Jamnia and of Judas' attack on Azotus, but not of any attack by Judas on Joppa and Jamnia, though 2 Maccabees links these with the period of Judas' campaign in Gilead (i.e. 163 B.C.). 2 Maccabees is particularly concerned to highlight the activities of Judas as the protector of the Jews against aggression.

3. *Joppa*, modern Tel Aviv-Jafo about 50 km (32 miles) from Jerusalem, was an open 'roadstead' (Ezra 3: 7). In pre-exilic times it belonged to the Philistines, and did not come under Jewish control until Simon took it (1 Macc. 12: 33–4).

4. The Jews, as aliens, would have no part in making any *public decision* in the assembly. It is perhaps a sign of how much they were disliked that no rumour of the plot was allowed to reach their ears. *two hundred:* 1,000 men were massacred in the region of Tubias (1 Macc. 5: 13).

6–7. Judas, attacking *by night* when the *town gates* would be *closed*, could destroy only the *harbour* and the *shipping*, which were separate from the town (compare Gaza; see the note on 1 Macc. 11: 61).

8. *Jamnia* (see the note on 1 Macc. 5: 58) was in fact inland, quite separate from its harbour, about 17 km (10 miles) south of Joppa. *

THE CAMPAIGN IN GILEAD

When they had marched more than a mile further in 10 their advance against Timotheus, they were set upon by not less than five thousand Arabs, with five hundred cavalry. A violent combat ensued, in which by divine 11 help Judas and his men were victorious. The defeated nomads begged Judas to make an alliance with them, and promised to supply him with cattle and to give the Jews every other kind of help. Judas realized that they could 12 indeed be useful in many ways; so he agreed to make peace with them, and, after receiving assurances from him, they went back to their tents.

Judas also attacked Caspin, a walled town, strongly 13 fortified and inhabited by a motley crew of Gentiles. Confident in the strength of their walls and in their store 14 of provisions, the defenders behaved provocatively towards Judas and his men, abusing them and also uttering

15 the most wicked blasphemies. But they invoked the world's great Sovereign who in the days of Joshua threw down the walls of Jericho without battering-rams or
16 siege-engines. They attacked the wall fiercely and, by the will of God, captured the town. The carnage was indescribable; the adjacent lake, a quarter of a mile wide, appeared to be overflowing with blood.

✶ The narrative of 12: 10–31, describing a campaign against Timotheus in northern Transjordan, is clearly parallel to that of 1 Macc. 5: 24–54. The date is early summer 163 B.C.

10. In verse 9 Judas is at Jamnia, and here, *more than a mile further* on, he is among Arab nomads. Clearly these verses had some context other than their present one, as the reference to Timotheus, whose death is recorded in 10: 37, also shows. (See the note on 10: 24–38.) *Arabs:* in 1 Macc. 5: 25, peaceful Nabataeans. But cp. 1 Macc. 5: 39, which mentions Timotheus' Arab mercenaries. There is nothing unlikely in the skirmish recorded here, or in its result.

13. *Caspin:* probably the Casphor occupied by Judas (1 Macc. 5: 26, 36), about 15 km (9 miles) east of the Sea of Galilee.

14. *blasphemies:* 2 Maccabees emphasizes, as 1 Maccabees does not, the religious nature of the campaign, as also in 10: 34, 36. Both Antiochus (9: 28) and Nicanor (15: 32) are 'blasphemers' above all.

15. See Josh. 6. For a similar invocation before battle coupled with a reference to previous divine assistance, cp. 15: 20–4. The Greek word for *Sovereign* (*dunastes*), used of God, occurs several times in 2 Maccabees, but only once in the New Testament (1 Tim. 6: 15: N.E.B. 'who alone holds sway'), where it is otherwise used of lesser mortal rulers, e.g. Acts 8: 27, 'a high official of the Kandake'. The use of the word for God comes from a non-Palestinian Jewish background. ✶

THE DEFEAT OF TIMOTHEUS

Advancing about ninety-five miles from there, they 17
reached Charax, which is inhabited by the Tubian Jews,
as they are called. They did not find Timotheus there; he 18
had by that time left the district, having had no success,
but in one place he had left behind an extremely strong
garrison. Dositheus and Sosipater, Maccabaeus's generals, 19
set out and destroyed the garrison, which consisted of
over ten thousand men. Maccabaeus for his part grouped 20
his army in several divisions, appointed commanders for
them,[a] and hurried after Timotheus, whose forces numbered a hundred and twenty thousand infantry and two
thousand five hundred cavalry. When he learnt of Judas's 21
approach, Timotheus sent off the women and children
with all the baggage to a town called Carnaim, this being
an inaccessible place, hard to storm because all the approaches to it were narrow. But when Judas's first divi- 22
sion appeared, terror and panic seized the enemy at the
manifestation of the all-seeing One. In their flight they
rushed headlong in every direction, so that frequently
they were injured by their comrades and were run through
by the points of their swords. Judas pressed the pursuit 23
vigorously and put thirty thousand of these criminals to
the sword. Timotheus himself was taken prisoner by the 24
troops of Dositheus and Sosipater. With much cunning,
he begged them to let him go in safety, pointing out that
most of them had parents, and some of them brothers,
who were in his hands, and might never be heard of

[a] *Probable meaning, based on one Vs.; Gk.* appointed them to command
the divisions.

25 again. He pledged himself over and over again to restore these hostages safe and sound; and so they let him go in order to save their relatives.

26 Judas moved on Carnaim and the sanctuary of Atar-
27 gatis, and killed twenty-five thousand people there. After this victory and destruction he next marched on Ephron, a fortified town inhabited by a mixed population.[a] Stalwart young men took up their position in front of the walls and fought vigorously, while inside there was a
28 great supply of engines of war and ammunition. But the Jews invoked the Sovereign whose might shatters all the strength of the enemy. They made themselves masters of the town and killed twenty-five thousand of the defen-
29 ders. Leaving that place, they advanced to Scythopolis,
30 some seventy-five miles from Jerusalem. The Jews who lived there testified to the goodwill shown them by the people of Scythopolis and the kindness with which they
31 had treated them in their bad times; so Judas and his men thanked them, and charged them to be equally friendly to the Jewish race for the future. They returned to Jerusalem in time for the Feast of Weeks.

* The account of the campaign in Gilead continues. Judas marches to the region of the Tubian Jews, destroys a garrison, defeats Timotheus at Carnaim, and returns to Jerusalem. For this section the reader should consult the map on p. 50.

17. *Charax* is in the region of Tubias, where Jews have been massacred, and could be the fortress where Jewish survivors had taken residence (cp. 1 Macc. 5: 11–13). The Greek word *charax* means a sharpened stake used in fortifying a camp site, and so the camp itself, and may not be the real name of the

[a] *Some witnesses add* where Lysias had his headquarters.

place. Some suggest the place was Dathema, whose unsuccessful (cp. verse 18) siege by Timotheus' army is described in
1 Macc. 5: 29–34. Others place it south-east of Dathema
towards Bozrah. *ninety-five miles* (154 km): this is probably
the equivalent of the three days' march of 1 Macc. 5: 24, and
calculated from Jerusalem, not from Caspin (Casphor, 1 Maccabees), which was only about 40 miles (64 km) from the
region of Tubias. Thus, as 1 Macc. 5: 36 suggests, the paragraph about the capture of Caspin (verses 13–16) is probably
misplaced by the author of 2 Maccabees.

18. *garrison:* perhaps one of those mentioned in 1 Macc. 5 –
Bozrah, Alema, Maked, Bezer, or one of 'the other towns of
Gilead' (1 Macc. 5: 36).

19. *Dositheus* was a Tubian Jew (verse 35), bearing, like
Sosipater, a Greek name.

20–5: these verses describe a battle immediately prior to
the capture of Carnaim; 1 Macc. 5: 37–43 sets this battle across
a ravine at Raphon, a few miles north-east of Carnaim.

20. 1 Macc. 5: 37–9 gives no figures, but notes large local
reinforcements and Arab mercenaries in Timotheus' new
army.

21. *Carnaim:* see the note on 1 Macc. 5: 43. The *approaches*
were restricted by the course of the river Yarmuk and its
tributaries.

22. *the manifestation of the all-seeing One* may imply something like the apparition of the horsemen which confused the
enemy in 10: 29–30.

24. For the chronological problem raised by this passage
and 10: 37, see the commentary on 10: 24–38. *their relatives:*
probably the captured wives and children of the Tubian Jews
(1 Macc. 5: 13).

26. Carnaim's sanctuary went back to Canaanite times (see
the note on 1 Macc. 5: 43). *Atargatis* was a compound of two
divine names, '*Athar* (= Astarte) and '*Atti*, and personified
the fertility that comes from water; she was a Syrian goddess
of hellenistic times, the consort of the Syrian god Hadad.

Busts of Atargatis, both as a grain-goddess and as a fish-goddess, have been discovered at a Nabataean temple at *khirbet tannur* south-east of the Dead Sea, though these date from the second century A.D.

27. *Ephron:* cp. 1 Macc. 5: 46. For its *mixed population*, compare Caspin's (verse 13). The reference of some witnesses to Ephron as the headquarters of Lysias is hard to account for, though the place might have been a supply base for Timotheus' army.

28. *Sovereign:* see the note on verse 14.

29. *Scythopolis* was the Greek name of Bethshan (1 Macc. 5: 52). The site was inhabited as far back as 3000 B.C., and it was a flourishing city with several temples in the mid-second millennium B.C. The Philistines once held this area; they nailed Saul's body to the wall here (1 Sam. 31: 10). Solomon incorporated the city into his kingdom (1 Kings 4: 12), but we hear nothing else of it until the hellenistic period; in 218 B.C. it exchanged Egyptian rule for Syrian. Why Bethshan should have shown goodwill and kindness to resident Jews when similar hellenistic cities did not is uncertain; perhaps Bethshan, like other trading cities such as Ascalon (1 Macc. 10: 86), preferred making friends to making enemies. Bethshan's behaviour is clearly contrasted here with that of the cities of Gilead.

31. *Feast of Weeks:* June 163 B.C. It was also called 'the pilgrim-feast of Harvest' (Exod. 23: 16) or 'the day of Firstfruits' (Num. 28: 26), and marked the beginning of the wheat harvest. It was one of the three ancient feasts of Canaan (cp. Exod. 23: 14–17). *Pentecost* was, as verse 32 shows ('as it is called'), a relatively new Greek name, meaning 'fiftieth' day after Passover. Judas' campaign, therefore, took place between Passover (April) and Pentecost (June) 163 B.C. ✻

A CAMPAIGN IN IDUMAEA

32 After celebrating Pentecost, as it is called, they advanced
33 to attack Gorgias, the general in charge of Idumaea, who

met them with three thousand infantry and four hundred
cavalry. When the ranks joined battle, a small number of 34
the Jews fell. But a cavalryman of great strength called 35
Dositheus, one of the Tubian Jews, had hold of Gorgias
by his cloak and was dragging the villain off by main
force, with the object of taking him alive, when a Thracian horseman bore down on him and chopped off his
arm; so Gorgias escaped to Marisa.

Esdrias and his men had been fighting for a long time 36
and were exhausted. But Judas invoked the Lord to show
himself their ally and leader in battle. Striking up hymns 37
in his native language as a battle-cry, he put the forces of
Gorgias to flight by a surprise attack.

Regrouping his forces, he led them to the town of 38
Adullam. The seventh day was coming on, so they purified themselves, as custom dictated, and kept the sabbath
there. Next day they went, as had by now become neces- 39
sary, to collect the bodies of the fallen in order to bury
them with their relatives in the ancestral graves. But on 40
every one of the dead, they found, under the tunic, amulets sacred to the idols of Jamnia, objects which the law
forbids to Jews. It was evident to all that here was the
reason why these men had fallen. Therefore they praised 41
the work of the Lord, the just judge, who reveals what is
hidden; and, turning to prayer, they asked that this sin 42
might be entirely blotted out. The noble Judas called on
the people to keep themselves free from sin, for they had
seen with their own eyes what had happened to the fallen
because of their sin. He levied a contribution from each 43
man, and sent the total of two thousand silver drachmas
to Jerusalem for a sin-offering – a fit and proper act in

44 which he took due account of the resurrection. For if he had not been expecting the fallen to rise again, it would have been foolish and superfluous to pray for the dead.
45 But since he had in view the wonderful reward reserved for those who die a godly death, his purpose was a holy and pious one. And this was why he offered an atoning sacrifice to free the dead from their sin.

* See the commentary on 1 Macc. 5: 66–7, which describes a not entirely successful campaign near Marisa. 2 Maccabees heavily emphasizes the religious nature of the struggle.

32. *Gorgias... in charge of Idumaea:* Gorgias is mentioned alongside the Idumaeans in 10: 14. *Idumaea* was the hellenistic name for the region to Judaea's south and south-west now occupied by descendants of the ancient Edomites. Its centre was Hebron, but it seems at this time to have stretched westwards towards the coastal regions of Azotus and Jamnia, though these places were in Philistia (cp. 1 Macc. 5: 65–8).

33. The figures sound plausible and may be accurate; 1 Maccabees gives no figures.

35. *Dositheus:* see the note on verse 19. *a Thracian horseman:* Thrace, on the European side of the Bosporus, was notoriously uncivilized, but well known for its horses and soldiers. *Marisa:* cp. 1 Macc. 5: 66.

36. *Esdrias:* see the note on 8: 22.

37. The *hymns* were probably psalms, such as Ps. 20, in whole or part, or similar compositions now lost to us. The author of 2 Maccabees makes a point of referring to their being sung in the *native language* (cp. 7: 8; 15: 29), by which he probably means Hebrew, though Aramaic may have been more generally spoken at this time. The author of 2 Maccabees, or Jason of Cyrene (cp. 2: 19), writing from the standpoint of a Jew living abroad, is perhaps more conscious of the national importance of the Jews' native language than the author of 1 Maccabees, for whom Jewish nationalism is brought

out by Jewish political success. This element is less pronounced in 2 Maccabees.

38. In spite of the surprise attack which put Gorgias to flight, the Jews were not clear victors on this occasion, and Judas retired to *Adullam* (David had retired to this area from Saul, 1 Sam. 22: 1), 15 km (9 miles) north-east of Marisa – far enough away to avoid a return surprise attack on the coming sabbath. The men *purified themselves* after battle because they had been in contact with blood or corpses or both; Num. 31: 13–30 describes procedures to be followed after battle, including purification, which lasted seven days, though 2 Maccabees here restricts it to one day.

39–45: this story does not occur in 1 Maccabees, though 1 Macc. 5: 68 does refer to the burning of divine images from Azotus. The author of 2 Maccabees perhaps intends his Jewish readers living abroad to learn a lesson from the fate of these soldiers, who had secretly adopted the cult practices of Jamnia. The narrative also affords some explanation of Jewish casualties on this occasion: 1 Maccabees refers, perhaps more factually, to priests 'who had ill-advisedly gone into action wishing to distinguish themselves' (5: 67).

39. *ancestral graves* would be chambers cut out of the limestone for the wealthier families; the poorer folk would have a more humble burial. But family solidarity in Israel was thought to extend beyond the grave: thus Bathsheba can speak to David of the time 'when you, sir, rest with your forefathers' (1 Kings 1: 21).

40. *amulets:* worn as a protective charm, and probably bearing a representation of Dagon of Azotus (cp. 1 Macc. 10: 84). Foreign idols were banned in Israel (cp. Deut. 7: 25–6); in place of protective amulets the Israelite was instructed to bind the commandments 'as a sign on the hand and wear them as a phylactery on the forehead' (Deut. 6: 8).

41–5. In spite of their sin, the soldiers had died fighting for the Maccabaean cause; their example has served its purpose, and the people can now pray that *this sin might be . . . blotted out.*

Judas therefore collected money for a *sin-offering . . . to free the dead from their sin*. The expectation was that those who had died fighting on the Maccabaean side would be raised to share in the now imminent kingdom which is to replace the Syrian domination. This is *the wonderful reward reserved for those who die a godly death* (verse 45); cp. Dan. 12: 1–3. So Judas *took due account of the resurrection*; the *sin-offering* (the laws for which are laid down in Lev. chs. 4–5) was to make expiation for the inadvertent sins of those who had died, who are thought of as still belonging to God's holy people. Judas' intention perhaps also included the expiation of the inadvertent sins of the living. ✶

EUPATOR CAMPAIGNS AGAINST JUDAS

13 In the year 149,[a] information reached Judas and his men that Antiochus Eupator was advancing on Judaea 2 with a large army; he was accompanied by Lysias, his guardian and vicegerent, bringing in addition a Greek force, consisting of one hundred and ten thousand infantry, five thousand three hundred cavalry, twenty-two elephants, and three hundred chariots armed with scythes. 3 Menelaus also joined them and urged Antiochus on; this he did most disingenuously, not for his country's good, but because he believed he would be maintained in 4 office. However, the King of kings aroused the rage of Antiochus against Menelaus: Lysias produced evidence that this criminal was responsible for all Antiochus's troubles, and so the king ordered him to be taken to Beroea and there to be executed in the manner customary 5 at that place. Now in Beroea there is a tower some seventy-five feet[b] high, filled with ashes; it has a circular device

[a] *That is* 163 B.C.   [b] some . . . feet: *Gk.* fifty cubits.

sloping down sheer on all sides into the ashes. This is 6
where the citizens take anyone guilty of sacrilege or any
other notorious crime, and thrust him to his doom; and 7
such was the fate of the law-breaker Menelaus, who was
not even allowed burial – a fate he richly deserved. Many 8
a time he had desecrated the hallowed ashes of the altar-
fire, and by ashes he met his death.

✻ Ch. 13 should be compared with 1 Macc. 6: 18–63. 2 Maccabees here describes the campaign of Antiochus V (Eupator),
and also the death of Menelaus (which 1 Maccabees does not
mention).

1. *the year 149:* see the note on 1 Macc. 6: 20. This campaign
probably took place in autumn 163 B.C., the end of year 149.
Eupator (cp. 1 Macc. 6: 17) was now about twelve years old.
1 Macc. 6: 21–7 says that the campaign was prompted by
hellenizers' complaints of Judas' attack on the citadel and other
activities.

2. *vicegerent:* see the note on 10: 11. *guardian:* cp. 1 Macc.
3: 33. *a Greek force:* i.e. mercenaries; see the note on 1 Macc.
6: 29, and for the numbers, compare 1 Macc. 6: 30. *chariots
armed with scythes:* chariots carried archers, and the scythes,
on the wheels (and according to the Roman historian Livy,
on the horses' yokes), prevented foot-soldiers from getting too
close.

3. Early in 164 B.C. *Menelaus* had been involved in diplomatic activity between Antiochus IV and the Jewish Senate
(cp. 11: 27–33). But he was an extreme hellenizer, and probably the spokesman for the 'renegade Israelites' (1 Macc. 6:
21) who complained of Judas' activities. While Syrian policy
remained one of subduing rebels by force, Menelaus *would be
maintained in office.*

4. *Lysias,* probably as a result of this campaign and of the
political problems in Antioch (cp. verses 23 ff.), seems to have
realized that the policy of force was not the answer. The

removal of Menelaus was part of the change in policy, and probably followed Lysias' withdrawal from Jerusalem (verses 23–4). Lysias could urge against Menelaus that his lack of hereditary right to the high-priesthood and his disposal of the temple treasures and his overbearing behaviour were largely *responsible for all Antiochus's troubles* with the Jews. *Beroea* is modern Aleppo.

5–6. This form of execution by asphyxiation was Persian in origin.

7–8. For the idea that punishment should fit the crime, see the note on 4: 16. The author of 2 Maccabees presumably thought that by his very presence in the temple as high priest the hellenizing Menelaus desecrated the *altar-fire*; no particular occasion is mentioned. ✳

JEWISH PREPARATIONS: A NIGHT ATTACK

9 So the king came on with the barbarous intention of inflicting on the Jews sufferings far worse than his father
10 had inflicted. When Judas heard this he ordered the people to invoke the Lord day and night and pray that now more than ever he would come to their aid, since they were on
11 the point of losing law, country, and temple; and that he would not allow them, just when they had begun to breathe again, to fall into the hands of blaspheming Gen-
12 tiles. They all obeyed his orders: for three days without respite they prayed to their merciful Lord, they wailed, they fasted, they prostrated themselves. Then Judas urged them to action and called upon them to stand by him.

13   After holding a council of war with the elders, he decided not to wait until the royal army invaded Judaea and took Jerusalem, but to march out and with God's
14 help to bring things to a decision. He entrusted the outcome to the Creator of the world; his troops he charged

to fight bravely to the death for the law, for the temple
and for Jerusalem, for their country and their way of life.
He pitched camp near Modin, and giving his men the 15
signal for battle with the cry 'God's victory!', he made a
night attack on the royal pavilion with a picked force of
the bravest young men. He killed as many as two
thousand in the enemy camp, and his men stabbed to
death[a] the leading elephant and its driver. In the end they 16
reduced the whole camp to panic and confusion, and
withdrew victorious. It was all over by daybreak, through 17
the help and protection which Judas had received from
the Lord.

* 2 Maccabees describes Judas' preparations for the Syrian
invasion, and his night attack on the Syrian camp near Modin.
This material does not appear in 1 Maccabees, which describes
a pitched battle by day at Bethzacharia, the occupation of
Bethsura, and the siege of the temple.

9. *So* looks back to verse 2, the narrative being interrupted
by reference to Menelaus' part in events and subsequent fate.
Antiochus V is somewhat unfairly portrayed; the prime
mover in any case was probably Lysias.

10. *losing law, country, and temple:* these were clearly threatened by a Syrian success and the consequent restoration of
control by the hellenizers. The importance of *law* and *temple*
has been more prominent in 2 Maccabees than that of *country*
(cp. 8: 21; the Greek word means 'fatherland'); perhaps to
Jason of Cyrene and his epitomist, as Dispersion Jews, the idea
of the Jewish *country* mattered a little less than the focal ideas
of *law* and *temple*. But the idea of the land as an 'inheritance'
from God was and is important to Judaism; see the note on
1 Macc. 15: 33-4.

12. For the preparation for battle, compare 1 Macc. 3: 44-7.

[a] stabbed to death: *probable reading, based on one Vs.*

13. The strategy is typical of Judas' constant attempt to take the initiative. He moves north from Jerusalem to prevent any Syrian contact with the besieged citadel (cp. 1 Macc. 6: 20).

14. *Creator:* cp. 1: 24; 7: 23. *for the law . . . and their way of life:* see the note on verse 10. *Modin,* the home town of the Maccabaean family, lay on the edge of the plain of Aijalon which was the obvious route into Judaea for an army coming south down the coastal plain.

15. Compare the battle cry of 8: 23, 'God is our help'. *The signal for battle,* the battle-cry, the *picked force,* and the night attack on the *enemy camp* remind us of Gideon's famous attack (Judg. 7). The stabbing of the *leading elephant* seems strange in a situation where, presumably, the elephants were not drawn up in battle line, and reminds us of Eleazar's action at Bethzacharia (1 Macc. 6: 43–6). There may be some confusion here. ✳

THE KING'S WITHDRAWAL AND TREATY

18 Now that he had had a taste of Jewish daring, the king
19 tried stratagems in attacking their strong-points. He advanced on Bethsura, one of their powerful forts; he was
20 repulsed; he attacked, he was beaten. Judas sent in supplies
21 to the garrison, but a soldier in the Jewish ranks, Rhodocus by name, betrayed their secrets to the enemy. How-
22 ever, he was tracked down, arrested, and put away. The king parleyed for the second time with the inhabitants of Bethsura, and, when he had given and received guarantees, he withdrew; he then attacked Judas and his men,
23 but had the worst of it. He now received news that Philip, whom he had left in charge of state affairs in Antioch, had gone out of his mind. In dismay he summoned the Jews, agreed to their terms, took an oath to respect all their rights, and, after this settlement, offered a sacrifice,

paid honour to the sanctuary and its precincts, and received 24
Maccabaeus graciously. He left behind Hegemonides as
governor of the region from Ptolemais to Gerra, and 25
went himself to Ptolemais. Its inhabitants were furious
at the treaty he had made, and in their alarm wanted to
repudiate it. Lysias mounted the rostrum, made the best 26
defence he could, won the people over, calmed them down,
and, having thus gained their support, left for Antioch.

Such was the course of the king's offensive and retreat.

---

* This passage parallels 1 Macc. 6: 47–50, 55–63, but there
are some notable differences, particularly in the account of the
siege of Bethsura (verses 18–22). According to 1 Macc. 6: 31,
49–50, Bethsura was besieged and capitulated, after some
resistance, for lack of food; here, Judas succeeds in getting
supplies to the garrison and two Syrian attacks are repulsed.
Yet the two accounts have in common that the defenders did
make a successful attack on the besiegers (verse 19, cp. 1 Macc.
6: 31) and that the siege ended with an agreement (verse 22,
cp. 1 Macc. 6: 49), not with a successful Syrian assault. If 2
Maccabees had noted that a Syrian garrison was left at Bethsura (cp. 1 Macc. 6: 50), there would be less apparent difference
between the two accounts.

20–1. *Rhodocus:* the name, perhaps Persian in origin, is
otherwise unknown. *put away* means 'killed', which was the
fate of the traitors mentioned in 10: 22.

22. *he then attacked Judas* probably refers to the attack on
the temple (1 Macc. 6: 51–2); *but had the worst of it:* cp. the
words of Lysias in 1 Macc. 6: 57.

23. *Philip:* cp. 9: 29, and see the note on 1 Macc. 6: 14.
The parallel narrative in 1 Macc. 6: 63 does not suggest that
Lysias had left Philip in charge at Antioch but rather that
Philip had taken possession for himself, as regent nominated
by Antiochus IV for his son. *had gone out of his mind* may be

one interpretation of Philip's attempt to seize power. The king – or, more probably, Lysias – *agreed to their terms*; cp. the 'agreed terms' of 1 Macc. 6: 61 and the commentary on that passage. The letter of Antiochus V to Lysias (11: 22–6) officially ratifies these terms, by which the hellenistic constitution of the city was revoked, the temple restored, and the Jewish law reinstated. Hence Antiochus (or Lysias) promises *to respect* the Jewish *rights*, offers *a sacrifice*, and honours *the sanctuary*. He further *received Maccabaeus graciously*: this would hardly please the hellenizing Jews of the Jewish government, who regarded Maccabaeus as a rebel. (There is no mention here, however, of the demolishing of the temple defences; cp. 1 Macc. 6: 62.)

24–5. *the region from Ptolemais to Gerra* means the coastal plain from modern Haifa to the Egyptian border (Gerra was near Pelusium; see the note on 1 Macc. 1: 19). The area was later put under Judas' brother Simon by Antiochus VI in 145 B.C. (1 Macc. 11: 59). *Hegemonides* is otherwise unknown to us; he may have been Jewish or pro-Jewish, and hence, in part, the *alarm* of the people of *Ptolemais*. For Ptolemais' antipathy towards the Jews, which largely explains their alarm, cp. 6: 8 and 1 Macc. 5: 15. Demetrius I even offered to make over Ptolemais to the Jerusalem temple (1 Macc. 10: 39), but perhaps fortunately for all concerned the offer was never taken up. *

The victory of Maccabaeus over Nicanor

* For the events described in 2 Macc. 14 and 15, compare 1 Macc. 7. Antiochus V had ratified Lysias' agreement early in 162 B.C. (see the commentary on 2 Macc. 11: 22 ff.), but late

in 162 B.C. or early in 161 B.C. Demetrius, son of Seleucus IV, arrived in Syria and took power. This change of government in Syria prompted new appeals from the hellenizing party in Jerusalem. A new campaign against the Maccabees began. The Syrian general, Nicanor, was finally defeated and killed, and 2 Maccabees makes this the climax of the book, thereby suggesting that this was the victorious climax of the whole rebellion. In fact it was not, as 1 Macc. 8–16 clearly show. ✳

DEMETRIUS AND ALCIMUS

AFTER AN INTERVAL of three years, information **14** reached Judas and his men that Demetrius son of Seleucus had sailed into the harbour of Tripolis with a powerful army and fleet, and, after disposing of Antio- 2 chus and his guardian Lysias, had taken possession of the country.

There was a man called Alcimus, who had formerly 3 been high priest but had submitted voluntarily to pollu- tions at the time of the secession. This man, realizing that there was not now the slightest guarantee of his safety, or any possibility of access to the holy altar, came to King 4 Demetrius, about the year 151,[a] and presented him with a gold crown and palm, and also some of the customary olive branches from the temple. On that particular occa- sion he kept quiet; but he found a chance of forwarding 5 his own mad scheme when Demetrius summoned him to his council and questioned him about the attitude and plans of the Jews. He replied: 'Those of the Jews who are 6 called Hasidaeans and are led by Judas Maccabaeus are keeping the war alive and fomenting sedition, refusing to

[a] *That is* 161 B.C.

7 leave the kingdom in peace. Thus, although I have been deprived of my hereditary dignity – I mean the high-
8 priesthood – I am here today from two motives: first, a genuine concern for the king's rights; and secondly, a regard for my fellow-citizens, since our whole race is suffering considerable hardship as a result of the folly of
9 the people I have just mentioned. I would advise your majesty to acquaint yourself with every one of these matters and then make provision for our country and our beleaguered nation, as befits your universal kindness and
10 goodwill. For the empire will enjoy no peace so long as Judas remains alive.'

∗ 1–2. For a full discussion of these events, see the commentary on 1 Macc. 7: 1–11.

3–4. *who had formerly been high priest:* this may mean that his elevation to office (on the death of Menelaus) had preceded Demetrius' arrival. He would therefore be a moderate hellenizer (he *had submitted voluntarily to pollutions at the time of the secession,* 167–164 B.C.), perhaps approved of, and appointed by, Lysias. Insecure in Jerusalem (for the Maccabees would hardly approve of him) he would be insecure at Antioch with the change of régime, so he came to present tokens of loyalty to the new king (cp. 1 Macc. 13: 37 ff. for similar tokens sent by Simon to Demetrius II).

5. This verse suggests a second appearance before Demetrius, and Alcimus' speech, especially the reference to his being deprived of the high-priesthood (verse 7), suggests that the first complaints of Alcimus and his party and the campaign of Bacchides (1 Macc. 7: 5–20) are omitted from 2 Maccabees. The present situation is that described in 1 Macc. 7: 25: 'When Alcimus saw... he returned to the king and accused them of atrocities.' Demetrius may well have *summoned him,* wishing to understand more clearly why the province was so trouble-

some. His *council* would consist of his Friends and army officers (cp. I Macc. 6: 28).

6. *Hasidaeans:* see the commentary on I Macc. 2: 42; 7: 12 ff. They would have been hardened against Syria by the executions carried out by Alcimus and Bacchides (I Macc. 7: 12–20). For Judas' activity, cp. I Macc. 7: 23–4.

7. *deprived:* Alcimus was in fact a refugee from Judas and his party; cp. I Macc. 7: 25. *hereditary dignity:* see the note on I Macc. 7: 14.

8. Alcimus wanted peace under Syrian rule, and saw Judas and his party as men of violence bringing *hardship* on the people. His solution to the problem seems to have been a simply military one (see verse 10, and I Macc. 7: 12–20).

9. *kindness and goodwill:* Greek *philanthropia*; see the note on 6: 22. ✲

THE ARRIVAL OF NICANOR

When he had spoken to this effect, the other Friends, 11 who were hostile to Judas, immediately inflamed Demetrius still more. The king at once selected Nicanor, com- 12 mander of the elephant corps, gave him command of Judaea, and sent him off with a commission to dispose of 13 Judas himself and disperse his forces, and to install Alcimus as high priest of the great temple. The gentile 14 population of Judaea, refugees from the attacks of Judas, now flocked to Nicanor, thinking that defeat and misfortune for the Jews would mean prosperity for themselves.

When they learnt of Nicanor's offensive and the gentile 15 attack, the Jews sprinkled dust over themselves and prayed to the One who established his people for ever, who never fails to manifest himself when his chosen are in need of help. At their leader's command, they immediately struck 16

camp and joined battle with the enemy at the village of
17 Adasa.[a] Simon, the brother of Judas, had fought an engagement with Nicanor, but, because the enemy came
18 up[b] unexpectedly, he had suffered a slight reverse. In spite
of this, when Nicanor learnt how brave Judas and his
troops were and how courageously they fought for their
19 country, he shrank from deciding the issue in battle. So
he sent Posidonius, Theodotus, and Mattathias to negotiate a settlement.

✷ The military solution is now tried; Nicanor is told 'to
dispose of Judas himself and disperse his forces, and to install
Alcimus as high priest'. After a minor engagement and a
battle, however, Nicanor tried to find a more diplomatic
solution. 1 Macc. 7: 26–32 presents Nicanor as a smiling villain who tries force only when deceit fails, but the fuller
presentation of 2 Maccabees seems more likely. See the com
mentary on 1 Macc. 7: 26–32.

12. Nicanor had campaigned previously in Judaea (cp. 8:
9–36), as also had his elephants (cp. 13: 15) which appear in
15: 20 (though not in 1 Maccabees) in the account of Nicanor's
final battle. Where these elephants had come from is not clear,
for the Romans had destroyed Syria's elephants in 162 B.C.

14. *gentile population of Judaea*: probably Syrian civil servants and businessmen from Egypt and the towns of the coast.

15. *sprinkled dust... prayed*: cp. 10: 25. The prayer appeals to
Israel's special relationship with God as *his chosen*. The Greek
words mean 'his part' or 'share' and the idea is stated in
Deut. 32: 9,

> but the LORD's share was his own people,
> Jacob was his allotted portion.

[a] Adasa: *probable reading; compare 1 Macc. 7: 40.*   [b] came up: *probable
reading, based on one Vs.*

The prayer expresses the hope that God will *manifest himself:*
cp. 2: 21 and the note on that verse, and compare also the
prayer in 1: 24–9.

16. *Adasa:* the Greek actually reads 'Dessaou' which has
been taken to be a corrupt version of the name of the place
where Nicanor, according to 1 Macc. 7: 40, fought his last
battle. As Adasa is only 3 km (1¾ miles) from Capharsalama
which 1 Macc. 7: 31 gives as the place of Nicanor's minor
engagement with Judas, possibly the Capharsalama battle is
meant here in 2 Maccabees. But another reading is 'Lessaou',
possibly the Laish of Isa. 10: 30 near Anathoth just north-east
of Jerusalem. In this case the battle is distinct from those
described in 1 Maccabees.

17. We know nothing else of this previous skirmish.

18–19. Probably the battle (verse 16) was inconclusive, both
sides losing a number of men; hence both sides (verses 19–20)
were ready to come to terms. ✲

NICANOR'S POLICY OF FRIENDLINESS

After a lengthy consideration of the proposals, Judas 20
informed his men of them; they were unanimous in
agreeing to make peace. A day was fixed for a private 21
meeting of the leaders. A chariot advanced from each of
the two lines, and seats were placed for them; but Judas 22
posted armed men at strategic points ready to deal with
any unforeseen treachery on the enemy's part. The discussion between the two leaders was harmonious. Nicanor 23
stayed some time in Jerusalem and behaved correctly;
he dismissed the crowds that had flocked round him, and 24
kept Judas always close to himself. He had acquired a real
affection for him, and urged him to marry and start a 25
family. So Judas married and settled down to the quiet
life of an ordinary citizen.

26 Alcimus noticed their friendliness and got hold of a copy of the agreement they had concluded. He went to Demetrius and said that Nicanor was pursuing a policy detrimental to the interests of the empire, by appointing that
27 traitor Judas King's Friend designate. The king was furious and was provoked by these villainous slanders to write to Nicanor expressing his dissatisfaction with the agreement and ordering him to arrest Maccabaeus and send him at
28 once to Antioch. This message filled Nicanor with dismay; he took it hard that he should have to break his agreement although the man had committed no offence,
29 but since there was no going against the king, he watched for a favourable opportunity of carrying out the order
30 by means of some stratagem. Maccabaeus, however, observed that Nicanor had become less friendly towards him and no longer showed him the same civility. He realized that this unfriendliness boded no good, so he collected a large number of his followers and went into hiding from Nicanor.
31 When Nicanor recognized that he had been outmanœuvred by the resolute action of Judas, he went to the great and holy temple at the time when the priests were offering the regular sacrifices, and ordered them to
32 surrender Judas to him. The priests declared on oath that they did not know the whereabouts of the wanted man.
33 But Nicanor stretched out his right hand towards the shrine and swore this oath: 'Unless you surrender Judas into my custody, I will raze God's sanctuary to the ground, I will destroy the altar, and on this spot I will build a
34 temple to Dionysus for all the world to see.' With these words he left; but the priests with outstretched hands

prayed to Heaven, the constant champion of our race: 35 'Lord, thou hast no need of anything in the world, yet it was thy pleasure that among us there should be a shrine for thy dwelling-place. Now, Lord, who alone art holy, keep this 36 house, so newly purified, for ever free from defilement.'

* Compare 1 Macc. 7: 27–32. 2 Maccabees, which elsewhere describes Nicanor as 'impious' or 'double-dyed villain' (8: 14, 34), here shows Nicanor acting with sincere friendliness towards Judas, while 1 Maccabees emphasizes Nicanor's insincerity. 2 Maccabees is unlikely to invent such an attitude for Nicanor, and the portrayal of Nicanor as an enlightened army officer seeking a practical solution is most convincing. But the inevitable happens; Nicanor's apparent sympathy with the rebels offends the government party, which regards Nicanor's behaviour as tantamount to a betrayal. Nicanor's reaction is understandable (verses 31–6).

20. *proposals:* at these we can only guess. Probably Alcimus was to be accepted as high priest, while Judas was appointed 'King's Friend designate' (verse 26). As King's Friend Judas would have considerable personal honour and the chance to speak in the king's council; that is, the Maccabaean party had the promise of representation at Antioch.

26. *detrimental to the interests of the empire:* Alcimus might have argued that such recognition of Judas merely encouraged other rebels to take up violence and weakened the pro-Syrian government in Judaea.

27–30. Cp. 1 Macc. 7: 29–30. The king follows Alcimus' counsel, as earlier.

31–6. Cp. 1 Macc. 7: 33–8 and the commentary on that passage.

33. *a temple to Dionysus:* Nicanor goes further than Antiochus, who had dedicated the temple to Olympian Zeus and forced the Jews to join in the celebrations of the feast of Dionysus (see 6: 2, 7).

34 ff. The priests pray for the preservation of the temple's holiness, but not for vengeance (as in 1 Maccabees) on Nicanor.

35. *no need of anything:* for a similar idea, see Ps. 50: 9–15. *dwelling place* translates a Greek word (*skenosis*) whose verbal form means 'to live in a tent'; compare the Hebrew *shakan*, 'to encamp', 'to tent'. The predecessor of the temple in Israel was probably some form of tent-shrine, a 'tabernacle', and it came to be said that while God dwelt in heaven he on occasion 'tented' with men for the purpose of revealing himself. Thus in Ps. 76: 1–2:

> In Judah God is known,
> his name is great in Israel;
> his tent is pitched in Salem,
> in Zion his battle-quarters are set up.

The idea is preserved in the prologue of John's gospel, which says that the Word 'came to dwell (Greek "tent") among us'.

36. *who alone art holy:* cp. 'the only King', etc., in the prayer of 1: 24 ff. *newly purified:* see 10: 1–8, and the note on 2: 19. ✻

A PATRIOTIC SUICIDE

37 A man called Razis, a member of the Jerusalem senate, was denounced to Nicanor. He was very highly spoken of, a patriot who for his loyalty was known as 'Father of
38 the Jews'. In the early days of the secession he had stood his trial for practising Judaism, and with the utmost
39 eagerness had risked life and limb for that cause. Nicanor wished to give clear proof of his hostility towards the Jews, and sent more than five hundred soldiers to arrest
40 Razis; he reckoned that his arrest would be a severe blow
41 to the Jews. The troops were on the point of capturing the tower where Razis was, and were trying to force the outer door. Then an order was given to set the door on

fire, and Razis, hemmed in on all sides, turned his sword on himself. He preferred to die nobly rather than fall into 42 the hands of criminals and be subjected to gross humiliation. In his haste and anxiety he misjudged the blow, and 43 with the troops pouring through the doors he ran without hesitation on to the wall and heroically threw himself down into the crowd. The crowd hurriedly gave way 44 and he fell in the space they left. He was still breathing, 45 still on fire with courage; so, streaming with blood and severely wounded, he picked himself up and dashed through the crowd. Finally, standing on a sheer rock, and now completely drained of blood, he took his entrails 46 in both hands and flung them at the crowd. And thus, invoking the Lord of life and breath to give these entrails back to him again, he died.

* This story has much in common with the stories of 6: 18 – 7: 42. One notes in particular the superhuman heroism, the gory details, the resurrection hope, and the loyalty to the laws of the fathers.

37. The name *Razis* was perhaps Persian in origin; one of his ancestors might have been a Persian civil servant in Judaea who adopted the Jewish faith. It would seem that the *senate* still had some orthodox, un-hellenized members. '*Father of the Jews*'; 'father' was often used as an honorific title indicating a man's protective concern for or office over a group of people – e.g. 'father of the fatherless', Ps. 68: 5; 'father to the needy', Job 29:16. Jehoash of Israel called Elisha 'My father, the chariots and the horsemen of Israel!' (2 Kings 13: 14).

38. *secession*: cp. verse 3. *Judaism*: cp. 8: 1.

41 ff. Suicide is rarely mentioned in the Old Testament (cp. Ahithophel, 2 Sam. 17: 23), but in later times and in a similar context to the present case we know of the suicide of the Jews at Masada in A.D. 73. The Jewish historian Josephus himself

proposed a suicide pact on one occasion and survived it with one other(*Jewish War* III. 9. 7).

46. *to give these entrails back to him:* cp. 7: 11. ✳

NICANOR'S ARROGANCE

15 Nicanor received information that Judas and his men were in the region of Samaria, and he determined to attack them on their day of rest, when it could be done
2 without any danger. Those Jews who were forced to accompany his army said, 'Do not carry out such a savage and barbarous massacre, but respect the day singled out
3 and made holy by the all-seeing One.' The double-dyed villain retorted, 'Is there a ruler in the sky who has
4 ordered the sabbath day to be observed?' The Jews declared, 'The living Lord himself is ruler in the sky, and
5 he ordered the seventh day to be kept holy.' 'But I', replied Nicanor, 'am a ruler on earth, and I order you to take your arms and do your duty to the king.' However, he did not succeed in carrying out his cruel plan.

✳ The story of Nicanor's last battle is prefaced by a dialogue which the author puts into the mouths of Nicanor and 'Jews who were forced to accompany his army'. The intention is clearly to show up Nicanor as a 'bragging blasphemer' (cp. verse 32).

1. Judas has moved north from Jerusalem, held by Nicanor and the citadel garrison, to *the region of Samaria* and the borders of his own country area of Modin, in order to control the northern approaches to Jerusalem (cp. 1 Macc. 7: 39). Nicanor's threat to attack the Jews on the sabbath does not appear in 1 Maccabees, and is probably introduced to emphasize the deceitful nature of Nicanor. *without danger:* Nicanor (or the

author) is wrong, for the Maccabees had agreed to defend themselves if need be on the sabbath; cp. 1 Macc. 2: 41.

2. The dialogue is artificial; see above.

4. Nicanor's somewhat contemptuous reference to 'a ruler in the sky' is answered by the Jewish reference to *The living Lord* and to the fourth commandment (Exod. 20: 8 ff.).

5. Nicanor's arrogant demand is made to appear futile. ✳

JUDAS PREPARES THE JEWS FOR BATTLE

Now Nicanor, in his pretentious and extravagant con- 6 ceit, had resolved upon erecting a public trophy from the spoils of Judas's forces. But Maccabaeus's confidence 7 never wavered, and he had not the least doubt that he would obtain help from the Lord. He urged his men not 8 to be afraid of the gentile attack, but to bear in mind the aid they had received from heaven in the past and so look to the Almighty for the victory which he would send this time also. He drew encouragement for them from 9 the law and the prophets and, by reminding them of the struggles they had already come through, filled them with a fresh enthusiasm. When he had roused their courage, he 10 gave them their orders, reminding them at the same time of the Gentiles' broken faith and perjury. He armed each 11 one of them, not so much with the security of shield and spear, as with the encouragement that brave words bring; and he also told them of a trustworthy dream he had had, a sort of waking vision, which put them all in good heart.

What he had seen was this: the former high priest 12 Onias appeared to him, that great gentleman of modest bearing and mild disposition, apt speaker, and exponent from childhood of the good life. With outstretched hands

he was praying earnestly for the whole Jewish commu-
13 nity. Next there appeared in the same attitude a figure of
great age and dignity, whose wonderful air of authority
14 marked him as a man of the utmost distinction. Then
Onias said, 'This is God's prophet Jeremiah, who loves
his fellow-Jews and offers many prayers for our people
15 and for the holy city.' Jeremiah extended his right hand
and delivered to Judas a golden sword, saying as he did
16 so, 'Take this holy sword, the gift of God, and with it
crush your enemies.'

17   The eloquent words of Judas had the power of stimu-
lating everyone to bravery and making men out of boys.
Encouraged by them, the Jews made up their minds not
to remain in camp, but to take the offensive manfully
and fight hand to hand with all their strength until the
issue was decided. This they did because Jerusalem,
10 their religion, and their temple were in danger. Their
fear was not chiefly for their wives and children, not to
mention brothers and relatives, but first and foremost for
19 the sacred shrine. The distress of those shut up in Jerusalem was no less, for they were anxious at the prospect
of a battle on open ground.

✶ Once again, the material is absent from 1 Maccabees.
2 Maccabees devotes much space and dramatic art to the Jewish
spiritual preparation for battle, for the author sees this battle
as the grand climax of Judas' career.
    6. Nicanor's presumption is again underlined (cp. 8: 10–11).
The word *trophy* is derived from the Greek word meaning the
turning or rout of the enemy; a trophy, often a mound topped
by a pile of armour taken from the dead, was set up on the
battle-field by the victor.

8. *aid... in the past:* cp. 10: 28; 13: 14 ff.

9. *the law and the prophets* were the two main parts of the Jewish bible, referred to also by the prologue of Ecclesiasticus as having been studied by the writer's grandfather, Jesus son of Sirach (about 180 B.C.). See the companion volume, *The Making of the Old Testament*, pp. 105–32.

10. *the Gentiles' broken faith and perjury* refers in the first instance to the Syrian change of policy that had led to the renewed fighting, but perhaps also to such behaviour as that of the people of Joppa (12: 3–9).

12. Both *Onias* (cp. 3: 1 ff.) and Jeremiah (verse 14), though dead, are seen as interceding for the Jewish nation and Jerusalem. *Onias* had made expiation for Heliodorus, the enemy of the temple (3: 32–3), and Jeremiah had been prevented from interceding for Jerusalem (Jer. 11: 14), though both men felt deeply for Jerusalem. For the description of Onias, see the note on 3: 1.

13. *authority... distinction:* the *figure* is thus reminiscent of Eleazar (6: 23).

14–15. Jeremiah seems to have been a prophet dear to Jason of Cyrene or his abbreviator (cp. 2: 1–8). His prophecies were also used by the author of Daniel (9: 2 ff.). Jeremiah is an appropriate prophet to offer the Maccabees the encouragement of the vision of a *sword*, for Jeremiah frequently threatens the sending of a sword on Israel or her enemies; e.g. Jer. 50: 35–7:

> A sword hangs over the Chaldaeans...
> A sword over the false prophets, and they are made fools,
> a sword over her warriors, and they despair,
> a sword over her horses and her chariots
>   and over all the rabble within her.

The *sword*, like the armour of the rider in the visions (3: 25; 5: 2; 11: 8) or their bridles (10: 29), is golden.

17. *their religion:* the Greek *ta hagia* may be a doublet of *the temple*, and should perhaps be omitted.

18. The temple had been directly threatened by Nicanor
(14: 33), who controlled Jerusalem. But the real threat was a
relapse to religious control by the hellenizing party, if Judas
lost.

19. *those shut up in Jerusalem* perhaps means those Maccabaean relatives and supporters in the city awaiting the outcome
of the *battle*. Judas, with his smaller numbers, had usually
avoided *open* battle, where the large, professional Syrian forces
had an advantage. ✳

THE BATTLE

20 All were waiting for the decisive struggle which lay
ahead. The enemy had already concentrated his forces;
his army was drawn up in order of battle, the elephants
stationed in a favourable position and the cavalry ranged
21 on the flank. When Maccabaeus observed the deploy-
ment of the troops, the variety of their equipment, and
the ferocity of the elephants, with hands upraised he
invoked the Lord, the worker of miracles; for he knew
that God grants victory to those who deserve it, not
because of their military strength but as he himself decides.
22 This was his prayer: 'Master, thou didst send thy angel in
the days of Hezekiah king of Judah, and he killed as many
as a hundred and eighty-five thousand men in Senna-
23 cherib's camp. Now, Ruler of heaven, send once again a
good angel to go in front of us spreading fear and panic.
24 May they be struck down by thy strong arm, these
blasphemers who are coming to attack thy holy people!'
Thus he ended.

25 Nicanor and his forces advanced with trumpets and
26 war-songs, but Judas and his men joined battle with
27 invocations and prayers. Fighting with their hands and

praying to God in their hearts, they killed no fewer than thirty-five thousand men, and were greatly cheered by the divine intervention.

* The final preparations are made. A contrast is drawn between the Syrians who trust in their troops, cavalry, elephants and equipment and advance 'with trumpets and war-songs', and the Jews, who trust in God and join battle 'with invocations and prayers'. The battle itself is briefly summarized in verse 27. Compare 1 Macc. 7: 39–46.

20. This verse and verse 19 suggests a battle on open ground, though this is not suggested by the reference of 1 Macc. 7: 39 to the Beth-horon region with its steep ascent into the hills. The picture here of a massive battle-array with elephants, cavalry and vast numbers may be misleading.

22. See the note on 8: 19–20.

27. 1 Macc. 7: 40 credits Judas with a mere 3,000 men. *divine intervention* translates the Greek *epiphaneia*, 'manifestation', and reminds us of 2 Maccabees' continual reference to heavenly manifestations at such moments of crisis (cp. 2: 21 and the commentary there). *

NICANOR'S DAY

The action was over, and they were joyfully disbanding, 28 when they recognized Nicanor lying dead in his armour. Then with tumultuous shouts they praised their Master in 29 their native language. Judas their leader, who had always 30 fought body and soul on behalf of his fellow-Jews, never losing his youthful patriotism, now ordered Nicanor's head to be cut off, also his hand and arm, and taken to Jerusalem. On arrival there he summoned all the people 31 and stationed the priests before the altar. Then he sent for the men in the citadel, and showed them the head of 32

the blackguardly Nicanor and the hand which this bragging blasphemer had extended against the Almighty's
33 holy temple. He cut out the tongue of the impious Nicanor, and said he would give it to the birds bit by bit; and
he gave orders that the evidence of what Nicanor's folly
had brought upon him should be hung up opposite the
34 shrine. They all made the sky ring with the praises of the
Lord who had shown his power: 'Praise to him who has
35 preserved his own sanctuary from defilement!' Judas
hung Nicanor's head from the citadel, a clear proof of
36 the Lord's help, for all to see. It was unanimously decreed
that this day should never pass unnoticed but be regularly
celebrated. It is the thirteenth of the twelfth month,
called Adar in Aramaic, the day before Mordecai's Day.
37 Such, then, was the fate of Nicanor, and from that
time Jerusalem has remained in the possession of the
Hebrews.

* The author ends his work with the death of Nicanor and
the establishment of a festival to mark the event. Compare
the much briefer account in 1 Macc. 7: 47–50. 2 Maccabees
omits any reference to the pursuit of the enemy (1 Macc. 7:
44–6) – the enemy has already been completely vanquished
by 'the divine intervention' – and concentrates on the grand
climax (as he sees it) and the lessons to be drawn from it.

29. *in their native language*: see the note on 7: 8.

31. *the men in the citadel* are the Syrian garrison, who are
still very much in charge of Jerusalem, militarily, in spite of
Nicanor's death.

32. Compare 14: 33.

35. Similarly Judith hung the head of Holofernes on the
battlements (Judith 13: 15; 14: 1), and David took Goliath's
head back to Jerusalem (1 Sam. 17: 54), probably to expose it.

For the practice of leaving corpses to the birds (and other animals) to dispose of, see Ezek. 39: 4 or 2 Sam. 21: 10. Thus they were deprived of the normal right to proper burial.

36. The date is 17 March 160 B.C. See the note on 1 Macc. 7: 43, and 7: 48–9. *Mordecai's Day:* the story behind this is found in the book of Esther. 'On the thirteenth day of the twelfth month, the month Adar... the Jews united in their cities in all the provinces of King Ahasuerus to fall upon those who had planned their ruin... Mordecai... sent letters to all the Jews... binding them to keep the fourteenth and fifteenth days of the month Adar, year by year, as the days on which the Jews obtained relief from their enemies' (Esther 9: 1–2, 20–2). Nicanor's Day, whether by chance or by design, fell at an appropriate season.

37. *from that time:* 1 Macc. 7: 50 more accurately says that 'Judaea entered upon a short period of peace'. Jerusalem remained religiously under Maccabaean rather than hellenizing control. For an assessment of the political situation at this point, see the commentary on 1 Macc. 7: 50. ✲

THE AUTHOR'S CONCLUSION

At this point I will bring my work to an end. If it is 38 found well written and aptly composed, that is what I myself hoped for; if cheap and mediocre, I could only do my best. For, just as it is disagreeable to drink wine alone 39 or water alone, whereas the mixing of the two gives a pleasant and delightful taste, so too variety of style in a literary work charms the ear of the reader. Let this then be my final word.

✲ The author's conclusion matches his preface (2: 19–32). One notices that the author has literary rather than academic pretensions; he appears to want to charm *the ear of the reader* (in ancient times one read to oneself aloud) rather than to satisfy his curiosity. As evidence for the history of the early Maccabaean period, his work is valuable, but it must be used with care. *

* * * * * * * * * * * *

THE VALUE FOR US OF
1 AND 2 MACCABEES

The influence of the Reformation has relegated for a large
section of Christendom the books of the Apocrypha to a
place of secondary importance. The Church of England's
'Articles of Religion' say that the apocryphal books are read
'for example of life and instruction of manners', but not used
'to establish any doctrine'. But since that was written, our
knowledge of the nature of the biblical books has changed
and with it our approach to understanding their contents.
We now see that 1 and 2 Maccabees and the rest of the Apocrypha are enormously valuable to us for our knowledge of
Judaism in the inter-testamental period and therefore for our
understanding of Judaism in the following period of the New
Testament. If the protestant churches do not use 1 and 2
Maccabees 'to establish any doctrine', they certainly use them
to aid their understanding of the roots of Christian doctrine.
These books give us both the historical background to New
Testament Judaea (the Zealots, Pharisees and Sadducees have
their ancestors in the party groups portrayed in 1 and 2 Maccabees) and the theological background (the obvious example
is the idea of resurrection in 2 Maccabees).

But much more than this can be said. In Berlin in 1937 – the
place and date are significant – Elias Bickermann published in
German his book *The God of the Maccabees: studies in the
meaning and origin of the Maccabaean rising*. In two fascinating
opening chapters he shows how our ancient sources explain
the historical events of the Maccabaean period from quite
different theological or political viewpoints, and how through
the centuries since the Maccabees the explanations given of
Antiochus' persecution have reflected faithfully theological
and political trends of the times. Thus 2 Maccabees explains
events by saying that the Jews were being disciplined for their

345

sins by Antiochus, who would be punished for his pride. 1 Maccabees blames events simply on the pride of Greek imperialism and the hellenizing apostasy of some of the Jews. But there were also non-Jewish explanations of these events, which justified the behaviour of Antiochus by regarding it as punishment for the Jewish rebellion, and later by portraying Antiochus as a champion of Greek liberalism against Jewish barbarism. If many Jews disliked the hellenistic world, there were, after all, many hellenistic neighbours of the Jews who had good reason to dislike the Jews, first, on political and economic grounds, and then, inevitably, because culturally and religiously they were different. Bickermann goes on to point out how in the Christian world for sixteen centuries the Jewish explanation prevailed. The Maccabees were above all champions of the faith against tyrants (though there was some doubt as to whether one could follow their lead if the tyrant was a Christian and legally constituted head of state). But then came a change, and the Greek view prevailed; Antiochus was a cultivated monarch, the rightful king of Jerusalem, who needed to unify his empire, while the Jews were rebels who had to be dealt with for the sake of the whole empire. In the late nineteenth century A.D. Antiochus was seen as trying to remove local nationalism; the Jews were to give up their particularism and become fully integrated into the empire. This corresponded with the cry in Germany that the Jews should become fully German. The state was championing a culture which a stubborn minority were rejecting.

The historical Antiochus was certainly no Hitler, except perhaps in certain Jewish and Christian portrayal, as Bickermann demonstrated; but the publication of such studies 'in the meaning and origin' of the Maccabaean rising in Germany in 1937 was surely an act of courage. But the theme of these books does not concern Jews alone. The theme of the use of violence by a section of the community which has its own particular cultural history and deep-seated frustrations is a highly contemporary one. We hear much of 'urban guerrillas' today, and in the Maccabees and their supporters we see something very similar. The social and economic difficulties of the rebels, the inner struggles for power at the top, the difficulties of finding a policy that will keep the peace and satisfy everybody, the embarrassment of army commanders – all these appear in 1 and 2 Maccabees and are familiar sights in the world today.

But circumstances alter cases, and the presence of 1 and 2 Maccabees in the Apocrypha or the Bible does not compel us to adopt Maccabaean solutions for any apparently similar modern problems. What these books can do, however, is open our eyes to the feelings and passions that are bred in minorities with deep convictions, and help us to sympathize with them. Possibly these books will only take on full meaning for us if ever we ourselves are deeply involved in the fortunes of a persecuted minority. If that happens, then the faith and conviction so clear in both the Maccabees and their chroniclers might become a most effective source of inspiration.

A NOTE ON FURTHER READING

English commentaries on 1 and 2 Maccabees are mainly in large one-volume commentaries covering the whole Bible and Apocrypha. These include the commentaries of J. W. Hunkin, in C. Gore, H. L. Goudge and A. Guillaume (eds.), *A New Commentary on Holy Scripture*, Part II, *Apocrypha* (S.P.C.K., 1928); N. McEleney, in R. E. Brown, J. A. Fitzmyer and R. E. Murphy (eds.), *The Jerome Biblical Commentary* (Chapman, 1968); T. Corbishley, in R. C. Fuller, L. Johnston and C. Kearns (eds.), *The New Catholic Commentary on Holy Scripture* (Nelson, 1969); and G. A. F. Knight (1 Maccabees) and R. C. Dentan (2 Maccabees) in Charles M. Laymon (ed.), *The Interpreter's One-Volume Commentary on the Bible* (Abingdon, 1972). More detailed commentaries are those by W. O. E. Oesterley (1 Maccabees) and J. Moffatt (2 Maccabees) in R. H. Charles (ed.), *Apocrypha and Pseudepigrapha of the Old Testament*, Vol. 1, *Apocrypha* (O.U.P., 1913), and by J. C. Dancy, *Commentary on First Maccabees* (Blackwell, 1954). The standard commentary on 1 and 2 Maccabees is F-M. Abel, *Les Livres des Maccabées* (2nd ed., J. Gabalda et Cie., 1949), a shorter commentary by F.-M. Abel and J. Starcky is in the French *Jerusalem Bible* series (Les Éditions du Cerf, 3rd ed., Paris, 1961). No student of the Maccabaean period can ignore Josephus; the translation of his works made in 1737 by W. Whiston has been reprinted many times and is still available. (More recently G. Williamson has translated *The Jewish War* in Penguin Classics.) Political and social background is given by Sir William Tarn, *Hellenistic Civilization* (rev. ed., Methuen, 1966) and by V. Tcherikover, *Hellenistic Civilization and the Jews* (Jewish Pub. Soc., 1966). The geographical details raised by 1 and 2 Maccabees may be studied in G. A. Smith's famous *The Historical Geography of the Holy Land* (paperback ed., Fontana Library, 1966) or in Y. Aharoni and M. Avi-Yonah (eds.), *The Macmillan Bible Atlas* (Macmillan, 1968), which provides detailed maps illustrating the events of 1 and 2 Maccabees.

INDEX

349